WHO'S HIRING IN ATLANTA

- 3000+ of Atlanta's most active employers, compiled from our survey of more than 6,000 companies.
- 300+ permanent and temporary personnel agencies with specialties
- Local professional associations and Atlanta officers

Plus

The latest advancements in job search technology:
- **SmartFax Job Support**: Send your resume to any company from the convenience of your own phone.
- **CareerSource Resume Bank**: Include your resume FREE to be reviewed by interested employers.
- **SmartSearch Job Locator**: Fax your resume only to the companies looking for your specific job skills.

Plus

Job search strategy to . . .
- Make your resume stand out
- Mount a Direct Marketing Campaign
- Make personal contact with employers
- Respond to classified advertisements
- Network through professional associations
- Use permanent and temporary agencies
- Improve your interviewing skills
- Develop a job network

WHO'S HIRING IN ATLANTA HAS IT ALL!

Who's Hiring in Atlanta

Published by CareerSource Publications
P O Box 52291, Atlanta, GA 30355
(404) 262-7131; 842-1815 fax
email: JobGuru@aol.com

SMARTFAX technical support
P O Box 72725, Marietta, GA 30007-2725
(770) 952-2211; (770) 988-8855 fax

Manufactured in United States of America.

Text: Steve Hines
Research coordinator: Jamie Mount

ISBN 0-929255-19-4

TABLE OF CONTENTS

PART 3: INTERVIEWING TIPS ... p 41

- Preparing for your interviews
- Researching the companies
- Anticipate certain questions
- Evaluating each interview
- Questions to ask the interviewer
- Most frequently asked questions with suggested answers
- "Tell me about yourself."

PART 4: USING SMARTFAX... p 49

- What is SmartFax • Activating your SmartFax Card • SmartFax Questions and Answers • SmartFax Order Forms • SmartSearch Job Locator p 55 • SmartFax Broadcast Fax p 56 • SmartFax Employment Agencies p 75 • SmartFax Professional Associations p 78

PART 5: COMPANY LISTS ...

More than 3,000 of Atlanta's largest and fastest growing companies:

- **Business Services p 81**
Accounting • Architectural Services • Building Contractors • Interior Design • Engineering Services • Legal Services • Office Equipment • Transportation • Utilities
- **Human Services p 119**
Consulting • Education • Hospitals and Medical Services • Recreation and Sports • Security
- **Financial p 141**
Banks • Financial Services • Insurance • Stockbrokers • Commercial Real Estate • Residential Real Estate
- **Hospitality and Travel p 165**
Airlines • Hotels/Motels • Food Service and Restaurants • Travel Agencies
- **Marketing p 175**
Advertising • Marketing • Media • Public Relations • Printing and Publishing • Retail

Other job guides from
CareerSource Publications:

WHO'S HIRING series, featuring SmartFax:
Who's Hiring in Atlanta $14.95
Who's Hring in Houston (available 1997)
Who's Hiring in Dallas (available 1997)

THE CAREER SEARCH SYSTEM series
by Steve Hines
Atlanta Jobs $16.95
Charlotte Jobs $15.95
Raleigh-Durham Jobs $15.95

For information and to order, contact
CAREERSOURCE PUBLICATIONS
P O Box 52291, Atlanta, GA 30355.
(404) 262-7131; fax (404) 842-1815
e-mail: JobGuru@aol.com

To order and charge to MasterCard or Visa, call toll-free
1-800-598-8197

INTRODUCTION

You will never find a new job while you're chained to your desk!

Everyone knows that the least effective way to conduct a job search is to sit in front of your typewriter typing hundreds of cover letters and envelopes. Equally as wasteful is to call every permanent and temporary employment agency in the yellow pages to inquire if they can help you. And don't you have something more constructive to do on Sunday afternoon than to type a reply to all the classified want ads?

Career counselors all stress a dynamic approach to the job search – that is, getting out on the front line and actively beating the bushes for new leads, new contacts, and new ideas. You should concentrate your time on locating sources for interviews, expanding your job network, and conducting research for your upcoming interviews.

Who's Hiring in Atlanta offers you several choices in conducting your job search. Not only does the text help you plan your job search, but then the Company Directory gives you the names and addresses of Atlanta's major employers, which you can contact as you please. But *Who's Hiring in Atlanta* gives you even more: **SmartFax Job Support,** the most advanced technological innovation to become available to job seekers in many years. SmartFax does all of your office correspondence, freeing you up to follow through on the mechanics of your job search.

What is SMARTFAX?

SMARTFAX is a powerful new technology that allows you to immediately fax your resume to any employer from any touch tone phone, 24 hours a day, seven days a week - even from the convenience of your own home! With SmartFax, you can send your resume instantly to
- Atlanta's largest employers,
- Atlanta's permanent and temporary employment services
- companies in any of 50 industries
- classified want ads
- any one or more companies selected from a databank of more than 3000 companies.

And there is more:

SmartSearch Job Locator: SmartFax has contacted the 500 most active Atlanta employers regarding their specific needs, so you can allow SmartFax to pick the companies that frequently have job openings for your background! Your resume will be sent instantly, so you can be considered for any job needs, now or in the future. By sending your resume to selected groups of companies, industries, and personnel services at the beginning of your job search, you will never miss a job opening because you were too busy doing something else.

CareerSource Resume Bank: While you are searching for leads and job opportunities, you can have your resume available to prospective employers by including it free with the CareerSource Resume Bank.

With SmartFax you can eliminate the paperwork drudgery and rescue your time to do the things that will propel you to your new job. Plus you'll stay several steps ahead of your competition by adding a voice resume and the ability to make an immediate response to any opportunity you uncover.

For a more detailed description of the services provided by SmartFax and how to activate your SmartFax Card, refer to Part 4 (the blue pages) of this book.

Who's Hiring text

The text consists of a three-part, detailed explanation of the three major parts of your job search:

• "Part 1: Resumes, Etc." clarifies the preparation of the eight basic documents you will need.
• "Part 2: Marketing Yourself" explains how to make inroads with companies, either through direct marketing, personal contact, or responding to classified want ads. The advantages of using temporary and permanent agencies is discussed, followed by the procedure for developing a job network.
• "Part 3: Interviewing Tips" highlights the preparation necessary before each interview, and then offers some probable questions and suggested answers.

Who's Hiring in Atlanta gives you the choice of conducting a traditional job search or adding the convenience of SmartFax. And by combining the two, you can add new dimensions to your search.

PART 1
RESUMES, ETC.

This chapter details the eight basic documents you will use in your job search:

- written resume
- cover letters
- voice resume
- broadcast cover letter

- business cards
- references page
- salary history
- thank-you notes

WRITTEN RESUME

When preparing your resume, remember that a resume will not get you a job; that will come later from your interview. Rather, the sole purpose of a resume is to arouse enough interest to result in an interview. Try to imagine that you are the employer, reviewing many resumes: What would you want to see? What would bore you?

Since this resume may be your first contact with a company, spend enough time to prepare it well. You never have a second chance to make a first impression!

Content

Name and address: At the top of your resume, place your name, address and phone number. Professional certifications, such as C.P.A., should be included on the line with your name.

What makes a resume stand out?

• Most importantly, I look for a neat, well-organized, clean resume. A poor layout or smudges will take me to the next resume immediately. I also discard the flashy resumes that look more like a sales brochure.

• Misspelled words or other inaccuracies make me question the applicant's attention to detail, and I will put the resume aside.

• Since my time is limited, I prefer a one-page resume, especially if the applicant has only a few years experience. I also avoid verbose resumes that have too much information crammed onto the pages or those that have reduced the type size to squeeze in more information.

• I look for a clear job focus or objective. If I can't determine quickly why this job seeker has sent me a resume, I don't waste time trying to second guess the applicant.

• I scan for "buzz-words" — those acronyms, titles, hardware/software, certain degrees, etc. that relate specifically to the position for which I am recruiting. If one or more catch my attention, I likely will read the entire resume.

• Every company wants to know what you have accomplished thus far in your career. What have you contributed to the company's "bottom line"? What can you include to show that you have excelled in your jobs? I favor those resumes that contain actual figures or percentages that prove your achievements.

When composing your resume, constantly remind yourself that this piece of paper is the first impression a personnel or corporate recruiter will have of you. If it is too long or too wordy, you will be judged as longwinded. If the resume lacks focus, you will be perceived as undirected or uncertain of your career goals. If you fail to include achievements and accomplishments, the reader will question what you can contribute to their organization. Worst of all, if your resume is messy, you can bet you will never be called for an interview.

— by permission from Steve Hines, author of *Atlanta Jobs*, et al.

Objective: This will be the first section, after your name and address. If you are applying for a specific opening or in a specific industry, tailor your objective to fit. Remember, however, that if your resume states a specific objective (*e.g.*, sales) and you are applying for another (*e.g.*, management), you likely will not be considered. Thus, if you are not so sure about a specific objective, make it more open in nature.

Summary: A summary paragraph is optional, but it can be very effective, especially if you have some short, important data you wish the reader to see first, as an enticement to read further. Do not defeat its purpose by making it too long and thus lose its impact.

Employment: List your job title, company name, dates of employment, and description of job duties. Use reverse chronology (last job first), and be certain to include your achievements and accomplishments with each assignment.

Education: State the name of your college, the type of degree received, major and minor concentrations, and month/year you graduated. Definitely include honors, activities and elected positions. If you have more than one degree to include, list the most recent first.

Personal: This section is optional and the current trend now is to omit it, since your personal data should not affect your job performance, and therefore should not be a consideration in your job application.

Format

A resume should be only one or two pages, with a lay-out that is easy to understand. The traditional, chronological format is always acceptable, but topical formats are becoming increasingly popular. Topical formats allow you to summarize and emphasize your best experiences or achievements at the beginning of the resume. Select from three to five categories that summarize most of your experiences, and include these in an "Experience" section just before your "Employment" section.

You may use statements preceded by a "bullet" (a period or dot) rather than complete sentences, but don't have a resume that looks full of holes. Bullets are especially useful to emphasize accomplishments, but can be used to list responsibilities also. Italics, all capitals, and boldface print help break the monotony of a standard layout and also can add emphasis to outstanding achievements. However, don't overuse these devices, or you will dilute their effectiveness.

Appearance

Most important of all, your resume must be neat and clean. Do not adopt any style that looks gimmicky or like a sales brochure. Print your resume on single sheets, one side only. Use beige, cream, light gray, or plain white paper of good quality; never use a brightly colored paper. Do not use parchment paper, since it often does not photocopy or fax clearly.

Having prepared your resume, writing cover letters will be easy.

Where will you send the first copy of your resume?
As soon as you have your resume completed, send a copy into the **CareerSource Resume Bank**, following the instructions in Part 4, the blue pages. Your resume will be available for interested employers to review and to contact you when a job opening occurs. For your convenience, an addressed envelope is included at the end of this book.

COVER LETTERS

Remember that the purpose of a resume is to get you an interview and that it must be perfect since it is often the first material you will present to the company. The same is true of cover letters, and more:
- It will be read before your resume, and thus it establishes an even earlier impression of you than does your resume.
- Companies realize that you may have had your resume professionally prepared, and thus the cover letter could be a more accurate reflection of you than your resume.
- It serves as an introduction to your resume, an enticement to the reader to peruse your resume.
- It includes information not on your resume, but requested by the company, such as salary history, restrictions, and availability.

- It can zero in on specific experience you have that fits the needs of the company.
- It allows you to emphasize the accomplishments and achievements that illustrate your general qualifications.

It also can highlight information contained in your resume that is important to the job for which you are applying. However, the purpose of the cover letter is *not* to repeat the same information in your resume. That is not necessary, since your cover letter always will be accompanied by your resume. Rather, you should emphasize factors you feel will be important to the reader and will encourage him/her to read your resume and invite you for an interview. Examples are included at the end of this chapter.

Thus, the primary rule in writing a cover letter is this: Keep it brief and to the point. A short, concise cover letter is always more effective than a long, detailed one. Recruiters often feel that a long, wordy letter indicates an excessively verbose person. Don't trap yourself by trying to include too much information.

Format

All cover letters have the same basic format, with some variations to suit specific purposes.

1) *Purpose*: The Purpose paragraph explains why you are contacting the company and for what position(s) you would like to be considered. One or two sentences should be enough for this.

2) *Qualifications*: Although the Qualifications section will be the longest section, it should highlight only the best of your qualifications, not explain in detail. Stress your accomplishments and achievements, and the specific experience or background that qualifies you for your job objective.

This section may be one or two paragraphs, depending on your layout, but it should never be more than eight or ten sentences, preferably less. You are trying to make a strong first impression by emphasizing a few hard-hitting facts. If you dilute this with a lengthy description, you will lose the impact.

3) *Closing*: End your cover letter with a standard closing paragraph of two or three sentences, similar to this: "Thank you for

13

your time and consideration, and I will call you in a few days to confirm that you have received this. I am available for an interview at your convenience."

If you have been asked for other information such as current salary or relocation status, include it here. "My current salary is $45,000 and I am seeking compensation in the $50,000 range." Or, "I lived in Chicago a few years ago and my knowledge of the city would be very helpful for your sales position there. I also am available for relocation elsewhere."

VOICE RESUME

During your job search, you will encounter many opportunities when you will be called upon to relate your qualifications and objectives. Some of these situations you will have created through your specific networking efforts, but there also will be other times when someone simply will turn to you and ask, "What do you do?"

You should be prepared for these opportunities with your "voice resume," a short oral synopsis of your full, written resume. Since you may have only a few moments of your listeners' time, you need an answer that will quickly stress the most important factors you want your listeners to know while you have their undivided attention.

Composing your Voice Resume

What should you include? First answer these questions:
- What are the requirements for the job I am seeking?
- What in my background fits those requirements?

Armed with that information, you can begin to separate relevant material from information that can be discussed later. Probably the worst mistake job seekers make with their written resume is making it too long and detailed, and the same is true regarding your voice resume. Keep it short and relevant to your job objective, saying just enough to show you are qualified and to keep your listener's attention.

Here are some factors to consider:

Job objective: In as few words as possible, explain the field or type of job you are seeking.

Education and training: Some professions emphasize academics, and if you have the right degree, you should mention it. Familiarity with computer hardware and software programs is becoming a necessity in most professions, and certification is nearly always an important asset. Career-related seminars and training programs also may be added, if they are well-known.

Qualities: Some examples are good communicator, self-motivated, well-organized, aggressive, etc.

Accomplishments and achievements: This is an integral part of both your written and oral resumes, and must always be included. Remembering that corporations are all "bottom-line"-oriented, you should also stress any increases in revenue or decreases in expenses due to your efforts.

Prior employment: If you seek to advance your current career path, then your past and current employment may be the most important information to stress. Condense it into a few sentences, stating job titles or descriptive titles and the responsibilities you have had.

Other experience: If your objective is to change careers, mention specific experiences that relate to your new field.

Organize your information into a clear, concise 30-second "voice resume." Practice it aloud many times until you are comfortable repeating it and try it with a friend for critique.

SmartFax Job Support

Who's Hiring in Atlanta offers you advantages and opportunities not available to other job seekers, one of which is SmartFax Job Support. As part of this support system, you can have your voice resume available for potential employers to access by phone. Not only will they have your written resume to review, but in addition they can hear you in your own words explain your qualifications. This powerful tool is not available to other applicants, and you should take full advantage of this opportunity to impress a potential employer. SmartFax cover sheets can direct employers to your voice resume.

Throughout *Who's Hiring in Atlanta,* more uses for SmartFax will be suggested. The blue pages of Part 4 will explain how to incorporate SmartFax into your job search, and your SmartFax card is on the inside cover of this book. Once you have activated your SmartFax file, your job search will take a quantum leap!

OTHER DOCUMENTS

References page: List your references with their name, company, title, address, and phone numbers on a separate page. Three references are sufficient, probably one professional, one personal, and one academic (for recent grads) or former employer. Key clients, former supervisors, or peers are also good choices.

Salary history: Companies often require your salary history, especially when responding to classified ads. Construct a separate page that includes each of your employers and the positions you held with the corresponding salary. However, if you are a recent grad or have only a few years employment, you can include your salary information in your cover letter or fax cover sheet.

Thank-you notes: Send a short note to thank interviewers for their time and consideration after an interview. Emphasize in one or two sentences why you fit the position, and make your note more personal by referring to a topic you discussed in the interview. Also send thank-you notes to individuals who help you during your job search by supplying a lead, a contact, or some other useful information.

Business cards: On those occasions when you have the opportunity to discuss your job search with someone, you should exchange business cards. These cards contain your contact data as well as brief information or your job objective. Do not attempt to condense your resume onto this small card, lest it look crowded and messy. As with your resume, do not design a flashy format or use colored paper.

Broadcast cover letter: The SmartFax broadcast cover letter is designed to create a positive initial impression of you by stating your abilities and career objective on one page, followed by your resume. The reader will appreciate this helpful summary, and then refer to your resume. SmartFax will design this page for you when you activate your SmartFax card (see instructions in Part 4).

Sample business cards

GEOFFREY WILLIAMS
BBA, University of Georgia, 1995
Marketing major, 3.4 GPA
Dean's List, Intramural Sports, Fraternity President
Sales experience

3445 Piedmont Road NE, #R-3
Atlanta, GA 30342
(404) 278-7873

Human Resources Generalist

LINDA B. ANALTO
Recruiting • Benefits • Employee Relations
12 years experience

3890 Little Tongue Road, San Antonio, TX 78204
(512) 898-5241

BS/MS, Mechanical Engineering
Seven years manufacturing experience

JAMES P. NELSON
PepsiCo (1992 - 1996)
Proctor & Gamble (1989 - 1992)

248 Main Street, Milwaukee, WI 78906
(888) 111-1111

Sample chronological/functional resume format

CHARLES G. PULLER
244 Mecklenburg Avenue
Greensboro, NC 28664
(919) 954-1042

Objective

Manufacturing Management, either in production, operations or administration, where education, abilities and experience can be best utilized.

Experience

JOHN H. HARLAND COMPANY, printer of bank stationery and other commercial printing. (1987 - Present)
PRODUCTION MANAGER, Greensboro, NC (1993 - present):
Have profit center responsibility for subsidiary involved in technical printing (forms, stationery, cards and mail order checks) and related direct mail operations. Direct the activities of four Supervisors managing a staff of 40 persons. Oversee inventory/quality control, efficiency, personnel, audit preparation and purchasing. Extensive involvement in overall company efficiency planning.
Accomplishments: Reduced labor costs by 5% per month. Boosted profit margin by 4% (from minus 2% to plus 2% level). Won "Best Quality Division" awards (1993 and 1994). Reduced turnover from over 50% to under 20%.

ASSISTANT PLANT MANAGER, Orlando, FL (1989 - 1992):
Supervised staff of 15 administrative employees in a check printing facility. Directed all daily operations in such areas as personnel management, accounting, safety, audit preparation, billing, customer service, purchasing, security, attitude surveys, customer relations and P&L statements. Served as Sales/Plant Coordinator for 13 Sales Representatives in Colorado, Wyoming, Utah and Montana.
Accomplishments: Heavily involved in planning and implementation of move into new printing facility. Received three "A's" on periodic plant audits. Developed new Employee Training Manual later utilized in three plants. Established procedure that reduced weekly billing errors by over 40%.

PLANT SUPERINTENDENT, Orlando, FL (1987 - 1989):
Directed activities of 50 production employees and five supervisors in a check printing facility. Managed production planning, scheduling, maintenance, quality control, inventory control and cost containment.
Accomplishments: Increased operational efficiency by 12% per year. Improved delivery time from 79% to 93%. Established quality standards for employees, reducing rerun rate from 3.4% to 2.6%.

Education

MASTER OF BUSINESS ADMINISTRATION, concentration in accounting, University of North Carolina at Greensboro, 1995. GPA 3.8/4.0.

BACHELOR OF SCIENCE in Industrial Management, North Carolina State University, 1986. GPA 3.7/4.0.

References available on request.

Sample topical resume format

SUSAN W. LINDSEY
5849 Bacchus Way
Richmond, Virginia 23226
(804) 355-0912

A results-oriented manager, with more than seven years of achievement in training, development and administration. Proficient in German and French. Available for travel and relocation.

OBJECTIVE
    A management position in training and development or product support.

EDUCATION
    BOSTON COLLEGE, Chestnut Hill, Massachusetts, 1986
    BACHELOR OF ARTS in Education, *magna cum laude*
    Dean's List, all semesters
    Most Valuable Player, Water Polo, Fall 1983. Varsity Letter in Swimming.

PROFESSIONAL ABILITIES

TRAINING:
- Received special recognition for superior technical training of co-workers in specialized instructional strategies.
- Trained and supervised more than 150 workers in basic skills competence, providing effective corrective and positive feedback.
- Documented detailed policies and procedures to enhance delivery of organizational objectives.
- Effectively analyzed causes of worker performance problems; recommended, implemented and monitored the alternatives.
- Conducted ongoing performance appraisals at regular intervals.
- Motivated and coached workers to improve productivity and to achieve successful performance.

PROGRAM DESIGN:
- Organized, developed, implemented courseware and systems for work management, basics instruction and training development.
- Analyzed job tasks, established measurable objectives, tracked performance and successful completion of assignments.
- Created successful performance feedback systems and established system to monitor and record results.
- Planned and produced audio-visual courseware.
- Organized, planned and conducted educational tours, related to increasing job knowledge and performance.

COMMUNICATION SKILLS:
- Developed and delivered presentations to groups of up to 100 people.
- Counseled, interviewed and negotiated with co-workers, management, public officials and the general public to enhance inter-communication and working relationships.
- Edited reports, researched, composed and distributed written information and materials.

EMPLOYMENT HISTORY

1991 - 1996	Educator, Stuttgart, West Germany Department of Defense Dependent Schools
1986 - 1991	Educator, Richmond City Public School System

19

(Sample Cover Letter)

879 Ridge Point Drive
Smyrna, GA 30339
April 7, 1995

Mr. John Thompson, Director of Personnel
Chicken Little Company
456 Corn Street
College Park, GA 30365

Dear Mr. Thompson:

Thank you for your time on the phone today and for the information regarding your current need for an Industrial Engineer. As you requested, I am enclosing my resume for your review.

During my three years with ABC Textiles, I have been responsible for implementing and managing projects very similar to the ones you described to me. A few of my recent assignments include these:
>   -- Organized and conducted a study to determine and document causes of dye department downtime.
>   -- Designed, estimated cost and proposed layout for relocation of maintenance shop, resulting in a 20% increase in efficiency.
>   -- Assisted Safety Department in training employees on the proper use of new machinery, resulting in a decrease of 25% in time lost due to accidents.

Thank you again, and I look forward to hearing from you soon. My current salary is $37,000 annually, and I am available for relocation.

Sincerely yours,

Lynn K. Parsons
(404) 433-4898

SUSAN B. SWIFT
3829 Helen Lane
Durham, NC 27702
(919) 282-4837

REFERENCES

HENRY C. ROBIN (client)
Purchasing Manager
North Carolina Food and Drug Distributors, Inc.
2173 Coventry Lane
Charlotte, NC 28760
(404) 822-9273

HAROLD T. HILL (former employer)
Southeast R
Sunshine F
7893 Chatt
Atlanta, GA
(404) 522-9

BETTY W.
Eastland, V
8384 Holcc
Chapel Hill
(919) 777-1
(919) 929-9

LURLINE C. HARRIS
231 E. Rock Springs Rd NE
Atlanta, GA 30324
(404) 876-2388

SALARY HISTORY

Synergism Systems (March 1992 - present)
 Director of Compensation and Benefits $65,000

Citizens and Southern National Bank (May 1989 - March 1992)
 Senior Compensation Analyst $50,000
 Compensation Analyst   45,000
 Exempt Recruiter   39,000

(Note: Income reduction accepted in order to enter
corporate Human Resources.)

Blinders Personnel Service (July 1986 - May 1989)
 Accounting Division Manager $49,000
 Senior Recruiter   40,000
 Staff Recruiter   18,000

Fax Transmission
Please Deliver to Recipient Immediately

To: Jane Snow	From: Job Seeker
Human Resource Director	123 Main Street
ABC Corporation	Atlanta, GA 30000
(404) 555-1212	(770) 555-1212

Dear Ms. Snow:

I am contacting you to explore placement opportunities with your company. My resume is included with this fax, and following is some additional information about my career goals that might be helpful:

Field of specialty: Accounting

Position desired: Accounting Manager

Years relative experience: 5 Years

Secondary position accepted: Staff Accountant

Education: B.S., Accounting, Georgia State, 1989

Travel acceptable: 2 Nights Per Week

Relocation: Prefer Atlanta, Will Consider Southeast

Thank you for your time and consideration. I look forward to hearing from you soon. I am available for an interview at your convenience.

PART 2

MARKETING YOURSELF

– How to Conduct a Direct Marketing Campaign –

Mass-mailing your resume is the oldest and simplest method of job search, and undoubtedly the most popular. It can be done at your convenience during evenings, weekends, or at any time you are not busy with other activities. Since it requires no face-to-face or verbal contact, it feels comfortable or at least non-threatening. Thus, this approach is tried by almost every job seeker.

There are two approaches to this method:

1) a selective mailing, in which you target companies in your industry or for your specialty, and

2) a "resume blanket," when you contact many companies, especially large, major corporations that hire hundreds of new employees annually.

Procedure

In planning to whom you will send your resume or other background information, imagine a "bulls-eye" target. In the center of the target, you will have large, major corporations that regularly hire hundreds of applicants annually. You will want to contact them at the onset of your job search, so that you can move on to other sources.

Now aim for the next ring, those industries in which you have experience, product knowledge, or some other useful information. Lastly, identify smaller companies that have job vacancies for which you are qualified. The best source to these companies is through some form of job networking, and how to develop a job network is explained later in this chapter.

"Part 7: Company Directory" details information on the largest local employers, including their employment figures and the types of backgrounds each hires on a regular basis, and that is followed by lists of smaller firms. Since the individuals handling personnel recruiting frequently change, specific names are not included. In fact, sending your resume to the wrong person or an ex-employee will delay your application, so you should phone the company to inquire to whom you should address your mail.

Using SmartFax Job Support

Who's Hiring in Atlanta offers you the option of faxing your information by using SmartFax instead of spending countless hours or days doing this direct marketing yourself. Your personal SmartFax card with ten free units is on the inside front cover of this book and complete instructions how to use this technology is included in Part 4.

SmartFax allows you to send your resume instantly to any of 3,000 Atlanta employers, freeing up your time to locate job vacancies with other companies. SmartFax is constantly updating the company addresses, fax numbers, and personnel recruiters, so that your information will always reach the appropriate person. As new companies open offices here, SmartFax will add them to its database.

You can select individual companies or choose to blanket many companies at once from several pre-packaged options:
- Atlanta's 50 or 100 largest employers
- The largest companies in 50 industries where your expertise may be highly regarded
- Atlanta's permanent and temporary employment services
- **SmartSearch Job Locator** (described below)

In addition, many of the smaller companies you identify through your networking efforts will be included in the 3000 companies in Part 7, and you can use SmartFax to contact any of them. Moreover, many companies have developed computerized files of applicants, and SmartFax can add your resume directly into these databases.

SmartSearch Job Locator

Would you like to send your resume to the Atlanta companies that most often hire for your specific job skills? Would you like to contact those companies overnight with little effort on your part, and cheaper than the cost of doing it yourself? **SmartSearch Job Locator** offers you this ability.

Who's Hiring has researched the personnel recruiting patterns of the 500 most active local employers and the specific job skills they frequently seek. Using SmartFax, you can choose from 25 job skills categories and have your resume faxed to the companies that often hire for your specific background and qualifications. How to use this feature is explained in Part 4, the blue pages of this book.

Conclusion

The Direct Marketing job search technique is included first because it is the most popular approach and the one most job seekers try at the beginning of their job search. Unfortunately, most applicants waste too much time determining which companies to contact, researching addresses and contact names, typing cover letters and envelops, licking stamps, and finally driving to the post office. That time could be spent in far more constructive efforts, especially networking. Remember, you will never find a job while you a chained to your desk with paperwork.

Use your time wisely – after all, "time is money," as the old cliché goes. Using SmartFax to handle the labor of sending your employment information will allow you to spend your time researching companies, developing leads, and preparing for interviews.

As part of your overall organization, you should maintain a record of every company you contact and the results. SmartFax will help with your organization by sending you a list of companies and phone numbers to which your information was sent, and you should make a similar list for the other companies you contact.

SmartFax will not do everything for you, but it will take over much of the time-consuming and mundane parts of your job search. In addition, you will gain the satisfaction that you are doing something constructive toward your job search. You may uncover an opportunity for an interview now or for a networking source later.

– How to Make Personal Contact with Companies –

Since making a personal contact is very time-consuming, don't waste your time by blindly calling companies that you know little about. That random approach generally is not effective, in time, cost, or results. Plan your time wisely, and concentrate your direct contact efforts on the companies that regularly hire for your specialty, on an industry that can use your specific experience, or to follow up on a job lead. Use the Direct Marketing method described earlier to approach other companies or to blanket a large number of companies.

First compile a list of the companies you plan to contact. Scan through the Employers' Directory in Part 7, and mark companies in which you have a special interest. Detailed information is given for the largest local employers, including the types of applicants frequently sought. Your general knowledge of the field you are targeting likely will give you more companies to contact. You also may wish to include reference materials you have obtained from local chambers of commerce, or information you found in the public library, such as manufacturers' guides, Dun and Bradstreet lists, etc.

Be certain to keep records of each company you contacted, the person with whom you spoke, the date of your contact, and any information you obtained. This organization is extremely important, since you may need to refer to it later.

Whom should I contact?

Most, if not all, career counselors would suggest that you should make your initial company contact with a "hiring authority," that is, a department manager who has control over the personnel requirements in that department. One reason is that this person may have current or projected personnel needs which have not been requisitioned from Human Resources or Personnel Recruiting. Secondly, this manager will most likely be the ultimate decision-maker with whom you would eventually interview, and thus you are a step ahead by starting here.

Most personnel managers strongly feel that you should contact them first. Their function within the company is to interview and screen applicants, following federal and local statutes, as well as company policies and procedures, which may be unknown to executives attempting to conduct their own hiring. Those personnel professionals have been trained to interview carefully and thoroughly, and they should be more in tune to the overall needs of the company, not just one department.

Your objective is to find the most direct route into a company and the source that can get you hired. Although personnel departments can be useful to you if you are unable to determine the appropriate department manager or hiring authority, your results generally will be better if you are able to identify a specific manager. Through research or networking, try to locate these decision-makers for your Direct Contact, but if you are unable to find this information, then go through personnel. In addition, you can increase your exposure by contacting both personnel and a hiring authority.

"Cold Calling" procedure

Many people have a fear of the phone, and if you are one of them, you must strive to overcome this problem. Preparing and rehearsing what you plan to say on the phone will help, as well as having your "voice resume" ready to use.

When the company receptionist answers your call, ask for the department or job title you wish to contact, or the individual you are seeking. When this person's secretary answers, you probably will be asked for the nature of your call, and you should explain your background, using your voice resume. Most likely at this point, you will be instructed to send your resume, in which case ask for the name of the person to whom you should address it, and record the name in your notebook. Don't be upset, however, if you are not given the name; some companies have a policy forbidding the disclosure of employee names.

If you actually do get the opportunity to speak with the person you seek, you must be prepared. This is your chance to make a positive first impression, have a brief telephone interview and also schedule a personal interview. Fortunately, you are a step ahead, because you already have composed and rehearsed a brief summary of your qualifications – your voice resume! You may have only one shot here, so make it count.

If your contact states that no job opportunities are available there, try to turn the call into a networking or information call. Ask for suggestions in your job search. Is he/she aware of openings with other

27

companies for your background? If you were instructed to send your resume, include a cover letter that refers to your conversation.

Although you should contact department managers whenever possible, this is not to say that you should ignore Human Resources or Recruiting. In fact, if you are told by the department manager that no opening currently exists, I suggest you also contact Personnel, either personally or through SmartFax. Individual departments and their managers seldom keep a resume file, but Human Resources often will, and another need for your background may arise later.

Using SmartFax for your Direct Contact

SmartFax Job Support can add several new possibilities to your direct contact approach. Many of the companies you identify as a potential employer will be included among the 3,000 companies in the Employers' Directory in Part 7, and you can fax your resume before you call the following day. This gives your source the opportunity to review your resume before you speak personally.

In addition, when you make contact with company officials who request that you send your resume, imagine the impact you can make by faxing your resume immediately after the conversation! They will be impressed with your promptness and may interpret that as an indication of your performance as an employee.

Summary

Be selective and don't attempt to reach too many companies, since making a personal contact is time consuming.

SmartFax will blanket the largest employers for you, but you still may wish to identify specific hiring authorities within those companies for a direct contact. Having your resume with both personnel and a specific department manager will increase your opportunities to be noticed. In addition, many Human Resources Departments have installed computer databases that will store your resume indefinitely, to be retrieved later when an opening for your background occurs.

Finally, by this point, you probably have begun to see the advantages of adding SmartFax Job Support to your job search, and as your job search progresses, you will find many more uses as well.

– How to Respond to Classified Help-Wanted Ads –

For obtaining employment in a specific city or region, the largest source of announced openings is the classified ads section of the Sunday edition of the primary newspaper for that area. In addition to newspapers, another excellent source of classified ads is in professional and trade magazines, usually on the last few pages of the publication.

Most newspapers group their job openings into many categories, such as "engineering," "data processing," "management," "sales," etc., and your background may fit into several. Examine the want-ads and determine the job categories that apply to you. Circle in red the openings, both company and personnel agency, for which you plan to apply.

As part of your organization, keep a folder or notebook for the classified ads to which you respond. After you have finished scrutinizing the ads, cut out the company (not agency) ads you circled and tape them onto blank pages in your notebook. Leave sufficient space around the ads to record information regarding your activity with each company.

Now, cut out the personnel agency ads. You may notice that one agency is advertising several jobs for which you will want to apply. Write the name of each agency at the top of a page and then tape the corresponding ads to the page. Leave space on the page to record activity with that agency.

Now go back to the company ads and contact each one. You will find that most ads request that you fax your resume, and fortunately for you, you have SmartFax! While other applicants are standing in line to fax their resume, you will already have your resume on the recruiter's desk.

If the company included its phone number or did not specifically forbid phone calls, I suggest you call them and ask if you can speak with someone regarding the opening. If you do get through to the recruiter, you must be prepared for an interview then, so before calling, you should practice your interviewing skills and voice resume. Also, here is another SmartFax opportunity to impress the interviewer by faxing your resume to the company immediately after your conversation.

Responding to personnel agency advertisements will be slightly different. Operating procedures vary from agency to agency, some requiring that you send a resume first, others requesting you to come in for a personal interview and bring your resume. If you are instructed to send your resume, ask to whom you should address it and record that name in your notebook on the page for that agency. Some agencies will have several persons handling the same opening, and so there may not be a specific contact person.

If you have utilized a SmartFax package that included personnel agencies, they already may have your resume. In this case, ask the status of your file and if they will be able to arrange interviews for you. Offer to come to their office for a personal interview if that will encourage them to work harder for you.

Just as you would prepare for a face-to-face interview, be ready for a phone screening whenever you contact a company or employment agency. Telephone interviews are usually short and cover only basic information. Typical questions will revolve around why you are seeking new employment and if you have the experience needed for the job. If you pass this quick test, you will be invited for an interview.

In addition to locating current job openings, scanning the want ads can yield other information. You can determine which disciplines and industries are growing, because these will be mentioned most often. Conversely, shrinking job categories will be conspicuous by their absence. If you are contemplating a career change or undecided on which career to pursue, reviewing these ads can help you decide. Further, if there is a retailer near you who sells many newspapers from across the country, you can compare the size of the want ads from several cities to get an idea of the job prospects in each city.

– How to Utilize Permanent Employment Services –

The number of job openings represented collectively by the various personnel agencies in large metropolitan areas can be numbered in the tens of thousands. There are literally hundreds of these agencies in many cities, filling the Yellow Pages in several different listing categories, including "employment," executive search," "personnel agencies," "temporary agencies," and more. Because they represent so many companies and opportunities, they should be an invaluable source for you.

Selecting your agencies

The best method for locating agencies is to call the personnel department (or a specific department manager) of a few major local companies and ask which permanent employment firms they use for your discipline and if they would recommend a specific recruiter there. This has the advantage of not only finding an agency, but also talking with a corporate personnel professional who may have other suggestions as well. In addition, when you then call the agencies that were recommended, be certain to mention the company and/or the individual who recommended them, and you will be guaranteed a warm reception!

Another good source is to network by asking friends and business associates which agencies they have used and would recommend. This is especially helpful if the person you ask has a background similar to your own.

Although you should not waste your time calling every agency in the phone book, nevertheless you should probe the Yellow Pages under the headings "Employment Agencies" and "Executive Search Consultants" to see if there are agencies who specialize in your field. Oftentimes these agencies will have your industry as part of their name (e.g., "Restaurant Recruiters" or "Insurance Personnel Search") or they may have a box ad that mentions your specialty.

Still another excellent source is the back pages of trade newspapers and magazines. Agencies who advertise in these specialized journals usually concentrate on that discipline in their recruiting.

But all this research takes time, and time is a priceless commodity when you're seeking employment. Your most effective approach is to have SmartFax send your resume to all the local employment agencies at the beginning of your job search. Agencies that have current job openings will call immediately, and you could have interviews scheduled long before you would have your research completed.

Procedure

When possible, you should visit with the agencies you have selected for two reasons:

    1) to determine if they can adequately represent you, and

    2) to make a personal impression on them, so they can better present you to their clients.

Interview with the agency as though it is the company with whom you hope to be employed. Many companies have established a strong rapport with the agency(s) they use and have great confidence in the agency's opinion. Thus, you must impress the agency enough to be referred on to these key clients.

At the end of your interview, ask how soon you can expect to hear from them and when you will be sent on an interview. Also, seek their frank appraisal of your resume and interviewing skills, and ask if they have any suggestions or recommendations for you to consider.

During this interview, you should ask questions that will help you to evaluate the agency, the agency interviewer, and the assistance they can offer you. Personnel agencies have notoriously high employee turnover, and it is not unlikely that this interviewer has been at the job for only a very short while. If this is the case, an opinion of your resume and interviewing skills may be totally useless. In addition, this trainee may not understand your background and experience, and will not be able to present you to potential clients.

Working with Agencies

You have every reason to expect the agencies you select to treat you honestly and fairly. They should never send you on interviews for which you are not qualified or refer you to positions in which you have no interest. You should be briefed before each interview regarding the nature of the position, promotional potential, salary range, and company background. The best agencies will maintain files in their office of company literature for you to study, including annual reports and recruiting information, especially for their best clients. Many agencies also know their client's interviewers and interviewing techniques.

In return, you should treat your agencies with the same respect you expect from them. If you are not interested in a specific interview, tell the agency why; this will help your recruiter to be more selective for future interviews. Always show up for your interviews or advise the agency well in advance to cancel; most agencies will not work with you once you have failed to show for an scheduled interview. Call your agency recruiter immediately after each interview to relay your impressions of the interview.

Before you accept a position through a personnel agency, determine your legal liability, if any, to the agency. For example, are there any circumstances under which you may be held responsible for all or part of their fee? If you are uncomfortable with any part of the agreement, obtain a written waiver from the agency before you accept the job.

Summary

Major metropolitan areas will have hundreds of employment agencies, and you cannot possibly contact all of them in a timely and cost effective manner. Again, this a job for SmartFax. Let SmartFax distribute your resume to the agencies for you while you seek out other leads or prepare for interviews.

Personnel agencies, both permanent and temporary, can be an excellent source and you should use them when possible, but recognize they do have limitations. If you are seeking employment in a very narrow field (e.g., public relations or staff marketing), they likely will be of little help. If there is something in your background that makes you less marketable than their other applicants, you will not have good results with them. As stated before, the best approach with agencies is to ask for a frank analysis of the help they can offer you.

– How to Work through
Temporary Employment Agencies –

Companies sometimes need additional help, but for many reasons are reluctant to take on new, permanent employees. An increasingly popular solution to this dilemma is to hire temporary employees, utilizing the services of a temporary employment agency. These "temps," as they are euphemistically termed, are hired only for as long as needed or to fill a short-term replacement.

Most often this is for hourly or clerical work, but some firms offer long-term contracts, especially for engineers and other specialized work. There are also temporary agencies specializing in short-term professional-level openings, most often in accounting and data processing.

Large cities will have at least as many temporary agencies as permanent, and you must not spend your valuable time attempting to contact each one. This is another job for SmartFax. While you work on developing other sources and preparing for interviews, SmartFax will send your resume instantly to all the local temporary agencies. When the agencies call with temp assignments, you can decide if they fit into your current plans.

Advantages of working "temp"

Working a temporary assignment offers you three new options for finding other employment:

(1) The position may be "temp-to-perm," that is, a job that may become permanent within a short period. These positions may be for any discipline, including clerical, accounting, engineering, data processing, marketing, etc., and can be for short- or long-term assignments. When applying through a temporary agency, always ask what they have available in "temp-to-perm."

(2) While on the assignment, you can job-network through other company employees, vendors, or clients. Comparing job search techniques and information with other temps can be a useful exchange of ideas. Permanent employees may be aware of vacancies within their company or openings they learned about through clients. You also may be able to discuss your job search with vendors or clients, but be discreet.

34

(3) Once inside the company, you can review the company's "in-house job postings" i.e., listings of jobs currently available with the company, including functional descriptions and basic requirements. You can review the information and then apply for positions for which you qualify.

Another reason for working temp is the opportunity to learn new skills, or maintain and improve existing skills. For example, if your background is in data processing, working a temp position in your field might expose you to new software or new applications for procedures you already knew. At the very least, you would preserve your current level of competency.

Many temporary agencies offer training classes in the new, "hot" fields, especially in data processing. These classes are free and you can include the added knowledge on your resume.

In the past few years, many large corporations have established in-house temporary services that staff positions primarily for their firm. Nearly all of these positions offer a route to permanent, full-time employment with that company, either through "temp-to-perm" or company job postings.

Conclusion

As you see, working temp offers many advantages. It provides you with income, skill and knowledge development, networking potential, and the possibility of permanent employment. Also, many temporary agencies now offer excellent benefits, including health insurance, retirement packages, profit sharing, etc. Best of all, you can continue your job search in your time off, showing that you are currently employed.

One major downside, however, is that you will lose your unemployment benefits while working temp. But if your unemployment benefits have already expired or if the amount is less than you can earn working temporary, you should consider using this tool.

– How to Develop a Job Network –

More people find their new jobs through networking than through all other sources combined! That is one of the major reasons for using SmartFax: SmartFax can handle much of your paperwork, freeing up your time to network.

First, understand what job networking is not. It is not an excuse to abuse your friends and relatives by bombarding them with constant calls for contacts or by pressuring them to use their influence when you sense their reluctance. Certainly you will want to include them in your job networking, but there are so many other potential networking sources at your disposal that you should not test the patience of any person. If you find yourself calling the same people, then you are not conducting a correct job search.

There are several approaches to job networking, all of which can generate many leads and interviews. Before starting to network, however, you already must have developed your "voice resume," described in Part 1. If for some reason, you skipped that discussion, refer to it now. You will be using this oral resume often, and now is still another of those times.

Developing A Job Network

Start by compiling a list of individuals you want to contact, beginning with the friends and relatives who will be the most sympathetic and supportive. They will be less critical, and the mistakes you make with them will be learning experiences. With these close associates, you should ask for a critique of your phone manner before you continue on with more calls. Stress that you are seeking constructive criticism and you would appreciate their frank appraisal. Practice your voice resume with them and ask their opinion.

Now expand this list to include business associates, then social, professional, civic, and church contacts, and anyone else you think could help. However, if you are currently employed and discretion is utmost, you may wish to contact only close, trusted associates.

In compiling this list, you also should predetermine why you are including each person. How can they help you? What information do you think they might share with you?

36

Now develop other networking sources.

• Establish new contacts by volunteering your free time with a non-profit charity or other organization.

• Attend the meetings of professional associations that pertain to your field, and discuss your job search with the local officers. (See next section for more discussion of this source.)

• College alumni groups are an outstanding source. Locate the local chapter president and attend the alumni meetings, planning to job-network there.

• When at social gatherings, listen out for people who might lead you to a source.

• Call the appropriate academic department head at a local college and ask for suggestions.

• If possible, discuss your situation with current or former clients.

• When attending job fairs, network with other job seekers. Ask for recommendations for personnel agencies, compare job search techniques, exchange business cards, etc.

• Use information interviews with industry experts to gain the "inside information."

• Attend trade shows and conventions. Exchange business cards with company representatives and then call them later for job leads with their company or other job search suggestions.

As you see, networking has infinite possibilities. Think about it, and you surely will come up with many more potential sources for contacts.

Phone each one and let them know that you are actively seeking new employment. What questions can you ask that will produce the information you seek? Have your questions written down in front of you, so you will be certain to cover everything you planned.

- "Do you have any job search suggestions?"

- Do you know of someone else who has recently conducted a job search?" You can call that person to ask for more suggestions.

- "Do you have any contacts or know of anyone in my field who could be helpful?"

- "Is there a career consultant, personnel agent, or advisor you know and would recommend?"

- "Are you aware of any professional associations or job network groups that I should contact?"

Conclusion

Don't expect instant results or that all of your efforts will be productive. Accept the fact that although most of your leads will not be useful, you must follow through on all of them anyway. That is the slow, time-consuming part of job networking, but by having SmartFax to handle so much of your other work, you will have more time to apply to this source.

Since networking is the most effective source overall, you should plan to spend much of your time cultivating leads and contacts, and then following through on them. Don't let all the dead ends deter you; sooner or later, one or more of your leads will bear fruit. It only takes the one "right" lead to land your new job!

– How to Network through Professional Associations –

Too few job seekers are aware of the excellent job search potential found in their professional associations. Not only do these groups offer excellent opportunities for networking, but also they frequently have well-developed career placement and career enhancement programs, and some even sponsor job fairs.

There is an organization covering virtually every conceivable job description, industry, or academic discipline. *National Trade and Professional Associations of the United States* is a catalogue that lists thousands of trade and professional associations and labor unions with national memberships. Even more complete is the *Encyclopedia of Associations*, a multi-volume work that includes detailed information. These publications are available at most public libraries.

"Part 6: Professional Associations" includes the largest and most active local associations and their officers, and you may wish to determine others. Some of the larger associations also sponsor smaller, specialized sub-groups. In many cases, you may fax your resume to the association's job coordinator using SmartFax.

Most associations meet monthly and welcome visitors and potential members, in addition to their current membership. With a little preparation beforehand, you can successfully job-network at any meeting – professional association, alumni group, business meeting, or whatever.

Contact the national headquarters of your association and ask for the local chapter president, and then inquire about their direct career assistance, if any. Call one of those officers to confirm the meeting date, place, fee, and program of the next meeting, and then indicate that you would like to attend. Ask this person to meet you and introduce you to a few members.

Now set your objectives for the meeting. What do you hope to accomplish? You will want to meet some officers, certainly the president and/or the job coordinator. Ask if there are members who recently completed a job search, and then try to locate them to discuss your current search and to ask for suggestions.

Plan what you will wear – business attire, of course. Carry enough business cards to hand out, as well as a few resumes to give to key people. Take a small, pocket-size notebook to record quick information. Plan to use your "voice resume" often at the meeting.

At the meeting, remember your objectives. Don't spend too much time with one person, or you may run out of time. Ask open-ended questions, and then listen; people are always more impressed with good listeners than they are with good talkers! Do not pass out too many resumes, three at the most, or you will seem too opportunistic. Record names and information in your notebook, but don't waste time recording too much now; you can do that later.

If you have the inclination and the time available, volunteer to help on a committee or such. You will make some valuable contacts and begin to feel more comfortable at the meetings.

Immediately after the meeting, record your results. Whom did you meet (name, company, job title, association function, etc.)? What follow-up do you plan? Is there someone you met and with whom you would like to schedule an "information interview"? What would you want to do differently at the next meeting?

You should send a thank-you note to the person who introduced you at the meeting and enclose your business card. Are there others you need to write and/or send a resume?

Planning what you will do at these meetings will make you less nervous and self-conscious, plus you will accomplish more. You can use this procedure to network at other meetings as well (e.g., college alumni groups, social gatherings, etc.) As with so much of your job search, it only takes organization and preparation.

PART 3

INTERVIEWING TIPS

The most important factor in interviewing well is <u>preparation</u>:

<u>Research the company,</u> and when possible, research the job and interviewer. Learn as much about the company as timely possible, but don't feel that you must know more than the interviewer.

• Most importantly, know the company's products or services. What do they offer, provide, manufacture, or sell?

• What is their annual growth and how profitable are they?

• What can you find out about their industry in general, including competitors?

• What is their ranking within their industry?

• Research the company's history.

• Try to determine their reputation. Are they considered aggressive? What is their personnel turnover rate? How are they regarded by their customers?

Researching most of the company data is easy, and there are many sources. The simplest method is to call the company and ask for an annual report, information brochure, or recruiting information to be mailed to you. If the company declines, as many privately-held companies will, or if you are short on time, go to your college placement center or the public library. Some good reference books include *Standard and Poor's, Moody's, Million Dollar Directory, American Corporate Families* and *Thomas Register of American Manufacturers.*

Networking is also a good source. Ask friends or business contacts if they are familiar with the company; however, keep in mind you may be hearing biased information or rumor, and treat this information accordingly. If you know some of the company's clients, you can carefully and discreetly call them for information.

Anticipate certain questions and be ready with your answers. Before your first interview, sit at your desk and write down at least 25 possible questions an interviewer might ask you. Plan your response to each question, then rehearse those answers aloud; even better, audio or video tape your response and then critique your performance. After each interview, add to your list new questions you were asked, so you will be prepared for them on your next interview.

Although you cannot possibly plan for every question you might be asked, knowing what your interviewers are seeking with their questions will help you plan your responses. Of course, you must have the technical expertise required for the position. Excluding that, interviewers look for three primary factors:

1) Clear and certain job focus. You know what job you are currently seeking and how it fits into your career plans.

2) Your life patterns — that is, demonstrated patterns of success, accomplishment, over-achievement, etc., and the opposites.

3) Your ability to "sell yourself" — that is, convincing the interviewer you are the one to hire! Probably more applicants are rejected for failing this, than for any other reason.

Determine your past accomplishments and achievements. This personal inventory is a very important part of your preparation, and you should plan how you can mention them during your interview. Write them down and then review them before each interview. Include not only major feats you can document, but also problems you encountered in your job and how you solved them.

Plan questions of your own. For most of the interview, you will be asked questions which will allow the interviewer to determine if you will be a good match for the company and the job vacancy. However, at some point in the interview, you must have several pertinent, well-conceived questions of your own.

Why? There are two reasons:

1) If you don't, the interviewer will think you are disinterested or unintelligent. Surely everything was not explained thoroughly.

2) Equally as important, you must evaluate the company and the position to decide if they fit into your career plans.

Some questions you can plan in advance, but you also need to have some spontaneous questions that show you have listened and comprehended what the interviewer has said. Choose some questions that reveal your research and preparation, and some others that show interest in the job, company, and career path. Although it is important to ask questions, it is more important to ask *good* questions! And make them flow logically and spontaneously, and not sound rehearsed or "canned."

Here are some suggestions, and you will want to add more:

• What are the projections for the growth of your company and its industry?

• What is a reasonable career path for me to expect?

• Why is the position open?

• What characteristics seem to be present in your most successful employees?

• Why has your company been so successful?

• What problems has the company encountered in the manufacturing process [or sales, accounting, engineering, etc.]?

• What do you want done differently by the next person to fill this job?

• What are the most challenging aspects of the job?

The second most important factor in interviewing is evaluation. Immediately after each interview, sit down with pen and paper, and think through the interview and your performance. Record specific questions you were asked and what a better answer from you might have been. List things you might have done better and how. What did you do well? What did you say that the interviewer seemed to like? Dislike? What have you learned from the interview that will be helpful in future interviews?

THE MOST FREQUENTLY ASKED INTERVIEW QUESTION IS

"Tell me about yourself."

What will you say?

Your answer should be no more than two minutes, and yet it will set the tenor for the remaining part of the interview. Plan your reply well in advance and rehearse it often. If you wait until you're sitting in front of the interviewer to come up with an answer, you have blown the interview!

Here are some guidelines:
• Be concise, and keep your response to a maximum of two minutes.
• Keep your conversation upbeat, and emphasize accomplishments and achievements.
• Include data you want to discuss further during the interview.

Other subjects to consider

Proper dress: Always dress conservatively and traditionally. Pay attention to details such as polished shoes, clean fingernails, limited cologne, etc. Do not wear anything distracting, such as tinted glasses or flashy jewelry. There is no excuse for failing an interview because you were inappropriately attired.

Punctuality: Always arrive a few minutes early, but never more than ten minutes. If you are not familiar with the area where the interview is to take place, make a practice trip the day or night before. As with proper dress, there is no excuse for failing the interview because you were late.

Body language: Sit up straight in the chair and do not slouch. Be appropriately animated and seem genuinely interested. Project a positive, optimistic mien.

First impression: Strive to make an excellent first impression. A truism to remember is that 90% of the interview occurs in the first minute! Offer a firm, dry handshake, and do not sit until told to do so. Be poised and with an air of self-confidence. Thank the interviewer for seeing you, and then wait for the session to begin.

Ending the interview: When you sense the interview is over, again thank the interviewer for the time and consideration, and shake hands as you leave. If you have not already been informed of their selection process, now is the time to ask. How many additional interviews will be required, and with whom? Ask when you can expect to hear from them, should you be selected for the position.

Thank-you note: As soon after the interview as possible, send the interviewer a short note expressing your interest and again thanking him/her.

Now consider these few admonitions:

• Never chew gum and do not smoke, even if offered. If having a luncheon or dinner interview, do not drink alcohol.

• Never use profanity. Even the mildest "four-letter word" could be offensive to the interviewer or may be interpreted as a lack of sensitivity on your part.

• Never "bad-mouth" former employers or teachers. Present a positive attitude and avoid making any negative statements.

• Don't make excuses for failures or mistakes. Avoid even mentioning them at all, but if you must, present them as positive learning experiences from which you gained much insight and knowledge.

- Be careful not to make statements that interviewers might view as "red flags." Try to imagine yourself on the other side of the desk, listening to your answers. Are you saying things that seem to disturb the interviewer?

- Unless specifically asked, not discuss salary and benefits, location of the job, or the first promotion on your initial interview. You should seem more interested in the job and potential with the company, than you are in immediate compensation or promotions.

Practice questions

Start your list of potential questions with these. Before you read the suggested answers, think what your response would be. In planning your reply, try to imagine you are sitting on the other side of the desk listening to your answer. Why do you think the interviewer is asking this question?

1) Why did you leave your past employers?

Never say anything derogatory about former employers. Rather, you left your previous employment for more responsibility, a greater challenge and a better career opportunity. If your departure was the result of a reduction-in-force, make that clear, and note that your position was not refilled. If you were part of a massive lay-off, your job performance is less likely to be an issue.

2) Pick three adjectives to describe yourself.

This is one of the oldest and simplest questions of all, but many applicants are stunned when asked this. There are other ways of phrasing this question, such as "What are your strong points?" or "How would your best friend (or employer) describe you?"

Remember, this is a business interview, so pick adjectives that are business-oriented: aggressive, ambitious, assertive, self-motivated, goal-oriented, self-disciplined, persistent, good communicator, competitive, team player, etc. Having chosen your adjectives, now think of specific instances illustrating how you have used those qualities, and be prepared to relate them.

3) Give me a specific example of a problem you overcame in your job.

The interviewer is asking you what you have accomplished in your job. Choose an achievement that best illustrates your results-orientation.

4) What constructive criticism have former bosses made to you, and what did you do in response?

In other words, how well do you take criticism? If your answer is that you never have been criticized, then the interviewer will think you are lying! Since we are all imperfect, we all have made mistakes and thus encountered criticism. You must freely and openly admit some shortcomings and give specific examples of what you have done to overcome them.

5) What did you like [or dislike] most about your last job? If you could change anything about your last job, what would it be?

You should have many items about your job that you like and only a few that you dislike, although these dislikes obviously outweigh the positive aspects of your job. Above all, do not blame your displeasure on any person, especially your supervisor; the interviewer will question your version of the conflict.

However, if you are seriously considering a job change, then you must have serious misgivings about your job. You should discuss them tactfully, yet frankly and forcefully, showing that you have given this considerable thought and have concluded that your talents would be best used elsewhere.

6) Evaluate your present and past supervisors. (Recent grads may be asked to evaluate their instructors.)

Using specific examples, mention a few good and bad points about current or former bosses, and how you might have acted differently. Most of your supervisors were probably good, so be certain that your praise is greater than your fault-finding, lest you be considered too negative. Also, do not be too derogatory and never personal – you are commenting on performance as a supervisor, not as a "person."

7) Why haven't you found a job after so many months?

The standard reply is this: "Finding a job is easy; finding the right job takes a while longer." Quite likely, this will not satisfy the interviewer, and you may be asked for more details regarding your prolonged job search. If you have received job offers that you declined, explain why – with good, logical reasons.

8) What interests you about this job?

If you don't have a good answer to this question, your interview is over. Your preparation should have given you at least some information about the job, and you must show how your qualities match the nature of this job.

9) What can you contribute to our organization?

If you can't sell yourself now, you never will. From your preparation, you should already know how your background and experience will benefit them, so tell them now. Show how their needs mesh closely with your own qualities, and include several examples.

10) If you were hiring for this position, what would you look for?

This is too easy. Describe yourself, mentioning several accomplishments and achievements.

Conclusion

Many job applicants become extremely nervous before interviews, and if you are one of those, preparation and evaluation will help to calm your nerves. Interviewing - and interviewing well - is a job in itself, and the more practice you have the better you will perform.

Section 4

Using SmartFax

♦ **Activating Your SmartFax Card**

Attached to the front inside cover of this book is a FREE Pre-Activated SmartFax Card, that allows you to sample the convenience of SmartFax by sending your resume to up to ten companies of your choice - absolutely FREE! To take advantage of this free offer, SmartFax must load your resume into its system. Once this is done, you can take advantage of all the benefits of the SmartFax Job Support System. Please make a note of your SmartFax Access Number and Password, found on the back of your new Card. Call (770) 952-2211 if you have questions or if your SmartFax Card is missing, or if you need additional cards.

♦ **Loading Your Resume Into SmartFax and The CareerSource Resume Bank**

This can be done in one of two ways:

1) Call (770) 984-5900 <u>from the handset</u> of any fax machine. Have your SmartFax Card and resume available. Follow the simple instructions to fax your resume into the system. After you hang up, your resume is available immediately to fax to employers!

    or

2) Mail your resume to SmartFax in the pre-addressed envelope provided in the back of the book. Be sure to include your SmartFax Access Number and Password <u>on the back</u> of your resume and on the envelope. SmartFax will load your resume <u>free</u> the day it is received.

♦ **What Is SmartFax?**

When your resume is loaded in the SmartFax System, you have several convenient options.

1) You may immediately fax your resume to any company or companies by simply calling (770) 984-5900 and entering your SmartFax Access Number and Password, then entering the Fax number of the company you wish faxed. SmartFax will even give you the option of dictating a personalized cover sheet.

49

2) You may use the SmartFax Job Locator on the following blue pages to fax your resume to a number of companies or agencies listed in this book. Simply fill out the following broadcast order form and mail it with your resume (if not already in the SmartFax system) and payment to SmartFax at 271 Village Parkway, Marietta, GA 30067. Call (770) 952-2211 for assistance.

3) Record your 30-second voice resume to be heard by recruiting companies by calling 984-5900 and following the prompts. Your voice resume can be referenced on your personalized cover sheet sent with your resume.

4) Your resume is automatically stored in the CareerSource Resume Bank for access by all companies registered with SmartFax. This can dramatically increase your exposure to hiring companies. (You also can choose to restrict your resume listing if you choose.)

◆ **What Does SmartFax Cost**.
The first ten units on your SmartFax Card are free! (A unit equals one faxed page.) After that, the cost depends upon the total number of units you anticipate using. For example, if you purchase 20 units, the cost is 85 cents per unit; but if you purchase 100 units, the cost drops to only 49 cents per unit. Higher unit purchases are even less! Refer to the price list on page 80. For additional information, call (770) 952-2211.

◆ **Smart Fax Quick Reference Guide**
(Call (770) 952-2211 for additional information.)

Questions	Answers
How Do I Get Started with SmartFax?	(1) Have your SmartFax Card and resume and either dial (770) 984-5900 from the handset of a fax machine (follow the prompts), or (2) mail your resume with SmartFax Access Code and pin number written on the back to SmartFax, L.L.C., 271 Village Parkway, Marietta GA 30067. If you need a SmartFax Card, call (770) 952-2211.

How do I get my resume into the SmartFax system?	See answer to previous question.
How do I send my resume to an employer?	Call the phone number on the back of your SmartFax Card and follow the voice instructions.
How many units does one fax cost?	Faxing your resume costs one unit per page, and faxing a cover letter costs one unit per page.
How do I send my resume with a personalized cover sheet?	Call the number on the back of the SmartFax Card, and follow the voice instructions.
How much does it cost to create a personalized cover sheet?	Creating a personalized cover letter cost one unit.
What is a "Voice Resume?"	A Voice Resume is a 30-second audio, recorded by you, giving a brief description of yourself and your work history. This is available for review by an employer, and many be referenced on your personalized cover sheet.
How do I record or change my voice resume?	Call the number on the back of your SmartFax Card and follow the voice instructions
How much does my Voice Resume Cost?	The Voice Resume service is Free! You may record or change your voice resume as often as you like, free of charge! You are charged one unit only when an employer listens to your Voice Resume..

How do I send my resume to many different companies?	You may choose to fax your resume to many different companies in your field of expertise. This is called SmartSend Broadcast Fax. You simply need to fill out the SmartSend Order Request Form in the following Blue Pages. Select the companies to which you want your resume sent and send in your request, SmartFax will do the rest. You also may call (770) 952-2211.
How do I verify that my resume was actually sent?	Call the number on the back of your SmartFax Card and follow the voice instructions to listen to your completed transactions. SmartSend Broadcast faxes will be confirmed in writing.
How do I check the units remaining on my SmartFax Card?	Call the number on the back of your SmartFax Card and follow the voice instructions to check your account.
How do I replenish my Card after I have used all of the units?	For credit card orders, call the number on the back of your SmartFax Card and follow the voice Instructions. Otherwise mail a check or money order along with your SmartFax number to SmartFax, L.L.C.. , 271 Village Parkway, Marietta, GA 30067.
How do I replace a lost Card?	Be sure to make a note of your access code and password. You can access the system without your Card.

SmartFax™
BROADCAST ORDER FORM
Enclose your resume with this order form and mail it to **SmartFax**
Jump Start Your Job Search!

Name _____ SmartFax Card #:_____

Address _____

City _____ State _____ Zip _____ Phone _____

Field Of Specialty _____

You have three options when we fax your resume. We can send to:

A) all the organizations that frequently recruit in your **Field of Specialty** using the "SmartSearch Job Locator",

B) the 50 or 100 **Largest Atlanta Employers**,

C) the specific **Hiring Companies, Employment Agencies** or **Associations** you select from this book.

*NOTE: you may select **one** or **all** of the options listed and **SmartFax** will automatically remove any duplications so no company will receive more than one resume.*

You will also receive by mail a written order confirmation listing all of the organizations that received your resume, including their telephone number for follow-up.

TO BEGIN, choose whether you want a personalized cover letter to be sent with your resume, then simply indicate the companies you would like us to contact for you.

Personalized Cover Letter

Do you want a cover letter sent with your resume?   ❑ Yes   ❑ No
If **yes**, complete the information requested in Step ONE.
If not, go to Step TWO.

Please note: We have the contact name for the hiring authority at each company. Our cover letter will insert his/her name, title and company name, as well as your contact information and career goals as completed on the next page.

271 Village Parkway ● Marietta, GA ● 30067 ● 770 952-2211 ● 770/988-8855 Fax

Tear out here

53

Step **ONE**
Personalized Cover Letter
If you do not want a cover letter, go to step TWO.

Field of Specialty _____ Years Experience _____

Position Desired _____

Secondary Position Accepted _____

Education _____ Willing To Travel? ❏ Yes ❏ No

Relocation Preference _____

Do you want to reference your voice resume ❏ Yes ❏ No

Step **TWO**

A) Select *all* the hiring companies, employment agencies, or associations that frequently recruit in your Field of Specialty, by checking the appropriate box using the SmartSearch Job Locator,

B) select the 50 or 100 Largest Atlanta Employers,

C) select from the specific **companies**, **employment agencies** and **associations** listed in this book by checking the box next to the organization name provided on pages 56-78.

*Mail this order form to us with your resume.
SmartFax will send you a confirmation list of the
companies and their phone numbers that received your
resume!*

*Note: **Your resume will be stored in the Career Source
Resume Bank unless declined here. I decline ❏**

Option A: <u>SmartSearch Job Locator</u>

Check the Box by each category you want your resume sent. The number next to the box indicates how many companies, agencies or associations have indicated a hiring need in that field of specialty.

Tear out here

FIELD OF SPECIALTY	Companies	Agencies	Associations
(01) Accounting/Finance/Bookkeeping	❏ 233	❏ 114	❏ 3
(02) Agriculture and Environmental	❏ 10	❏ 10	❏ 0
(03) Banking and Credit	❏ 33	❏ 49	❏ 0
(04) Building and Construction	❏ 24	❏ 23	❏ 0
(voice, data, wireless)			
(06) Customer Service	❏ 159	❏ 83	❏ 1
(07) Financial	❏ 36	❏ 21	❏ 0
(investment, real estate, stocks, etc.)			
(08) Food Service & Hospitality	❏ 48	❏ 34	❏ 0
(09) General Office Support	❏ 166	❏ 127	❏ 0
(includes secretarial, word processing, receptionist, clerical, data entry, etc.)			
(10) Graphic Design	❏ 38	❏ 37	❏ 2
(includes desktop publishing, illustration presentation graphics, etc.)			
(11) Human Resources and Education	❏ 68	❏ 37	❏ 2
(12) Insurance	❏ 46	❏ 38	❏ 1
(13) Journalism	❏ 17	❏ 2	❏ 0
(14) Legal	❏ 16	❏ 33	❏ 0
(includes office support, paralegal, attorneys, etc.)			
(15) Light Industrial (warehouse, etc.)	❏ 69	❏ 74	❏ 0
(16) Management	❏ 145	❏ 35	❏ 2
(17) Manufacturing & Distribution	❏ 74	❏ 47	❏ 0
(18) Marketing	❏ 112	❏ 25	❏ 2
(includes advertising, public relations, etc.)			
(19) Medical Health Care	❏ 43	❏ 40	❏ 1
(20) Packaging & Paper	❏ 15	❏ 34	❏ 0
(21) Retail	❏ 35	❏ 21	❏ 1
(includes merchandising, purchasing operations, etc.)			
(22) Sales & Sales Management	❏ 204	❏ 42	❏ 0
(23) Scientists/Research/Development	❏ 28	❏ 12	❏ 0
(including math, chem., bio., enviro., etc.)			
(24) Systems/Technical	❏ 239	❏ 101	❏ 2
(includes programmers, computer operators, technical support, etc.)			
(25) Technical	❏ 152	❏ 52	❏ 5
(includes engineers, designers, architects, drafters, CAD operators, etc.)			

Option B: Largest Employers
Please Send My Resume To the ❑ 50 ❑ 100 Largest Atlanta Employers.

Option C: Broadcast Fax
Please Check The Box Next To Each Company To Which You Want Your Resume Sent.

Tear out here

❑ 1-800-Database	5346	
❑ A & P Supermarkets	5997	
❑ A BoKay By JoAnn	7845	
❑ A&C Enercom	7135	
❑ A. Brown Olmstead Assoc	5348	
❑ A. Foster Higgins & Co.	7247	
❑ A.D.A.M. Software	5005	
❑ A.E.L. Cross Systems	5349	
❑ A.E.R. Energy Resources	5561	
❑ A.G. Edwards & Sons	7715	
❑ AAA Paging	8170	
❑ Aaron's Rental Purchase	5001	
❑ ABCO Builders, Inc.	7031	
❑ Aberdeen Marketing Inc.	7912	
❑ Absolute Communications	8171	
❑ Accurate Inv & Calculating Svc of GA	5002	
❑ Ace Mailing Svcs Inc	5003	
❑ Action Cellular	8172	
❑ Action Electric Company	8165	
❑ Active Parenting Publishers	5004	
❑ Ad Tranz	5353	
❑ Adair Greene Inc.	7913	
❑ Addison Corporation	7033	
❑ Adovation Inc.	7914	
❑ ADS Environmental Svcs Inc.	8270	
❑ ADT Security Systems-Customer Svc	5006	
❑ Advanced Computer Distributors	5007	
❑ Advanced Control Systems Inc.	8125	
❑ Advanced Drainage Systems	7042	
❑ Advanced Systems Technology	7136	
❑ Advantage Cellular	8173	
❑ Advantage Communication	8174	
❑ Advertising Technologies Inc	5667	
❑ Aeronautical Specialties, Inc.	8100	
❑ Aetna	5354	
❑ Aetna Health Plan of Georgia	7645	
❑ Aetna Insurance Co.	7646	
❑ Affairs To Remember	7846	
❑ Agape Consulting Group	7248	
❑ AGCO	6021	
❑ Age of Travel Inc.	7886	
❑ Agency For Toxic Substances & Disease Registry	5669	
❑ Agnes Scott College	7275	
❑ AIG Life Insurance Co.	7647	
❑ Airport Group International Inc	5009	
❑ Airtouch Cellular	5315	
❑ AirTouch Paging	8175	
❑ Akzo Coatings Inc.	5367	
❑ Alba Communications Assoc Inc.	7997	

❑ Albany Government Emp Fed Credit	7516
❑ Alcan Cable	8458
❑ Alexander & Alexander Cons Group	7250
❑ Alexander Communications	7998
❑ All American Communications	8176
❑ All American Gourmet Company	8561
❑ All Green	8649
❑ All In One Electronic Repair	5929
❑ All Metals Svcs & Warehouse Inc	5010
❑ Allgood Outdoors Inc.	8650
❑ Alliance Theatre Company	8089
❑ Allied Bank of Georgia	7517
❑ Allied Foods, Inc.	8557
❑ Allied Holdings	5989
❑ Allied Security	7510
❑ Allied Signal, Inc.(Friction Materials Div)	8331
❑ Allison-Smith Company	7134
❑ Allmerica Financial	6002
❑ Allstate Insurance	5358
❑ Alltel Information Svcs	8106
❑ Alpha Mortgage Bankers	5593
❑ Alpha Products	5360
❑ Alston & Bird	7206
❑ ALT Communications	8177
❑ Alta Telecom	8166
❑ Alternate Roots Inc	5012
❑ Alumax, Inc.	5361
❑ Amarlite Architectural Products	7043
❑ Amer. General Life & Accident Ins.	7649
❑ America's Favorite Chicken Company	5016
❑ American Airlines	7812
❑ American Cancer Society	5670
❑ American Child Care Center	7276
❑ American Coach Lines Inc	5011
❑ American Eagle Advertising	5363
❑ American Express Travel Related Svs	7887
❑ American Frozen Foods	6027
❑ American Megatrends	5671
❑ American Nonwovens	8374
❑ American Polycraft	8375
❑ American Radio & Cellular Commun.	8178
❑ American Recycling Co.	8271
❑ American Red Cross	5365
❑ American Security Group	5926
❑ American Signature	5366
❑ American Software USA Inc	5668
❑ American Sound & Video	7994
❑ American Sys & Programming Co, Inc.	5014
❑ American Water Broom	5015
❑ Americana Furniture Showroom	5369

56

Tear out here

Ames Taping Tool Systems Company	7044
Amoco Fabrics and Fibers Company	8352
Amoco Foam - Technology Center	5939
Amrep, Inc.	5556
AMS Distributors Inc	5013
Amsouth Bank of Georgia	7518
Anderson Communications	7999
Anderson Properties	7735
Anheuser-Busch	5371
Apac, Inc.	7035
Apache Mills	8376
Apartment Realty Advisors Inc.	7736
Apex Samples	8377
Apex Supply Company, Inc.	5468
Apostles Lutheran Child Dev Center	5017
Apparel Finishers	8378
Apple South, Inc.	5372
Applied Innovation, Inc.	5373
Aqualon Company	8496
Aramark Uniform Svcs	5018
Aratex Svcs	8379
ARC Security	7508
Archimedes Systems Inc	5019
Argenbright Security Inc	5038
Argus, Inc.	5616
Arizona Chemical Company	8497
Armco Advanced Materials Company	8459
Armknecht & Assoc	5020
Armor Kone Elevator	7141
Armour Cape & Pond Inc.	7142
Armstrong Relocation	5021
Arnall, Golden & Gregory	7207
Arthritis Foundation	5375
Arthur Andersen and Company	5376
Arthur J. Gallagher & Co -Atlanta	5022
Artlite Office Supply Co.	7232
Asbury Harris Epworth Towers	7412
Asea, Brown, Boveri, Inc.	7139
Asher School of Business	5023
Ashland Chemical	8498
ASI Svcs Corporation	5024
Associated Credit Union	7519
Associated Space Design Inc.	8623
Astechnologies Inc.	8126
AT & T Global Bus Comm Sys	8179
AT&T	5025
AT&T Global Info Solutions-Retail Prod & Sys.	5608
AT&T Global Info Solutions-World Svc Parts Ct	5379
AT&T Network Cable Systems	5380
AT&T Network Systems	5637
AT&T Phone Center	8181
AT&T Small Business Lending Corp.	7520
AT&T Tridom	5599
ATCO International	5026
ATCO Rubber Products	8499
ATEC Assoc, Inc.	5558
Athens First Bank and Trust Co.	7521
Athens Packaging	8566
Atherton Place	7413
Athlete's Foot, The	5027
Athletic Club Northeast	7476
Atlanta Airport Hilton & Towers	5028
Atlanta Airport Marriott	7822
Atlanta Area Technical Institute	7278
Atlanta Baking Company	8577
Atlanta Botanical Garden	8090
Atlanta Cardiothoracic Surgical Assoc	5927
Atlanta Casualty Co.	7650
Atlanta Catering Co.	7847
Atlanta Cellular Svcs	8183
Atlanta Chamber of Commerce	5672
Atlanta Christian College	7279
Atlanta Coca-Cola Bottling Company	5029
Atlanta College of Art	7280
Atlanta Cyclorama	8091
Atlanta Fish Market	7848
Atlanta Forklifts	5383
Atlanta Gas Light Company	5384
Atlanta Hilton Hotel and Towers	7823
Atlanta Journal-Constitution	5385
Atlanta Mariott Marquis	5386
Atlanta Marriott/Norcross	5030
Atlanta Medical Assoc	7414
Atlanta Metal Inc.	8273
Atlanta Metropolitan College	7281
Atlanta Mobile Communications	8184
Atlanta Mortgage Svcs	7522
Atlanta Motor Speedway	7475
Atlanta Offset	8062
Atlanta Parent-Child	7282
Atlanta Pension Funds	7252
Atlanta Pest Control	8500
Atlanta Postal Credit Union	7523
Atlanta Printing & Design	5031
Atlanta Regional Commission	8093
Atlanta Renaissance Hotel-Airport	7825
Atlanta Renaissance Hotel-Downtown	7826
Atlanta Research & Trading, Inc.	5917
Atlanta Satellites and Beepers	8185
Atlanta Testing & Engineering	7143
Atlanta Testing & Engineering	7145
Atlanta Thermoplastic Products	5032
Atlanta Union Mission, The	5033
Atlanta Urban League, Inc.	8095
Atlanta Voice Page, Inc.	8186
Atlanta Web Printer Inc	5034
Atlanta Wire Works, Inc.	8454
Atlantic Envelope Company	5388
Atlantic Southeast Airlines	5389
Atlantic Steel	5390
Attachmate Corporation	5035
Austell Natural Gas System	7140
Austin Kelley Advertising Inc.	7915
Australian Body Works	7477
Auto Chlor System	5036
Auto-Owners Insurance Co.	7651
Automated Fire & Protection Systems	5037
Automatic Data Processing	5391

Autosave Car Rentals	5675
Aviation Constructors Inc.	7045
Axiom Real Estate Management Inc.	7738
Aydlotte & Cartwright Inc.	7916
B & B Spirits Inc	5039
B B D O South	5392
Babush, Neiman, Kornman,& Johnson	7006
Bagcraft Corporation of America	8501
Bagel Break	5537
Bagel Palace Deli & Bakery	5042
Baldwin Paving Company	7146
Bally's Holiday Fitness Center	7478
Bandag	8502
Bank Atlanta	7524
Bank of Canton	7525
Bank of Covington	7526
Bank of Coweta	7527
Bank of North Georgia	7529
Bank South Investment Svcs Inc.	7716
Bank South Mortgage Inc.	7531
Bank South NA	7532
Banker's Bank	5394
Bankers First Savings Bank, FSB	7533
Barco/Chromatics Division	5395
Barco/Display Division	6011
Bard, C.R. Inc - Urological Division	5396
Barfield Instrument Corporation	8103
Barnett Bank of Southwest Georgia	7535
Baron, McDonald & Wells	8000
Barret Carpet Mills	8380
Barrow Manufacturing	8381
Barry Manufacturing Company	8370
Barton Malow Co.	7046
Barton Protective Svcs	7511
Basinger & Assoc Inc.	7917
Bass Pro Shops Warehouse	5040
Batchelor & Kimball NC	7147
Bates Assoc	8002
Bates Fabrics	8382
Batson-Cook Co.	7047
Bauder College	7283
BBA Communications	8187
BBDO South	7918
BCD Inc.	7048
BDO Seidman LLP	7007
Bear Stearns & Co.	7717
Bearings & Drives Inc	5041
Beaulieu of America	8383
Beaver Manufacturing	8384
Beazer Homes Georgia Inc.	7049
Beech Street	7652
Beepers Etc.	8188
Beers Construction Company	7032
Bekaert Steel Wire Corporation	8452
BEL Tronics	5397
Bell Northern Research (BNR)	5676
Belles & Beaus Bridal & Formalwear	5043
Bellsouth Advertising & Pub Corp	5398
Bellsouth Cellular/Bellsouth Mobility	5677
BellSouth Communication Systems	8189
Bellsouth International	5399
Ben Carter Properties	7739
Bennett Kuhn Varner Inc.	7919
Bennett Thrasher & Co.	7008
Benton Advisory Group Ltd.	7740
Berlitz Language Center	7284
Berry College	7285
Best Buy	8190
Bibb Teachers Federal Credit Union	7536
Bigelow & Eigel Inc.	7920
Bill Harbert Construction	5044
Biolab, Incorporated	5519
Birnbrey, Minsk & Minsk LLC	7009
Black & Veatch Waste Science Inc.	7148
Blackeyed Pea Restaurants	5045
Blaze Recycling & Metal	8275
Bleyle	8385
Blockbuster Music	5400
Blockbuster Video	5559
Blue Cross / Blue Shield of Georgia	5401
BlueChoice Healthcare Plan	7654
Bockel & Co.	7921
Boehm Travel Co.	7888
Bone's Restaurant	7850
Borden Packaging	8503
Borg-Warner Protective Svcs	5046
Bowen & Bowen Homebuilders	7051
Boy Scouts of America	8096
Boys & Girls Clubs of America	5402
Braceland	8063
Branan Towers	7415
Branch Realty Management Inc.	7741
Brand Banking Co.	7537
Brannen/Goddard Co.	7742
Brasfield & Gorrie General Contract	7052
Bremen City School District	7286
Bremen-Bowdon	8361
Brenau University	7287
Bressler & Loftis Advertising	7922
Brickery Grill & Bar, The	5956
Broadus & Assoc Inc.	7923
Brock Control Systems	5336
Brookes & Assoc	5549
Brookstone	5678
Brookwood High School	7288
Brown & Bigelow Inc	5047
Brown and Caldwell	8276
Brown Realty Advisors	7743
Brown Reporting	7233
Brown Steel Contractors	8457
Browning-Ferris Industries of Ga	8277
Brownlow & Sons Co.	7053
Bryant & Assoc	7744
Bryant Electric Company	8167
BTI	8191
BTI Americas Inc.	7889
Buck Consultants Inc.	7253
Buckhead Brokers	7802
Buckhead Diner	7851
Buckhead Towne Club	7479

Tear out here

59

Tear out here

☐ Cleveland Group Inc.	7056
☐ Clockwork Advertising Inc.	7928
☐ Clorox Company	8507
☐ Clowhite Company	8508
☐ Cluett, Peabody & Co, Inc.	5937
☐ CMI Industries	8344
☐ CNA/Private Healthcare Systems	7657
☐ CNM Management Assoc	7751
☐ Coats American	8366
☐ Cobb America Bank & Trust Co.	7544
☐ Cobb Home Health	7427
☐ Cobb Wire Rope & Sling Company	8462
☐ Coca-Cola Enterprises	5413
☐ Cohn & Wolfe/Atlanta	5992
☐ Coldwell Banker	7803
☐ Cole Henderson Drake Inc.	7929
☐ Collier Cauble & Co	5070
☐ Collins & Aikman Floor	8386
☐ Colonial Pipeline	5414
☐ Colony Homes	7057
☐ Color Burst	8652
☐ Color Graphics Inc.	8065
☐ Colormasters	8387
☐ Columbia High School	7302
☐ Columbia Theological Seminary	7303
☐ Columbian Chemicals Company	8487
☐ Columbus Bank & Trust Co.	7545
☐ Columbus Rubber & Gasket	8509
☐ Command Control Inc	5071
☐ Commercial Bank	7546
☐ Commercial Bank of Georgia	7547
☐ Commercial Electric	5921
☐ Commercial Landscape & Design Inc	8653
☐ Communications 21, Inc.	5072
☐ Communications Central, Inc.	5577
☐ Community Federal Savings Bank	7548
☐ Compass Management and Leasing	5416
☐ Compass Marketing Research	5339
☐ Compass Retail Inc	5074
☐ Complete Health of Georgia	7658
☐ Comptroller of the Currency	5680
☐ Compubiz/Downtown Computers	6031
☐ Computer Communications Spec	8128
☐ Computer Horizons Corporation	5333
☐ Computone Corp.	8129
☐ Conagra	8558
☐ Concourse Athletic Club	7482
☐ Confederation Life Insurance Co	5614
☐ Confidential Security Agency	7512
☐ Connell & Assoc	7930
☐ Consolidated Stainless	7058
☐ Constangy, Brooks & Smith	7208
☐ Constar International	5418
☐ Consultec Inc	5078
☐ Continental Airlines	7814
☐ Continental Casualty Co.	7659
☐ Convergent Media Systems Corp.	8130
☐ Cook's Pest Control	8510
☐ Cookerly & Co.	8004
☐ Coolray Heating & AC	7150

☐ Cooper Carry & Assoc Inc.	8587
☐ Coopers & Lybrand L.L.P.	5419
☐ Coosa Valley Technical Institute	7304
☐ Copithorne & Bellows Public Relat.	8005
☐ Cornerstone Communications Group	8006
☐ Coronet Industries, Inc.	8353
☐ Corp. Sports Exec. Mgd. Health Club	7483
☐ Corporate Express of The South Inc.	7234
☐ Corporate Image Group Inc.	8007
☐ Corporate Printers Inc.	8066
☐ Coston Warner	7931
☐ Cotton States Insurance Group	5527
☐ Cotton States Mutual Insurance Co.	7660
☐ Country Club of Roswell	5079
☐ Cousins Properties	5612
☐ Covington Moulding Company	8324
☐ Cowan & Joseph	7932
☐ Cowan Supply	7059
☐ Cox Enterprises	5420
☐ CPC Group	8333
☐ CPI, Inc.	5538
☐ CrafCo	7060
☐ Crawford and Company	5421
☐ Crawford Long Hosp. of Emory Univ.	7305
☐ Creditor Resources, Inc.	6000
☐ Creekside High School	7306
☐ Creme De La Creme	5080
☐ Crescent Communications	7933
☐ Crown Andersen Inc.	8131
☐ Crown Cork & Seal Company	8463
☐ Crown Crafts, Inc.	8358
☐ Crowne Plaza Ravinia	5081
☐ Crumbley & Assoc	7934
☐ CryoLife Inc.	8132
☐ Crystal Farms, Inc.	8556
☐ CSI Advertising Inc.	7935
☐ Curry & Assoc	7755
☐ Curtis 1000	5423
☐ Cushman & Wakefield	7756
☐ Custer Gamwell Communications Inc.	8009
☐ Custom Cellular	8205
☐ Custom Graphics	8388
☐ Cytrx	5651
☐ D & B Software	5112
☐ D.R. Horton	7061
☐ Dabney & Assoc	7757
☐ Dailey's Restaurant and Bar	7856
☐ Dames & Moore	7151
☐ Daniel Dodson Inc./National Promo.	7936
☐ Darby Printing Company	5113
☐ Dargan Whitington & Maddox Inc.	7758
☐ Dart Container Corporation	8511
☐ Data General Corporation	5434
☐ DataMatx	8123
☐ Dateq Information Network Inc.	8133
☐ Daugherty Systems Inc	5335
☐ David Bock Homes L.P.	7062
☐ David H. Kistner Day Care Center	7307
☐ David Houser & Assoc, Inc.	5435
☐ Davis Advertising Inc.	7937

60

Dawn Electronics, Inc.	5114
Dawnville Tufters	8389
DayStar Digital Inc.	8134
Dean Witter	7720
DeKalb College	7308
DeKalb County Merit System	5115
DeKalb County Schools Transportation	5443
DeKalb Employee Retirement System	7255
DeKalb Medical Center	7309
DeKalb Office Environments, Inc.	5995
DeKalb Office Supply	7235
DeKalb Technical Institute	7310
Dellinger	8390
Delmar Gardens of Smyrna	5645
Deloitte and Touche	5681
Deloitte and Touche Mgmt Cons Grp	5436
Delta Air Lines	7815
Delta Employees Credit Union	7549
Delta Environmental Consultants Inc	8287
Deming, Parker, Hoffman, Green Campbell, PC	5666
Denney Construction Co.	7063
Design Benefit Plans, Inc.	5446
Designer Rugs Limited	8391
Devry Institute of Technology	5930
Diagnostic Imaging Specialists	7428
Dial Call Communications	5624
Dial Page	8206
Dickens Data Systems	8135
Diedrich Architects & Assoc	8588
Digital Communications Assoc	8136
Digital Equipment Corporation	5492
Digital Pathways	7513
Digitel Corp.	8207
Digitel Corporation	5448
Dillard Smith Construction Company	7152
Discovery Zone	7484
Dittler Brothers, Inc.	5437
Diversified Communications	8208
Dixie Plywood & Lumber	7064
Dobbs International Svcs	5438
Dollar Rent A Car	5439
Dominion Companies, The	5340
Donino & Partners Inc.	7938
Donzi Lane Landfill	8288
Doors & Building Components	7065
Dorsett Carpet Mills	8392
Doty & Assoc Inc	5341
Doubletree Hotel at Concourse	7828
Douglas & Lomason Company	8327
Douglas High School	7312
Douglasville Health & Athletic Club	7485
Dowling, Langley & Assoc	8010
Dresser Industries	7066
Drew, Eckl & Farnham	7209
Du Shaw Management Group Inc	6026
DuCharme Communications Inc.	7939
Duckett & Assoc Inc.	8626
Duffey Communications	8012
Dulmison, Inc.	5342

Duluth Middle School	7313
Dundee Mills, Inc.	8354
Dunwoody Medical Center	7314
Dunwoody Medical Svcs	5919
Dunwoody Mortgage Co.	7550
DuPont	8393
Duren Grading Contractors	7153
Durkan Pattern Carpet	8394
Duron Paints & Wallcoverings	5682
Dyer & Dyer Volvo	6007
Dykes Paving & Construction Co	7067
Dynamic Metals Inc.	8289
Dynamic Resources Incorporated	5343
Dynatron Bondo Corporation	8512
E.C.C International	5932
E3 Assoc Ltd.	8137
East Hampton Community Center	7486
Eastside Medical Center	7315
Easy Communication	8209
Eberly & Assoc Inc.	8589
EBS/Atlanta	7256
Eckerd Drugs	6001
Economy Forms Corporation	7068
EDAW Inc.	8590
EDC Pickering	8591
Edelman Public Relations Worldwide	8013
Edwards Baking Company	5986
Egleston Children's Hospital/ Emory University	7316
Electrolux Corporation	5441
Electromagnetic Sciences	5082
Electronic Power Technology, Inc.	5661
Electronic Realty Assoc	7804
ELG Creative Svcs	8014
Elkay Plastics Company	8513
Ellis-Don Construction Inc.	7069
Embassy Suites Hotel - Buckhead	5463
Emcon	7154
Emerging Market Technologies Inc	5085
Emory Clinic	7429
Emory Egleston Pediatric Care	7430
Emory University	5954
Emory University Hospital	5954
Employers Insurance of Wausau Mut.	7661
Encore Systems	5444
Ender Partners	7940
Enforcer Products	8449
Engineered Fabrics Corporation	8102
Enplas U.S.A., Inc.	8489
Enterprise Rent-A-Car	5086
Enterprise Sales Solutions	5087
Entrust	7551
Environmental Design Group	8654
Environmental Engineering Const	5088
Environmental Science & Engineering	8291
Environmental Tech. of North Amer.	8292
Epi De France Bakery	5089
Epstein School	7319
Equifax Information Svcs Center	5445
Equifax, Inc.	5963

61

❏ Equitable Real Estate Invest Mgmt	5925
❏ Equitable Variable Life Insurance	7662
❏ ER Snell Contractor	7070
❏ ERB Industries	8493
❏ ERDAS Inc.	8139
❏ Ernst & Young	5447
❏ Estex Manufacturing Company	8395
❏ Etowah Bank	7552
❏ Euramex Management Inc	5090
❏ Evanite Fiber Corporation	8514
❏ Evans, Porter, Bryan & Co.	7010
❏ Evco Plastics	8515
❏ Events	7858
❏ Everest Travel Inc.	7894
❏ Executive Printing Inc.	8069
❏ Executive Travel Inc./First Travel	7895
❏ Executone Information Systems Inc.	8210
❏ Extended Community Home Health	7431
❏ Facility Constructors	7155
❏ Fairchild Communication Svcs	8212
❏ Faison Atlanta Inc.	7760
❏ Falcon Sports & Fitness Complex	7487
❏ Farmers & Merchants Bank	7553
❏ Farrington Design Group	8627
❏ Fastenal Company	5953
❏ Fayette County High School	7320
❏ Fayette First Builders	7156
❏ Fayette Medical Clinic	7432
❏ Federal Deposit Insurance Corporation	5955
❏ Federal Employees Credit Union	6003
❏ Federal Home Loan Bank of Atlanta	5449
❏ Federal Home Loan Mortgage Corp	6025
❏ Federal Insurance Co.	7663
❏ Federal National Mortgage Association (Fannie Mae)	5946
❏ Federal Reserve Bank of Atlanta	5947
❏ Federated Department Stores	5452
❏ Federated Mutual Insurance	5118
❏ Federated Systems Group	5999
❏ Fennell Promotions Inc	5122
❏ Fenwal Safety Systems	7157
❏ Fernbank Museum of Natural History	5945
❏ Fidelity Acceptance Corp.	5683
❏ Fidelity Federal Savings Bank	7555
❏ Fidelity National Bank	7556
❏ Financial Svc Corporation	5119
❏ Fine Products Company, Inc.	8559
❏ Fireman's Fund Insurance Co	5120
❏ First Alliance Financial Processing	5121
❏ First American Health Care of GA	7433
❏ First Bulloch Bank and Trust Co.	7557
❏ First Class Inc.	8015
❏ First Colony Bank	7558
❏ First Data Corporation	5123
❏ First Federal Savings & Loan Assoc.	7559
❏ First Financial Bank	7560
❏ First Financial Management Corp.	8140
❏ First Georgia Bank	7561
❏ First Health	7664
❏ First Health Svcs	5455

❏ First Image	8070
❏ First Liberty Bank	7562
❏ First National Bank of Northwest Ga	7563
❏ First National Bank of Paulding County	7564
❏ First National Bank-Cherokee	7565
❏ First North American National Bank	5125
❏ First Railroad Community Fed Credit	7567
❏ First State Bank & Trust Co.	7568
❏ First Union National Bank of Georgia	5685
❏ Fiserv, Inc.	5126
❏ Fishback Stultz Ltd.	7941
❏ Fisher & Phillips	7210
❏ Fitness International Inc.	7488
❏ Fitness Today	7489
❏ Fitzgerald & Co.	7942
❏ Five Forks Middle School	7321
❏ Five Star Federal Credit Union	7571
❏ Fleet Finance, Inc.	5686
❏ Fleishman-Hillard International Com	8016
❏ Flexel Inc.	5531
❏ Flexible Products Company	8490
❏ Floral Hills Memory Gardens	5127
❏ Floyd College	7322
❏ Focal Point	8516
❏ Focus Carpet Company	8396
❏ Ford & Harrison	7211
❏ Ford Motor Co	5687
❏ Formed Metal Prdocuts Corporation	7037
❏ Foster Company	8464
❏ Foster Wheeler Environmental	8293
❏ Four Points Hotel / Atlanta NW	5124
❏ Frank M. Hall Construction Company	7158
❏ Franzman/Davis & Assoc Ltd.	8592
❏ Frazier & Deeter LLC	7011
❏ Free-Flow Packaging Corp.	8294
❏ Freebairn & Co.	7943
❏ Freeman & Hawkins	7212
❏ Fricks Advertising Inc.	7944
❏ Frito-Lay, Inc.	8576
❏ Frontier Communications	8214
❏ Full Spectrum Communications	8215
❏ Fulton Communications Inc	5129
❏ Fulton County Employees' Pension	7257
❏ Fuqua Enterprises	8372
❏ Future Cellular Inc.	8217
❏ Futurepage	8218
❏ GA Baptist Children's Homes	5095
❏ Gainesville College	7323
❏ Galaxy Scientific Corporation	5688
❏ Galaxy Telecommunications Inc.	8219
❏ Gay & Taylor, Inc	5526
❏ Gay Construction Company	7159
❏ GCI/Atlanta	8018
❏ GCTV (Georgia TV & Comm)	5477
❏ GE Capital Computer & Telecommunication Svcs	5458
❏ GE Capital Technology Mgmt Svcs	8111
❏ GE Capital-Retailer Financial Svcs	5091
❏ GEC Avionics	8101
❏ GEC Marconi Avionics	5585

Tear out here

63

Tear out here   Tear out here

64

Intermec Corporation	5696
Intermet Corporation	8456
International Personnel Resources Ltd	5145
International Safety Instruments Inc	5146
International Svc Systems	8267
Internet Communications	8227
Interserv Svcs Corporation	5147
Interstate Distributors, Inc.	8552
Interstate/Johnson Lane	7721
Intl. Telecommun. Exchange Corp.	8228
Inventory Locator Svc	8143
IPD Printing & Distributing Inc.	8074
IQ Software	5581
ISA/Sungard	5483
Isolyser Co.	8145
ISS Cleaning Svcs Group	7911
ISS Landscape Management Svcs	8659
IT Corporation of America	5697
ITT Automotive	8335
Ivan Allen	5149
Ivory Communications	7949
J & M Concrete Construction Inc	5150
J&J Industries	8411
J&P Supply	7084
J. Belk	8412
J. Walter Thompson	5152
J.C. Bradford & Co.	7722
J.C. Penney Catalog Distribution Ctr	5507
J.F. Kennedy Community Ctr Daycare	7342
J.M. Tull Metals Company, Inc.	8451
J.P. Atkinson & Assoc, Inc.	5915
J.W. Marriott	5338
Jackson National Life Insurance Co.	7674
Jackson Spalding Ledlie	8024
Jenny Craig Personal Weight Mgmt	5153
Jenny Pruitt & Assoc	7806
Jere Via Day Care Center	7343
JGA/Southern Roof Center	5151
Jim Palmer Trucking	5337
John Day & Co.	8025
John Hancock Mutual Life Ins. Co.	7675
John Wieland Homes Inc.	7085
Johnny Rockets	5916
Johnson High School	7344
Johnson Yokogawa	5451
Jones & Askew	7216
Jones and Kolb	7017
Jones Motor Group, The	5154
Jones, Day Reavis & Pogue	7217
Jonesboro High School	7345
Jordan Jones & Goulding Engineers	7167
Jordan, Jones & Goulding Inc.	7168
Joseph L. Walker & Assoc	7766
Josephthal, Lyon and Ross Inc.	7723
Jova/Daniels/Busby	8599
JTM Industries, Inc.	8269
Judy Harmon & Assoc	8026
Julian LeCraw & Co.	7767
Julie Davis Assoc	8027
Junior Achievement of Georgia	5156

K Mart	8229
Kaiser Found. Health Plan of GA Inc	7676
Kaiser Permanente	5987
Kajima Construction Svcs Inc.	7086
Kane Industries	8413
Kato Spring	8469
Kawneer Company, Inc.	8494
KC Travel	5493
KCM Incorporated	5320
Keane, Inc.	5495
Kearney Company	5157
Keebler Company	8562
Keller Graduate School	7346
Kellogg Company	8555
Kennesaw St. College/ Office of Personnel Svcs	5551
Kennesaw State College	7347
Ketchum Public Relations Worldwide	8028
Key Four Inc	5158
Kids 'R' Kids #16	5159
Kilpatrick & Cody	7218
Kimberly-Clark Corporation	5498
King & Assoc	7951
King & Spalding	7219
King Packaging Company	8522
King Springs Village Smyrna	7439
King's Bridge Retirement Community	7440
Kings Communications	8230
Kinnaird & Franke Carpets	8414
Kirkland & Co.	7768
Kleber & Assoc Advertising Inc	7952
Klockner Pentaplast America	8523
Knapp Inc.&The Knapp	8029
Knox Company	8470
Koger Equity Inc	5160
Koll	7769
KPMG Peat Marwick	5909
Kraft General Foods, Inc.	8572
Krane Products Inc	5655
Kroger Supermarkets	5499
Kudzu Cafe	7863
Kudzu Communications	8030
Kuppenheimer Manufacturing Co	8415
Kuppenheimer Men's Clothiers	6017
Kurt's	5162
Kym Company	8416
La Petite Academy	7348
Label America	8075
Lady Madison	8417
LaGrange College	7349
LaGrange Moulding Company	8326
LaGrange Plastics	8336
Laing Landscape	8660
Laing Properties Inc	5163
Lamar Manufacturing Company	8362
Lambis & Eisenberg Advertising	7953
Land Development Technologies	8582
Landauer Assoc Inc.	7770
Landmark Communications	8031
Landmark Communications, Inc.	6019

65

Tear out here

67

Tear out here

Newnan High School	7363	Olsonite Corporation	8488
Newnan Savings Bank, FSB	7599	Omni Hotel	7867
Newsletters Plus	5221	One Source Supply Inc.	7243
Newsmakers	8042	Oneda Corporation	8474
Newsome Pest Control	8529	Oppenheimer & Co.	7727
Newton County High School	7364	Optimage	5329
Newton Federal S&L Assoc	7600	Osgood & Assoc Inc.	8640
Nichols Carter Grant Architects Inc	8603	Outside Carpets Internationsl	8427
Night Magazine	5934	Overlook Communications Int'l	5206
Nightrider	5528	Owen of GA	8475
NIIT (USA) Incorporated	5332	Owen Steel Company of Georgia, Inc.	8453
Niles Bolton Assoc Inc.	8604	Owens-Brockway Plastic Products	8532
Nix, Mann and Assoc	8605	Oxford College of Emory University	7372
Noble Wealth Inc	5222	Oxford Industries	5949
Nobles Construction	7182	P&F Sales	8476
Noland Company	7183	P.M. Architects Inc.	8606
Nolen & Assoc Inc.	7961	Paces Ferry Apartments	7450
Nonpareil Finish Division	8425	Pacesetter Steel Svc	8477
Norcross High School	7365	Pacific Mutual Life Insurance Co.	7692
Nordson Corporation	5223	Page Express	8247
Norfolk Southern Corporation	5974	Page One	8248
Norrell Corporation	7246	Pagemart Wireless	5207
Norrell Svcs, Atlanta	1041	Pagenet	5208
North American Mortgage Co.	7601	Pain & Health Mgmt Center	5539
North Fulton Regional Hospital	7366	Paine Webber	7728
North Hall Middle School	7367	Palm Soft, Inc.	5976
North Metro Technical Institute	7368	Pameco Corporation	5540
North Springs High School	7369	Pamela A. Keene Public Relations	8043
Northeast Georgia Health Svcs Inc	5224	Panasonic/Matsushita Electronics	5490
Northern Telecom Atlanta	5610	Papp Clinic	7451
Northside Anesthesiology Consultant	7448	Paragon Protective Svcs, Inc.	5541
Northside Athletic Club	7491	Parisian Town Center	5209
Northside Hospital	7370	Park 'N Fly, Inc.	5210
Northside Hospital Home Health Svs.	7449	Park-N-Ticket Travel	7899
Northside Realty	7809	Parkview Community School	7373
Northwest Airlines, Inc.	5951	Parkway Medical Center	7374
Northwest Georgia Bank	7602	Parmalat New Atlanta Dairies, Inc.	8551
Northwest Georgia Girl Scout Council	5950	Parsons Engineering Science	8304
Northwest Georgia Health Systems	5534	Patercraft	8428
Northwestern Mutual Life Insurance	7691	Paul, Hastings, Janofsky & Walker	7224
Nova Information Systems Inc.	8150	Paulding County School District	7375
Novi American	8530	Paulding Properties Inc.	7097
Novus International	8531	Pave-Mark Corporation	8533
NPC South	8426	Pax Industries	8534
Nustar International Inc	5225	PCA Health Plans of Georgia Inc.	7693
Oakwood Landscaping Inc./APCI	8665	PD Communications	8044
OAO Svcs, Inc.	5205	Peace Corps	5305
Office Depot	7240	Peach State Cablevision	7995
Office Max	8246	Peachtree Center Athletic Club	7492
Office of Thrift Supervision	5964	Peachtree Federal Credit Union	7603
OfficeMax	7241	Peachtree Mobility	5542
OfficeWorx Inc.	7242	Peachtree Peddlers Flea Market	5212
Ogilvy & Mather	5536	Peachtree Publishers Ltd	5961
Oglethorpe Power	5473	Peachtree Software	6020
Oglethorpe University	7371	Peachtree Travel Management Inc.	7900
OHM Remediation Svcs Corp.	8303	Peachtree Windows & Doors	7098
Ohmeda, Inc. - Med Engineering Sys	6006	Peasant Restaurants, Inc.	5962
OK Cafe	7866	Peasant Uptown	7868
Oldcastle, Inc.	5975	Peds Products	8429
Olde Discount Stockbrokers	7726	Pelham Manufacturing Winer Ind	8430

68

Tear out here

69

Tear out here

70

Tear out here

71

Tear out here

72

Tear out here

❑ TNT & WTBS	5897
❑ Toccoa Clinic	7468
❑ Tortorici & Co.	8058
❑ Total Mobile Commun. of Stockbridge	8264
❑ Total Supply	7122
❑ Total System Svcs, Inc.	8122
❑ Towers High School	7405
❑ Towers Perrin Companies	5942
❑ Toys "R" Us	5267
❑ Trammel Crow Company	5268
❑ Trans World Airlines	7818
❑ Transus	5898
❑ Traton Corp.	7123
❑ Travel Inc.	7907
❑ Travelers Insurance Co.	7711
❑ Travelways, Inc.	5322
❑ Treasure Chest Advertising Company	5309
❑ Treco-Jones Public Relations	8059
❑ Trent Tube	8455
❑ Trindel America Corporation	5271
❑ Trinity Towers	7469
❑ Trintex Corporation	8486
❑ Troutman Sanders LLP	7230
❑ Trust Company Bank	5899
❑ TSW International	8120
❑ Tucker & Assoc Inc.	7982
❑ Tucker Federal Savings & Loan Assoc	7637
❑ Tucker Wayne / Luckie & Co.	5938
❑ Tune Up Clinic	5272
❑ Tunnell-Spangler & Assoc Inc.	8621
❑ Turfgarde Lawn & Shrub Care	5326
❑ Turknett Assoc Leadership Group	5474
❑ Turner & Turner Communications	7984
❑ Turner Construction Co.	7124
❑ Turner-Prichard Clothing	8446
❑ Tyson Foods, Inc.	8573
❑ U.S. Communications Inc.	8265
❑ U.S. Healthcare	7712
❑ U.S. Realty Consultants Inc.	7792
❑ UCB, Inc.	5607
❑ UniComp Inc.	8161
❑ Uniglobe Technology Travel Inc	5276
❑ Uniglobe Travel Southeast Inc.	7908
❑ Unimast	8481
❑ Union Camp Corporation	5277
❑ Union Camp Savannah Fed Crdt Un	7638
❑ Union County Bank	7639
❑ Unisys - Marketing Regional HQ	5900
❑ Unisys Corporation - Atlanta Dev Ctr	5515
❑ United Airlines	7819
❑ United Consumers Club of Nw Atlanta	5280
❑ United Energy Svcs Corporation	7137
❑ United Equipment Sales Co., Inc.	8325
❑ United Family Life Insurance	5281
❑ United Food & Commercial Workers	7272
❑ United HealthCare of Georgia	7713
❑ United Parcel Svc, Doraville	5984
❑ United Parking, Inc.	8675
❑ United Promotions, Inc	5282
❑ United Svcs Automobile Assoc.	7714
❑ United Waste Svc Inc.	8320
❑ United Way of Metro Atlanta	8098
❑ Unity Mortgage Corp.	7640
❑ Universal Security Systems, Inc.	5931
❑ University of Georgia	7406
❑ Upton Assoc	7793
❑ Upton's Department Stores	5656
❑ US FoodSvc of Atlanta	5275
❑ US General Construction	7201
❑ USAir	7820
❑ USG Interiors	8482
❑ UT Automotive	8342
❑ Val Pak	5286
❑ Valley Crest Landscape Inc.	8671
❑ Valuation Counselors Group Inc.	7794
❑ Valuation Group Inc.	7795
❑ ValuJet Airlines	7821
❑ Van Winkle & Assoc Inc.	7985
❑ Vankirk & Assoc	5318
❑ Vantage Products Corporation	8546
❑ Vargas Flores & Amigos	7986
❑ VBxtras	5284
❑ Venture Construction Company	7125
❑ Venture Homes Inc.	7126
❑ Veritec	8367
❑ Vidalia Federal Savings & Loan Asso	7641
❑ Video Display Corporation	6008
❑ Vimpah Corporation	5287
❑ Visions USA Inc.	7987
❑ Visiting Nurse Health System	5306
❑ Voltelcom	7202
❑ Volvo of North America	5623
❑ Von Roll, Inc.	5631
❑ Voxcom Inc.	8085
❑ VSC Communications Inc	5285
❑ VSI Enterprises Inc	5288
❑ W.C.C Incorporated	5331
❑ Wachovia Bank of Georgia	5488
❑ Wachovia Mortgage	7644
❑ Waddell & Reed Inc	5289
❑ Waddell,Smith,Magoon, O'Neal & Saul	7024
❑ Waffle House Inc	5290
❑ Wakefield Beasley & Assoc	8622
❑ Walk Thru The Bible Ministries Inc	5291
❑ Walton Fabrics, Inc.	8365
❑ Walton Manufacturing Company, Inc.	8363
❑ Walton Press Inc.	8086
❑ Wang Laboratories Inc	5292
❑ Warner Summers Ditzel Benefield	8648
❑ Warren Clark & Graham Inc.	7988
❑ Washington Evening Comm School	7407
❑ Waste Management of Atlanta	8321
❑ Waste Recovery Inc.	8322
❑ Waterford Homes	7127
❑ Wattyl Paint Corporation	8547
❑ Wausau Insurance Companies	5933
❑ Weatherly, Inc.	8581
❑ Webb,Carrlock,Copeland,Semler,Stair	7231
❑ Weeks Construction Svcs Inc.	7128
❑ Weeks Corp.	7796

73

Tear out here

74

Employment Agencies I Would Like To Have Receive My Resume:
(Please Check The Box Next To Each Agency To Which You Want Your Resume Sent.)

Agency	Code
☐ A Temporary Solution	1169
☐ A-One Service Personnel	1532
☐ A.R.M. Search	1541
☐ AAA Employment	1535
☐ Access, Inc.	1001
☐ Accountants & Bookkeepers	1002
☐ Accountants On Call	1520
☐ AccounTemps	1003
☐ Accounting Alliance Group	1005
☐ Accurate Medical Placement	1007
☐ Action Temporaries Inc	1008
☐ Ad Options	1547
☐ Ad-Vance Personnel Services	1010
☐ Adia Personnel Services	1009
☐ Agri Personnel	1530
☐ All Medical Personnel	1525
☐ Alternative Staffing, Inc.	1548
☐ America Employment Incorporated	1554
☐ AMH Employee Leasing Inc	1058
☐ Anesthesia Solutions	1179
☐ Anne Williams/Omni Associates	1526
☐ Apex Technical Resources	1181
☐ Arthur Sloan & Associates	1180
☐ Ashford Management Group Inc	1303
☐ Ashley Staffing Services	1341
☐ Ashley-Nolan International	1015
☐ ATC Healthcare Services	1556
☐ Atlanta Technical Support Inc	1018
☐ Atlanta Temporary Personnel	1076
☐ Atlanta Temporary Staffing	1326
☐ ATS Staffing, Atlanta	1017
☐ ATS Staffing, Norcross	1372
☐ Automation Temporary Services Inc	1019
☐ Bailey & Quinn Inc	1020
☐ Bases Consulting Group, Inc.	1021
☐ Bell Oaks Company	1524
☐ Betty Thomas Associates	1186
☐ Boreham International	1187
☐ Bradley-Morris, Inc.	1380
☐ Brandt & Associates	1359
☐ Brannon & Tully	1382
☐ Briggs Legal Staffing	1022
☐ Brock & Associates	1023
☐ Business Professional Group	1334
☐ Butler Service Group, Inc.	1371
☐ C-Peck Company	1523
☐ Cad Cam, Inc.	1190
☐ Cadtech Staffing Service Inc	1024
☐ Caldwell Services	1191
☐ Caldwell Services/Atlanta	1025
☐ Caldwell Services/Lithia Springs	1026
☐ Cambridge Placements Inc	1027
☐ Carrie York Assoc/Hallmark Recruiting	1028
☐ Carson Associates, Inc.	1029
☐ Catherine Bishop Consulting	1165
☐ CDI Information Services	1193
☐ Cella Associates of Atlanta	1194
☐ Chandler Consultants	1527
☐ Charlotte Cody Consultants	1552
☐ Chart Consulting Group	1030
☐ Chase Medical Staffing	1013
☐ Childcare Resources Inc	1031
☐ Citicare, Inc.	1555
☐ Claims Overload Systems	1300
☐ Claremont-Branan Inc	1032
☐ Clientlink Corporation	1570
☐ CMA Consulting Services	1199
☐ Coe & Associates	1370
☐ Comms People Inc	1033
☐ Compaid Consulting Services Inc	1571
☐ Comprehensive Computer Cons	1198
☐ Computer Aid Inc	1572
☐ Computer People Inc	1329
☐ Computer Staffing Solutions Inc	1034
☐ Computer Xperts, Inc.	1016
☐ Comsys Technical Services	1573
☐ Corporate Recruiting Group, Inc.	1036
☐ Corporate Search Consultants	1037
☐ Corporate Solutions	1358
☐ Crown Temporary Services, Inc.	1385
☐ Cubbage & Associates	1172
☐ Datanomics, Inc.	1112
☐ David C. Cooper & Associates	1357
☐ DCW Group (The)	1379
☐ Dixie Staffing Services, St Mtn	1324
☐ Doctor's Choice, Inc.	1325
☐ Don Richard Associates of Georgia	1343
☐ Dorothy Long Search	1521
☐ DSA-Dixie Search Associates	1545
☐ Dunbar Associates	1536
☐ Dunhill Professional Search	1550
☐ Dunhill Temporary Services	1202
☐ Durham Staffing	1388
☐ DXI Corporation	1166
☐ Dynamic People	1529
☐ Ecco Staffing	1284
☐ Eden Group, Inc.	1203
☐ Elite Staffing Services, Inc.	1295
☐ Emerging Technology Search	1204
☐ Emjay Computer Careers	1205
☐ Engineering Group	1039
☐ Etcon, Inc.	1206
☐ Evans & James Executive Search	1040
☐ Evie Kreisler & Associates	1289
☐ Excel Technical Services	1042
☐ Excel Temporary Services	1043
☐ Executive Placement Services	1044
☐ Executive Resource Group, Atlanta	1045
☐ Executive Search Consultants	1542
☐ Executive Strategies Inc	1519
☐ Expressdata Corporation	1208
☐ First Impressions Staffing Agency	1294

Tear out here.

❑ First Investors Corporation	1210
❑ Firstaff	1211
❑ Focus Enterprises, Inc.	1293
❑ Fox-Morris	1114
❑ FSA Inc	1115
❑ G&K Services, Inc.	1213
❑ Garland Group (The)	1215
❑ General Employment Enterprises	1522
❑ General Personnel Consultants of Atl	1048
❑ George Martin Associates, Inc.	1049
❑ GMW Agency	1047
❑ Graphic Resources	1050
❑ Gynn Associates, Inc	1291
❑ H & H Consulting Group Inc	1537
❑ Hall Management Group	1332
❑ Happy Helpers, The	1120
❑ Hillary Group, The	1219
❑ Hire Intellect, Inc.	1168
❑ Home Health & Hospital Recruiters	1221
❑ Horizons Resources, Inc.	1121
❑ Howie and Associates	1333
❑ Huey Gerald Associates	1123
❑ Hygun Group, Inc.	1378
❑ Information Technology Resources	1052
❑ Information Technology Staffing Inc	1053
❑ Interim Personnel	1054
❑ International Medical and Dental	1557
❑ Intersource Ltd	1056
❑ Interstaff, Inc.	1226
❑ IOA Staffing	1057
❑ IPR	1055
❑ ISC of Atlanta, Inc	1381
❑ J E S Search Firm, Inc.	1292
❑ Jackie Glover Associates, Inc	1330
❑ Jacobson Associates	1159
❑ Jean Cody Associates, Inc.	1228
❑ Jim Nixon & Associates	1229
❑ Jordan Temporaries	1230
❑ JSA Inc	1231
❑ K. Murphy & Associates	1339
❑ Kauffman & Co	1061
❑ Kelly Services	1063
❑ Kelly Technical Services	1544
❑ Kelly Temporary Services	1081
❑ Key Temporaries	1065
❑ Keystone Consulting Group, Inc.	1167
❑ Kindercare Learning Center	1232
❑ KL Stevens & Associates	1233
❑ Knight & Associates	1234
❑ Lanier Employment Services	1235
❑ Lawstaf, Inc.	1301
❑ Leader Institute	1066
❑ Leafstone Staffing Inc	1067
❑ Legal Professional Staffing Inc	1068
❑ Lucas Associates	1236
❑ Lucas Financial Search	1069
❑ M A & A Group	1071
❑ M.S.I. Consulting	1518
❑ Mac Temps	1075
❑ Malcom Group, The	1077
❑ Management Analysis & Utilization	1078
❑ Management Decisions	1238
❑ Management Recruiters of Atl, North	1558
❑ Management Recruiters of Atl, West	1079
❑ Management Recruiters of NO. Fulton	1082
❑ Manpower International, Norcross	1239
❑ Manpower International, Perimeter	1080
❑ Manpower Temporary Svcs, Marietta	1240
❑ Maristaff, Atlanta	1085
❑ Maristaff, Forest Park	1086
❑ Martin & Assoc	1087
❑ Matrix Resources	1539
❑ Med Stat, Inc	1125
❑ Medical Office Staff/Dental Personnel	1243
❑ MedPro Personnel, Inc	1528
❑ MedWorld Staffing Services	1127
❑ Meridian USA, Inc	1244
❑ Merlin Services Group	1559
❑ Metro Empl/Medical Employ Grp	1128
❑ Michael Alexander Group	1327
❑ Milam Design Services, Inc.	1368
❑ Millard & Assoc	1130
❑ Monarch Services	1131
❑ More Personnel Services	1551
❑ MRC Resources	1344
❑ MSI (Formerly Temps & Co)	1245
❑ MSI Consulting	1072
❑ MSI Services, Atlanta	1328
❑ MSI Services, Duluth	1073
❑ MSI Services, Inc.	1074
❑ MSI Technical Services, Duluth	1083
❑ Mullinax Temporary Services	1538
❑ Mulling Group, The	1576
❑ National Labor Group Inc	1088
❑ National Personnel Recruiters	1089
❑ NBI Staffing	1090
❑ Nell Rich & Associates	1560
❑ New Boston Select Group	1091
❑ Norrell Financial Staffing	1092
❑ Norrell Services, Atlanta/Piedmont	1095
❑ Norrell Services, Lawrenceville	1093
❑ Norrell Services, Norcross	1094
❑ Norrell Services, Piedmont Road	1285
❑ NPS of Atlanta, Hammond Drive	1096
❑ NPS of Atlanta, Southlake	1383
❑ NPS of Atlanta, Tucker	1097
❑ Office Specialists, Buckhead	1531
❑ Office Specialists, Sandy Springs	1134
❑ Oliver Search	1540
❑ Olsten Staffing Services	1297
❑ Omni Recruiting Group	1553
❑ Outsource Staffing	1288
❑ P.J. Reda & Associates, Inc	1098
❑ Paces Personnel, Inc.	1249
❑ Paragon Resources	1360
❑ Pathfinders, Inc.	1251
❑ People Network Inc	1175
❑ Personalized Management Associates	1546
❑ Premier Staffing	1253
❑ Premier Staffing-The Lucas Group	1533

Tear out here

77

Trade Associations I Would Like To Have Receive My Resume:
(Please Check The Box Next To Each Association)

❑	Amer Assoc of Occupational Health Nurses	4030
❑	Amer Institute of Graphic Arts	4010
❑	Amer Production & Inventory Control Society	4031
❑	American Marketing Association	4011
❑	American Soc of Heating, Refrig & Air Cond.	4022
❑	American Soc of Mechanical Engineers	4012
❑	Assoc of Records Mgrs & Administrators	4032
❑	Association For Systems Management	4034
❑	Atlanta Ad Club	4013
❑	Creative Club of Atlanta	4015
❑	Financial Women International	4017
❑	GA Society of Professional Engineers	4004
❑	Institute of Management Accountants	4036
❑	Int'l Foundation of Employee Benefit Plans	4021
❑	Nat'l Assoc of Purchasing Management	4018
❑	Nat'l Contract Management Assoc.	4019
❑	National Assoc of Insurance Women	4005
❑	Society For Human Resource Management	4020
❑	Society of Logistics Engineers	4008

Calculating Amount Due

First, determine the number of pages you are sending in your Broadcast as follows:

1. Add the total number of companies you have selected to receive your resume. Enter here: _____

2. Enter the number of pages in your fax (A cover letter is consider a page. - e.g. 1-page resume + 1 cover letter = 2 pages) _____

3. **Multiply the number of companies you have selected by the number of pages in your fax.** This is the **total number of units** you must purchase: _____

Next, calculate amount due.

Refer to the price sheet on the next page to determine the cost per unit, then multiply the number of units needed by the cost for each unit as follows:

1. Enter total number of units needed to conduct your Broadcast (from above): _____

2. Enter the cost per unit (from Price Sheet on following page): _____

3. **Multiply the total number of units you need by the cost per unit.** This is the **total amount due:** $ _____

Please Select Your Desired Method of Payment:

❑ Check Enclosed   ❑ MasterCard   ❑ Visa   ❑ American Express

Card # _____ Exp. Date _____

Name on Card: _____ Total Amount:$ _____

*I hereby authorize and direct **SmartFax** to fax the my resume to the indicated recipients on my behalf.*

SIGNED:_____Date:_____

Mail to: SmartFax, L.L.C.,271 Village Parkway ● Marietta, GA ● 30067 Phone (770) 952-2211 ● Fax (770) 988-8855

SmartFax Price List

# of Units	Cost Per Unit	Retail Price
5 Units	$1.00	$ 5.00
10 Units	.90	9.00
20 Units	.85	17.00
30 Units	.80	24.00
40 Units	.75	30.00
50 Units	.70	35.00
100 Units	**.49**	**49.00**
200 Units	.47	94.00
300 Units	.45	135.00
400 Units	.43	172.00
500 Units	.40	200.00
600+ Units	$ .35 each unit	

Minimum Broadcast Order - 30 Units, Long Distance Fax - 2 Units

<u>Note:</u> All Broadcast fax orders will be confirmed in writing, including a list of all companies, agencies and associations faxed to along with their
telephone numbers for follow up.

Check as many categories as appropriate. **SmartFax** will automatically remove any duplications on your order so no company will recieve more than one resume. The number of faxes sent may therefore be less than calculated. Only charges for faxes actually sent will be debited from your SmartFax account. The balance will be credited to your **SmartFax** card for future use.

All **SmartFax** units purchased are non-refundable and are redeemable only for
SmartFax services.
All sales are final and are subject to conditions on the SmartFax Card.

80

Tear out here

BUSINESS SERVICES

Accounting

ARTHUR ANDERSEN AND CO., SMARTFAX #5376
133 Peachtree Street NE, 25th floor, Atlanta, GA 30303 (404) 658-1776. Profile: Big Six Certified Public Accounting firm, and the largest CPA firm in Atlanta, employing over 1300.

COOPERS & LYBRAND L.L.P., SMARTFAX #5419
1155 Peachtree S, Atlanta, GA 30309 (404) 870-1100. Profile: Big 6 CPA firm employing over 400 here in Atlanta.

DELOITTE AND TOUCHE, SMARTFAX #5681
100 Peachtree St NE,S1700, Atlanta, GA 30303-1943 (404) 220-1500. Profile: Third largest CPA firm in Atlanta, employing 450 here.

ERNST & YOUNG, SMARTFAX #5447
600 Peachtree St NE, Atlanta, GA 30308 (404) 817-5269. Profile: World's largest CPA and consulting firm, employing 730 in Atlanta.

KPMG PEAT MARWICK, SMARTFAX #5909
303 Peachtree Center Ave #2000, Atlanta, GA 30308 (404) 222-3000. Profile: Fourth largest CPA firm in Atlanta and one of the Big Six international CPA firms, employing over 400.

PHYSICIANS' FINANCIAL SVCS OF AMERICA, SMARTFAX #5584
11660 Alpharetta Hwy #145, Roswell, GA 30076 (770) 569-1333. Profile: Handles medical billing and insurance.

PRICE WATERHOUSE, SMARTFAX #5996
50 Hurt Plaza, Suite 1700, Atlanta, GA 30303 (404) 658-1800. Profile: International Big 6 CPA firm with three divisions.

Babush, Neiman, Kornman, & Johnson
SmartFax #7006
3525 Piedmont Rd, Suite 500, Atlanta, GA 30305. (404) 266-1900.

BDO Seidman LLP
SmartFax #7007
235 Peachtree St NE, Suite 700, Atlanta, GA 30303. (404) 688-6841.

Bennett Thrasher & Co.
SmartFax #7008
115 Perimeter Center Place, Suite 100, Atlanta, GA 30346. (770) 396-2200.

Birnbrey, Minsk & Minsk LLC SmartFax #7009
1801 Peachtree St, Suite 300, Atlanta, GA 30309. (404) 355-3870.

Clayton, Miller & Co.
SmartFax #5067
1117 Perimtr Center W #W405, Atlanta, GA 30338. (770) 394-3300.

David Houser & Associates, Inc.
SmartFax #5435
PO Box 72315, Atlanta, GA . (770) 951-1335.

Evans, Porter, Bryan & Co. SmartFax #7010
235 Peachtree St NE, Atlanta, GA 30303. (404) 586-0133.

Frazier & Deeter LLC
SmartFax #7011
1100 Harris Tower, Atlanta, GA 30303. (404) 659-2213.

Gifford, Hillegass & Ingwersen SmartFax #7012
233 Peachtree St, Suite 815, Atlanta, GA 30303. (404) 586-0036.

Grant Thornton
SmartFax #7013
2300 North Tower, 235 Peachtree St, Atlanta, GA 30303. (404) 330-2000.

Gross, Collins & Cress
SmartFax #7014
2625 Cumberland Pkwy, Suite 400, Atlanta, GA 30339. (770) 433-1711.

Habif, Arogeti & Wynne SmartFax #7015
1073 West Peachtree St NE, Atlanta, GA 30309. (404) 892-9651.

Hyatt, Imler, Ott & Blount SmartFax #7016
100 Ashford Center N, Suite 200, Atlanta, GA 30338. (770) 394-8800.

Jones and Kolb
SmartFax #7017
10 Piedmont Center, Suite 100, Atlanta, GA 30305. (404) 262-7290.

Mauldin & Jenkins
SmartFax #7018
1640 Powers Fy Rd, Building 26, Marietta, GA 30067. (770) 955-8600.

Metcalf Rice Fricke & Davis SmartFax #7019
950 East Paces Fy Rd, Suite 2425, Atlanta, GA 30326. (404) 264-1700.

Smith & Howard
SmartFax #7021
1795 Peachtree St NE, Suite 300, Atlanta, GA 30309. (404) 874-6244.

Smith & Radigan
SmartFax #7022
4151 Ashford-Dunwoody Rd, Suite 675, Atlanta, GA 30319. (404) 255-1300.

Tiller, Stewart & Co. LLC SmartFax #7023
780 Johnson Fy Rd, Suite 325, Atlanta, GA 30342. (404) 256-1606.

Waddell,Smith,Magoon, O'Neal & Saul SmartFax #7024
10892 Crabapple Rd, Suite 100, Roswell, GA 30075. (770) 993-6818.

Williams Benator & Libby SmartFax #7025
1040 Crown Pointe Pkwy, Suite 400, Atlanta, GA 30338. (770) 512-0500.

Windham Brannon
SmartFax #7026
1355 Peachtree St, Suite
200, Atlanta, GA 30309.
(404) 898-2000.

Architectural Services

ABCO BUILDERS, INC., SMARTFAX #7031
2680 Abco Court, Lithonia, GA 30058 (770) 981-0350. Profile: Construction firm.

ADDISON CORP., SMARTFAX #7033
PO Box 93285, Atlanta, GA 30377 (404) 355-0520. Profile: Distributor of building products.

APAC, INC., SMARTFAX #7035
900 Ashwood Pkwy, Suite 700, Atlanta, GA 30338 (770) 392-5300. Profile: Handles street and highway construction.

ARAMARK UNIFORM SERVICES, SMARTFAX #5018
2839 Paces Fy Rd #1120, Atlanta, GA 30339 (770) 434-1535. Profile: One of the leading uniform rental companies in America, employing 200 here.

BEERS CONSTRUCTION CO., SMARTFAX #7032
70 Ellis Street NE, Atlanta, GA 30303 (404) 659-1970. Profile: Construction firm.

BILL HARBERT CONSTRUCTION, SMARTFAX #5044
1827 Powers Fy Rd, Bldg 24, #300, Atlanta, GA 30339 (770) 859-0103. Profile: Construction of water and wastewater treatment plants in the Southeast.

DOTY & ASSOCIATES INC, SMARTFAX #5341
3220 Pointe Pkwy #200, Norcross, GA 30092 . Profile: Interior finish contractor.

FASTENAL CO., SMARTFAX #5953

5015 Bakers Fy Rd SW, Atlanta, GA 30336 (404) 699-7228. Profile: Distributor of industrial and construction supplies.

FORMED METAL PRODUCTS CORP., SMARTFAX #7037
1118 West Spring Street, Monroe, GA 30655 (770) 267-2551. Profile: Manufactures drywall and related structural materials for construction.

HEERY INTERNATIONAL, SMARTFAX #5133
999 Peachtree S NE, Atlanta, GA 30367 (404) 881-9880. Profile: Architectural, engineering and construction management firm, employing 300 in Atlanta.

HOME DEPOT, SMARTFAX #5562
2727 Paces Fy Rd NW, Atlanta, GA 30339 (770) 433-8211. Profile: Retailer of home improvement and building material supplies, employs more than 1700.

HORTON HOMES, SMARTFAX #7028
PO Box 4410, Eatonton, GA 31024 (706) 485-8506. Profile: Builder of mobile homes.

JGA/SOUTHERN ROOF CENTER, SMARTFAX #5151
2200 Cook Drive, Atlanta, GA 30340-3133 (770) 447-6466. Profile: Wholesale distributor of roofing and related building products, employing 50.

JOHN WIELAND HOMES INC., SMARTFAX #7085
1950 Sullivan Rd, Atlanta, GA 30337 (770) 996-1400. Profile: Construction company specializing in single family homes.

LATEX CONSTRUCTION CO., SMARTFAX #7036
PO Box 917, Conyers, GA 30207 (770) 760-0820. Profile: Manufactures construction pipelines and related materials.

LESLIE-LOCKE, SMARTFAX #7038
4501 Circle 75 Pkwy NW, Suite F6300, Atlanta, GA 30339 (770) 953-6366. Profile: Manufactures heating and ventilation equipment and supplies.

LITHONIA LIGHTING, SMARTFAX #5630
1335 Industrial Blvd, Conyers, GA 30207 (770) 922-9000. Profile: Nation's largest lighting firm, employing 1700 in Atlanta.

PINKERTON AND LAWS, INC., SmartFax #7030
1810 Water Place, Suite 220, Atlanta, GA 30339 (770) 956-9000. Profile: Construction firm specializing in retail and commercial services.

PURYEAR & SON'S GRADING CO, SmartFax #5598
8834 County Line Rd, Hiram, GA 30141 (770) 943-4929. Profile: Grading F sitework contractor handling underground utilities, roadway and site development.

PYRAMID MASONRY CONTRACTORS, INC., SmartFax #7040
2330 Mellon Court, Decatur, GA 30035 (770) 987-4750. Profile: Specialized contractor handling masonry and other related services.

RAINWATER CONSTRUCTION CO., SmartFax #7027
2555 Chantilly Drive NE, Atlanta, GA 30324 (404) 636-8615. Profile: A general contracting firm offering building services, supplies and equipment.

RAYTHEON ENGINEERS, SmartFax #7041
145 Technology Park, Norcross, GA 30092 (770) 662-2049. Profile: This subsidiary of its' international parent company provides engineering, construction and consulting services.

RUSSELL, H.J. & CO., SmartFax #5935
504 Fair Str SW, Atlanta, GA 30313 (404) 330-1000. Profile: Fourth largest minority-owned business in the US, with real estate, property management, construction and communications divisions.

STO CORP, SmartFax #5307
PO Box 44609, Atlanta, GA 30336 (404) 346-3666. Profile: Manufactures specialty construction related products.

W.C.C. INC., SmartFax #5331
PO Box 317, Kennesaw, GA 30144 (770) 974-0766. Profile: One of the largest plastering contracting companies in the Atlanta area.

WELDING SERVICES, INC., SmartFax #7039
2225 Skyland Court, Norcross, GA 30071 (770) 452-0005. Profile: Provides welding repair services for nuclear and fossil fuel power plants.

WINTER CONSTRUCTION CO., SmartFax #5983

530 Means Street, Suite 200, Atlanta, GA 30318 (404) 588-3300. Profile: General contractor handling commercial construction.

CHEM-TURF LANDSCAPES/ RUSSELL & CO INC, SMARTFAX #5061
PO Box 920695, Norcross, GA 30092 (770) 446-3552. Profile: Commercial landscape contractor.

HARTRAMPF ENGINEERING, INC., SMARTFAX #8580
180 Allen Rd, Suite 217N, Atlanta, GA 30328 (404) 252-2063. Profile: Full service architectural and engineering firm.

HEERY INTERNATIONAL, SMARTFAX #5133
999 Peachtree S NE, Atlanta, GA 30367 (404) 881-9880. Profile: Architectural, engineering and construction management firm, employing 300 in Atlanta.

LAND DEVELOPMENT TECHNOLOGIES, SMARTFAX #8582
200 Cobb Pkwy N, Suite 417, Marietta, GA 30062 (770) 971-0121. Profile: Land survey company.

LOCKWOOD-GREENE ENGINEERS, INC., SMARTFAX #8579
250 Williams Street, Suite 4000, Atlanta, GA 30303 (404) 818-8585. Profile: Architecture, engineering and construction firm.

ROSSER INTERNATIONAL, INC., SMARTFAX #5870
524 West Peachtree Street NW, Atlanta, GA 30308 (404) 876-3800. Profile: Offers architectural services for government and commercial projects.

WEATHERLY, INC., SMARTFAX #8581
1100 Spring Street NW, Suite 800, Atlanta, GA 30309 (404) 873-5030. Profile: Handles architectural and services related to constructing chemical processing plants.

Advanced Drainage Systems SmartFax #7042 6106 Buford Highway, Suite B, Norcross, GA 30071. (770) 416-1063.

Amarlite Architectural Products SmartFax #7043 3765 Atlanta Industrial Drive NW, Atlanta, GA 30331. (404) 691-5750.

Ames Taping Tool Systems Co. SmartFax #7044 3305 Breckinridge Blvd, Suite 122, Duluth, GA 30136. (770) 381-1212.

Aviation Constructors Inc. SmartFax #7045
2690 Cumberland Pkwy, Suite 200, Atlanta, GA 30339. (770) 431-0800.

Barton Malow Co. SmartFax #7046
1301 Hightower Trail, Suite 205, Atlanta, GA 30202. (770) 552-6300.

Batson-Cook Co. SmartFax #7047
817 Fourth Ave, West Point, GA 31833. (706) 643-2101.

BCD Inc. SmartFax #7048
PO Box 401, Buford, GA 30518. (770) 932-1187.

Beazer Homes Georgia Inc. SmartFax #7049
1927 Lakeside Pkwy, Suite 602, Tucker, GA 30084. (770) 934-9500.

Bowen & Bowen Homebuilders SmartFax #7051
430 Fairmount St, Norcross, GA 30071. (770) 446-1189.

Brasfield & Gorrie General Contract SmartFax #7052
5660 New Northside Drive, Suite 250, Atlanta, GA 30328. (770) 988-0996.

Brownlow & Sons Co. SmartFax #7053
1654 Roswell Rd NE, Marietta, GA 30062. (404) 977-8404.

Centex Homes SmartFax #7054
1150 Northmeadow Pkwy, Suite 100, Roswell, GA 30076. (770) 663-7670.

Centimark Corp. SmartFax #5053
2150 L Northmont Pkwy, Duluth, GA 30136. (770) 497-0844.

Choate Construction Co. SmartFax #7055
1640 Powers Fy Rd, Bldg 11, Suite 300, Marietta, GA 30067. (770) 644-2170.

Cleveland Group Inc. SmartFax #7056
2690 Cumberland Pkwy, Suite 200, Atlanta, GA 30339. (770) 436-0879.

Colony Homes SmartFax #7057
5134 Highway 92 E, Woodstock, GA 30188. (770) 928-0092.

Consolidated Stainless SmartFax #7058
829 Pickens Industrial Drive, Marietta, GA 30062. (770) 427-8477.

Cowan Supply SmartFax #7059
485 Bishop St NW, Atlanta, GA 30318. (404) 351-6351.

CrafCo SmartFax #7060
160 Belleau Woods Drive, Newnan, GA 30263. (770) 254-8435.

D.R. Horton SmartFax #7061
2434 Highway 120, Suite 210, Duluth, GA 30136. (770) 476-5786.

David Bock Homes L.P. SmartFax #7062
743 Washington Ave, Marietta, GA 30060. (770) 499-1188.

Denney Construction Co. SmartFax #7063
164 West Oak St, Lawrenceville, GA 30245. (770) 995-5733.

Dixie Plywood & Lumber SmartFax #7064
2803 Pleasant Hill Rd, Duluth, GA 30136. (770) 497-8331.

Doors & Building Components SmartFax #7065
4310 Industrial Acces Rd, Douglasville, GA 30134. (770) 944-6313.

Dresser Industries
SmartFax #7066
5672 Peachtree Pkwy,
Norcross, GA 30092.
(770) 840-8360.

**Dykes Paving &
Construction Co.**
SmartFax #7067
2775 Jones Mill Rd,
Norcross, GA 30071.
(770) 448-3392.

Economy Forms Corp.
SmartFax #7068
1545 Henrico Rd,
Conley, GA 30027. (404)
243-5400.

**Ellis-Don Construction
Inc.** SmartFax #7069
3100 Medlock Bridge Rd,
Suite 335, Norcross, GA
30071. (770) 409-9985.

ER Snell Contractor
SmartFax #7070
7800 Covington Hwy,
Lithonia, GA 30058.
(770) 482-5861.

**Georgia Fence
Wholesale** SmartFax
#7071
4180 Angellette Drive,
Austell, GA 30001-1006.
(770) 941-2761.

**Glenn Sims Remodeling
Co.** SmartFax #7072
1924 Tucker-Industrial
Rd, Tucker, GA 30084.
(404) 934-9576.

GT Architecture
SmartFax #7073
9344 South Main St,
Jonesboro, GA 30236.
(770) 478-0032.

H.J. Russell & Co.
SmartFax #7074
504 Fair St, Atlanta, GA
30313. (404) 330-1000.

**Halstead New England
Corp.** SmartFax #7075
1326 Witham Drive,
Atlanta, GA 30338. (770)
698-0345.

HammerSmith Inc.
SmartFax #7076
2103 North Decatur Rd,
Suite 101, Decatur, GA
30033. (404) 377-1021.

**Hardin Construction
Group Inc.** SmartFax
#7077
1380 West Paces Fy Rd
NW, Atlanta, GA 30327.
(404) 264-0404.

HCB Contractors
SmartFax #7078
3495 Piedmont Rd NE,
Bldg 10, Suite 510,
Atlanta, GA 30305. (404)
261-2200.

**Hedgewood Properties
Inc.** SmartFax #7079
5930 Post Rd, Cumming,
GA 30130. (770) 889-
3667.

Herman Homes Inc.
SmartFax #7080
333 Main St NW, Suite
100, Suwanee, GA
30174. (770) 271-8227.

Highland Homes Inc.
SmartFax #7081
302 Perimeter Center N,
Suite 400, Atlanta, GA
30346. (770) 698-0519.

**Holder Construction
Co.** SmartFax #7082
3333 Cumberland Cir,
Suite 400, Atlanta, GA
30339. (770) 988-3000.

**Homeland Communities
Inc.** SmartFax #7083
6251 Smithpointe Drive,
Norcross, GA 30084.
(770) 416-0634.

Homestar Industries
SmartFax #5694
12o Interstate N Pkwy E,
Atlanta, GA 30367. (770)
952-9552.

J&P Supply SmartFax
#7084
209 E Franklin Street,
Dalton, GA 30721. (706)
226-6597.

**Kajima Construction
Services Inc.** SmartFax
#7086
2859 Paces Fy Rd, Suite
1500, Atlanta, GA 30339.
(770) 431-6300.

Leslie Contracting Inc.
SmartFax #7087
213 Jeff Davis Place,
Suite 101, Fayetteville,
GA 30214. (770) 460-
7400.

**M.G. Patton
Construction Co.**
SmartFax #7088
5775 Peachtree-
Dunwoody Rd, Suite 400-
D, Atlanta, GA 30342.
(404) 303-1200.

Main Street Homes
SmartFax #7089
PO Box 1658, Kennesaw,
GA 30144. (770) 426-
5545.

**McCar Development
Corp.** SmartFax #7090
2941-D Piedmont Rd,
Atlanta, GA 30305. (404)
262-9234.

**McDaniel Remodeling
Co.** SmartFax #7091
1916 Tucker-Industrial
Rd, Tucker, GA 30084.
(404) 939-1621.

McDevitt Street Bovis
SmartFax #7092
7000 Central Pkwy, Suite
1400, Atlanta, GA 30328.
(770) 481-9380.

**Metric Constructors
Inc.** SmartFax #7093
1800 Pkwy Place, Suite
810, Marietta, GA 30067.
(770) 428-4999.

Mingledorffs SmartFax
#7094
6675 Jones Mill Court,
Norcross, GA 30092.
(770) 446-6311.

Moon Brothers Inc.
SmartFax #7095
1662 McLendon Ave NE,
Atlanta, GA 30307. (404)
377-6006.

**New South Construction
Co.** SmartFax #7096
1800 Phoenix Blvd, Suite
206, Atlanta, GA 30349.
(770) 996-5600.

Paulding Properties Inc.
SmartFax #7097
8585 Indian Lake Court,
Hiram, GA 30141. (770)
943-0949.

**Peachtree Windows &
Doors** SmartFax #7098
PO Box 720, Gainesville,
GA 30503. (770) 534-
8070.

**Piedmont Residential
inc.** SmartFax #7099
3023 Maple Drive,
Atlanta, GA 30305. (404)
841-9301.

R.J. Griffin & Co.
SmartFax #7101
5775 Peachtree-
Dunwoody Rd, Suite 400-
C, Atlanta, GA 30342.
(404) 255-0082.

Rawn Construction Co.
SmartFax #7102
3723 Clairmont Rd,
Atlanta, GA 30341. (404)
452-1295.

Richport Properties Inc.
SmartFax #7103
PO Box 427, Tucker, GA
30085. (770) 934-0710.

Robert Bowden
SmartFax #7104
850 White Cir Court,
Marietta, GA 30060.
(770) 429-9285.

Ruby-Collins SmartFax
#7105
4806 Wright Drive,
Smyrna, GA 30082. (404)
432-2900.

Ryland Homes SmartFax
#7106
1000 Holcomb Woods
Pkwy, Roswell, GA
30076. (770) 587-1667.

**S.G. Torrey Atlanta
Ltd.** SmartFax #7107
5400 Highlands Pkwy,
Smyrna, GA 30082. (770)
431-8311.

Sawhorse Inc. SmartFax
#7108
5600 Roswell Rd, Suite
368, Atlanta, GA 30342.
(404) 256-2567.

Shepherd Construction Co., Inc. SmartFax #7109
PO Box 8088, Atlanta, GA 30306. (404) 325-9350.

Southern Energy & Construction SmartFax #7110
1955 Cliff Valley Way, Suite 235, Atlanta, GA 30329. (404) 315-0445.

Southern Traditional Builders SmartFax #7111
635 Holmes St, Atlanta, GA 30318. (404) 355-1332.

Southlife Development Inc. SmartFax #7112
1875 Marietta Highway, Dallas, GA 30132. (770) 443-2444.

Summers & Sons Development Co.
SmartFax #7113
2853 Henderson Mill Rd, Suite 100, Atlanta, GA 30341. (404) 934-2700.

Tampella Power Machinery SmartFax #7114
2300 Windy Ridge Pkwy, Marietta, GA 30067. (770) 984-8871.

The Building Firm Inc. SmartFax #7115

4 Executive Park Drive, Suite 2203, Atlanta, GA 30329. (404) 636-4313.

The Conlan Co.
SmartFax #7116
1800 Pkwy Place, Suite 520, Marietta, GA 30067. (770) 423-8000.

The Flagler Co.
SmartFax #7117
305 Techwood Drive, Atlanta, GA 30313. (404) 522-3648.

The Home Rebuilders Inc. SmartFax #7118
1629 Monroe Drive, Atlanta, GA 30324. (404) 876-3000.

The Lennon Cos.
SmartFax #7119
5920 Roswell Rd, Suite B107-106, Atlanta, GA 30328. (404) 252-9848.

The Winter Construction Co.
SmartFax #7120
530 Means St NW, Suite 200, Atlanta, GA 30318. (404) 588-3300.

TLC Remodeling Inc.
SmartFax #7121
785-A Myrtle St, Roswell, GA 30075. (404) 642-8825.

Total Supply SmartFax #7122

4620 S Atlanta Rd, Smyrna, GA 30080. (404) 792-1696.

Traton Corp. SmartFax #7123
639 Whitlock Ave, Marietta, GA 30064. (770) 427-9064.

Turner Construction Co. SmartFax #7124
7000 Central Pkwy, Suite 650, Atlanta, GA 30328. (770) 551-2100.

Venture Construction Co. SmartFax #7125
5660 Peachtree Industrial Blvd, Norcross, GA 30071. (770) 441-2404.

Venture Homes Inc.
SmartFax #7126
5755 Dupree Drive, Atlanta, GA 30327. (770) 955-8300.

Waterford Homes
SmartFax #7127
5825 Live Oak Pkwy, Suite 2D, Norcross, GA 30093. (770) 448-2175.

Weeks Construction Services Inc. SmartFax #7128
4497 Park Drive, Norcross, GA 30093. (770) 923-4076.

Weidmann & Associates Inc. SmartFax #7129

110 Georgian Manor Court, Alpharetta, GA 30202. (404) 552-8396.

Wellons SmartFax #7130
8613 Roswell Rd, Atlanta, GA 30350. (770) 993-8015.

Westside Builders Inc. SmartFax #7131
2985 Cherokee St, Kennesaw, GA 30144. (770) 919-0695.

White Contracting Co. SmartFax #7132
3922 North Peachtree Rd, Chamblee, GA 30341. (770) 452-8778.

Zumpano Enterprises SmartFax #7133
7411 Tara Blvd, Jonesboro, GA 30236. (770) 471-0666.

Chapman Coyle & Associates SmartFax #8585
1225 Johnson Fy Rd, Building 800, Marietta, GA 30068. (770) 973-6644.

Chegwidden Dorsey Holmes Archit. SmartFax #8586
675 Tower Rd, Suite 200, Marietta, GA 30060. (770) 423-0016.

Cooper Carry & Associates SmartFax #8587
3520 Piedmont Rd NE, Suite 200, Atlanta, GA 30305. (404) 237-2000.

Diedrich Architects & Associates SmartFax #8588
3399 Peachtree Rd, Suite 820, Atlanta, GA 30326. (404) 364-9633.

Eberly & Associates Inc. SmartFax #8589
2308 Perimeter Park Drive, Atlanta, GA 30341. (770) 452-7849.

EDAW Inc. SmartFax #8590
3475 Lenox Rd, Suite 100, Atlanta, GA 30326. (404) 365-1110.

EDC Pickering SmartFax #8591
1372 Peachtree St NE, Suite 203, Atlanta, GA 30309. (404) 872-3910.

Franzman/Davis & Associates Ltd. SmartFax #8592
2675 Cumberland Pkwy, Atlanta, GA 30339. (770) 432-0731.

Greenberg Farrow Architecture Inc. SmartFax #8593

3927 Peachtree Rd, Atlanta, GA 30319. (404) 237-5297.

HOH Associates Inc. SmartFax #8596
1575 Northside Drive, Bldg 200, Suite 240, Atlanta, GA 30318. (404) 351-1592.

Howell Rusk Dodson Architects SmartFax #8597
3355 Lenox Rd NE, Suite 1190, Atlanta, GA 30326. (404) 266-9631.

Hughes, Good, O'Leary and Ryan SmartFax #8598
1708 Peachtree St, Atlanta, GA 30309. (404) 876-7726.

Jova/Daniels/Busby SmartFax #8599
1380 Peachtree St, Atlanta, GA 30309. (404) 892-2890.

Leo A. Daly Co. SmartFax #8600
1201 Peachtree St, Suite 1730, Atlanta, GA 30361. (404) 874-8333.

Lockwood Greene Architects SmartFax #8601
250 Williams St, Suite 4000, Atlanta, GA 30303. (404) 525-0500.

Lord, Aeck & Sargent Inc. SmartFax #8602
1201 Peachtree St, 400 Colony Square, Suite 300, Atlanta, GA 30361. (404) 872-0330.

Lynch, Kenneth & Associates SmartFax #8415
56 E. Andrews Dr NW, Atlanta, GA 30305. (404) 262-3762.

Nichols Carter Grant Architects Inc SmartFax #8603
1 baltimore place, Suite 401, Atlanta, GA 30308. (404) 892-4510.

Niles Bolton Associates Inc. SmartFax #8604
3060 Peachtree Rd, Suite 600, Atlanta, GA 30305. (404) 365-7600.

Nix, Mann and Associates SmartFax #8605
1382 Peachtree St NE, Atlanta, GA 30309. (404) 873-2300.

P.M. Architects Inc. SmartFax #8606
100 Galleria Pkwy, Suite 1120, Atlanta, GA 30339. (770) 980-0020.

Pieper O'Brien Herr Architects SmartFax #8607

2 Ravinia Drive, Suite 1700, Atlanta, GA 30346. (770) 512-6622.

R.L. Brown & Associates Inc. SmartFax #8608
101 West Ponce De Leon Ave, Suite 670, Decatur, GA 30030. (404) 377-2460.

Reece, Hoopes & Fincher SmartFax #8609
400 Perimeter Center Terrace, Suite 85, Atlanta, GA 30346. (770) 394-8313.

Rick Jack Designs
SmartFax #8610
851 Cedar Street, Carrollton, GA 30117. (770) 832-0004.

Robert & Co. SmartFax #7192
96 Poplar St NW, Atlanta, GA 30335. (404) 577-4000.

Robert H. Lee & Association SmartFax #8612
1901 Powers Fy Rd, Marietta, GA 30067. (770) 859-9868.

Robertson/Loia/Roof
SmartFax #8613
5780 Peachtree-Dunwoody Rd, Suite 195,

Atlanta, GA 30342. (404) 257-9790.

Roy Ashley & Associates Inc. SmartFax #8615
1212 Fowler St NW, Atlanta, GA 30318. (404) 874-7546.

Sizemore Floyd Architects SmartFax #8616
1700 Commerce Drive NW, Atlanta, GA 30318. (404) 605-0690.

Smallwood,Reynolds,Stewart,Stewart SmartFax #8617
3565 Piedmont Rd, Bldg 1, Suite 303, Atlanta, GA 30305. (404) 233-5453.

Stang & Newdow Inc.
SmartFax #8618
84 Peachtree St, Suite 500, Atlanta, GA 30303. (404) 584-0500.

Thompson,Ventulett,Stainback&Assoc.
SmartFax #8620
2700 Promenade Two, 1230 Peachtree St NE, Atlanta, GA 30309. (404) 888-6600.

Tunnell-Spangler & Associates Inc. SmartFax #8621

134 Peachtree St, Suite 1200, Atlanta, GA 30303. (404) 524-3835.

Wakefield Beasley & Associates SmartFax #8622
7840 Roswell Rd, Suite 400, Atlanta, GA 30350. (770) 396-3792.

Interior Design Services

Associated Space Design Inc. SmartFax #8623
50 Hurt Plaza, Suite 500, Atlanta, GA 30303. (404) 688-3318.

Carson Guest Inc. SmartFax #8624
1720 Peachtree St, Suite 1001, Atlanta, GA 30309. (404) 873-3663.

Cooper Carry & Associates Inc. SmartFax #8587
3520 Piedmont Rd, Suite 200, Atlanta, GA 30305. (404) 237-2000.

Duckett & Associates Inc. SmartFax #8626
3300 Highlands Pkwy, Suite 110, Smyrna, GA 30082. (770) 435-8868.

Farrington Design Group SmartFax #8627
3391 Peachtree Rd NE, Suite 300, Atlanta, GA 30326. (404) 261-6626.

Godwin & Associates Inc. SmartFax #8628
900 Ashwood Pkwy, Suite 200, Atlanta, GA 30338. (770) 804-1280.

Goodman Decorating SmartFax #8629
2335 Adams Drive NW, Atlanta, GA 30318. (404) 351-8922.

Harold E. Troy & Associates SmartFax #8630
3405 Piedmont Rd, Suite 575, Atlanta, GA 30305. (404) 233-3533.

Heery International Inc. SmartFax #5133
999 Peachtree St NE, Atlanta, GA 30367. (404) 881-9880.

Hendrick Associates Inc. SmartFax #8632
5 Piedmont Center, Suite 300, Atlanta, GA 30305. (404) 261-9383.

Hirsch/Bedner Associates SmartFax #8633

909 West Peachtree St NE, Atlanta, GA 30309. (404) 873-4379.

Image Design Inc. SmartFax #8634
1300 Parkwood Cir, Suite 450, Atlanta, GA 30339. (770) 952-7171.

Jova/Daniels/Busby Inc. SmartFax #8599
1389 Peachtree St, Atlanta, GA 30309. (404) 892-2890.

Loia/Budde and Associates SmartFax #8636
5076 Winter's Chapel Rd, Suite 100, Atlanta, GA 30360. (770) 396-3207.

Lord Aeck & Sargent Inc. SmartFax #8602
1201 Peachtree St, Suite 300, Atlanta, GA 30361. (404) 872-0330.

Niles Bolton Interior Design SmartFax #8604
3060 Peachtree Rd, Suite 600, Atlanta, GA 30305. (404) 365-7620.

93

Nix Mann Interiors
SmartFax #8605
1382 Peachtree St,
Atlanta, GA 30309. (404)
873-2300.

**Osgood & Associates
Inc.** SmartFax #8640
60 Peachtree Park Drive
NE, Atlanta, GA 30309.
(404) 605-8650.

**Rosser International
Inc.** SmartFax #5870
524 West Peachtree St
NW, Atlanta, GA 30308.
(404) 876-3800.

Ruys & Co. SmartFax
#8642
3333 Peachtree Rd, Suite
200, Atlanta, GA 30326.
(404) 231-3572.

**Smallwood, Reynolds,
Stewart, Interior**
SmartFax #8617
3565 Piedmont Rd, Suite
303, Atlanta, GA 30305.
(404) 233-5453.

**Smith Cave &
Associates Inc.** SmartFax
#8644
1275 Peachtree St, Suite
400, Atlanta, GA 30309.
(404) 881-1811.

**Stevens & Wilkinson
Interiors Inc.** SmartFax
#8645
100 Peachtree St, Suite
2400, Atlanta, GA 30303.
(404) 522-8888.

**Thompson, Hancock,
Witte & Assoc.**
SmartFax #8646
1720 Peachtree St, Suite
1001, Atlanta, GA 30309.
(404) 873-3663.

**Thompson, Ventulett,
Stainback Associates**
SmartFax #8620
1230 Peachtree St NE,
Atlanta, GA 30309. (404)
888-6600.

**Warner Summers Ditzel
Benefield** SmartFax
#8648
67 Peachtree Park Drive
NE, Atlanta, GA 30309.
(404) 351-6075.

Architectural/Landscaping Services

ALL GREEN, SMARTFAX #8649
1503 Johnson Fy Rd, Suite 150, Marietta, GA 30062 (770) 973-1600. Profile: Offers
lawn care services.

Allgood Outdoors Inc.
SmartFax #8650
5235 Union Hill Rd,
Cumming, GA 30130.
(770) 442-3305.

**Chem-Turf/Russell &
Cos.** SmartFax #5061

6264 Crooked Creek Rd,
Suite 5, Norcross, GA
30092. (770) 446-6364.

Color Burst SmartFax
#8652
PO Box 450265, Atlanta,
GA 30145. (770) 822-
9706.

**Commercial Landscape
and Design Inc**
SmartFax #8653
5130 Piney Grove Rd,
Cumming, GA 30130.
(770) 271-0808.

**Environmental Design
Group** SmartFax #8654

5324 Old Norcross Rd, Norcross, GA 30071. (770) 448-3365.

Gibbs Landscape Co.
SmartFax #8655
4055 Atlanta Rd, Smyrna, GA 30080. (770) 432-7761.

Greenscape Environmental Services
SmartFax #8656
11100 Jones Bridge Rd, Alpharetta, GA 30202. (770) 475-1226.

Greentree Inc. SmartFax #8657
1640 Rdhaven Drive, Stone Mountain, GA 30083. (770) 938-8080.

Habersham Gardens
SmartFax #8658
2067 Manchester St, Atlanta, GA 30324. (404) 873-4702.

ISS Landscape Management Services
SmartFax #8659
1445 Marietta Blvd NW, Atlanta, GA 30318. (404) 355-6693.

Laing Landscape
SmartFax #8660
5901-B Peachtree-Dunwoody Rd, Suite 525, Atlanta, GA 30328. (770) 551-5970.

Landscape Services Inc.
SmartFax #8661
6268 Oakdale Rd, Mableton, GA 30059. (404) 691-9310.

Landscape Techniques Inc. SmartFax #8662
440 Fowler Rd, Alpharetta, GA 30201. (770) 751-7041.

Lifescapes Inc.
SmartFax #8663
6202 Hickory Flat Highway, Canton, GA 30105. (404) 524-4300.

Nature Scapes Inc.
SmartFax #8664
1307 Turner Rd, Lilburn, GA 30247. (770) 923-7023.

Oakwood Landscaping Inc./APCI SmartFax #8665
4455 Business Park Court, Suite D, Lilburn, GA 30247. (770) 381-2456.

Phillips Landscape
SmartFax #8666
3380 Hardee Ave, Chamblee, GA 30341. (770) 986-0475.

Post Landscape Services Inc. SmartFax #8667
3350 Cumberland Cir, Suite 2100, Atlanta, GA 30339. (770) 850-4301.

Ruppert Landscape Co.
SmartFax #8668
4425 Lilburn Industrial Way, Lilburn, GA 30247. (770) 381-2300.

SKB Industries Inc.
SmartFax #8669
467 Inland Way, Lilburn, GA 30247. (770) 564-2186.

The Morrell Group Inc.
SmartFax #8670
PO Box 620245, Atlanta, GA 30362. (770) 662-8775.

Valley Crest Landscape Inc. SmartFax #8671
3315 Peachtree Rd NE, Atlanta, GA 30326. (404) 266-3660.

Weeks Landscape
SmartFax #8672
4497 Park Drive, Norcross, GA 30093. (770) 717-3272.

White Oak Landscape Co. SmartFax #8673
3220 Moon Station Rd, Kennesaw, GA 30144. (770) 427-0524.

Wolf and Co. SmartFax #8674
2552 Baker Rd, Acworth, GA 30101. (770) 975-1049.

Building Contractors, Supplies and Service

ABCO BUILDERS, INC., SMARTFAX #7031
2680 Abco Court, Lithonia, GA 30058 (770) 981-0350. Profile: Construction firm.

ADDISON CORP., SMARTFAX #7033
PO Box 93285, Atlanta, GA 30377 (404) 355-0520. Profile: Distributor of building products.

APAC, INC., SMARTFAX #7035
900 Ashwood Pkwy, Suite 700, Atlanta, GA 30338 (770) 392-5300. Profile: Handles street and highway construction.

ARAMARK UNIFORM SERVICES, SMARTFAX #5018
2839 Paces Fy Rd #1120, Atlanta, GA 30339 (770) 434-1535. Profile: One of the leading uniform rental companies in America, employing 200 here.

BEERS CONSTRUCTION CO., SMARTFAX #7032
70 Ellis Street NE, Atlanta, GA 30303 (404) 659-1970. Profile: Construction firm.

BILL HARBERT CONSTRUCTION, SMARTFAX #5044
1827 Powers Fy Rd, Bldg 24, #300, Atlanta, GA 30339 (770) 859-0103. Profile: Construction of water and wastewater treatment plants in the Southeast.

DOTY & ASSOCIATES INC, SMARTFAX #5341
3220 Pointe Pkwy #200, Norcross, GA 30092 . Profile: Interior finish contractor.

FASTENAL CO., SMARTFAX #5953
5015 Bakers Fy Rd SW, Atlanta, GA 30336 (404) 699-7228. Profile: Distributor of industrial and construction supplies.

FORMED METAL PRODUCTS CORP., SMARTFAX #7037
1118 West Spring Street, Monroe, GA 30655 (770) 267-2551. Profile: Manufactures drywall and related structural materials for construction.

HEERY INTERNATIONAL, SMARTFAX #5133

999 Peachtree S NE, Atlanta, GA 30367 (404) 881-9880. Profile: Architectural, engineering and construction management firm, employing 300 in Atlanta.

HOME DEPOT, SMARTFAX #5562
2727 Paces Fy Rd NW, Atlanta, GA 30339 (770) 433-8211. Profile: Retailer of home improvement and building material supplies, employs more than 1700.

HORTON HOMES, SMARTFAX #7028
PO Box 4410, Eatonton, GA 31024 (706) 485-8506. Profile: Builder of mobile homes.

JGA/SOUTHERN ROOF CENTER, SMARTFAX #5151
2200 Cook Drive, Atlanta, GA 30340-3133 (770) 447-6466. Profile: Wholesale distributor of roofing and related building products, employing 50.

JOHN WIELAND HOMES INC., SMARTFAX #7085
1950 Sullivan Rd, Atlanta, GA 30337 (770) 996-1400. Profile: Construction company specializing in single family homes.

LATEX CONSTRUCTION CO., SMARTFAX #7036
PO Box 917, Conyers, GA 30207 (770) 760-0820. Profile: Manufactures construction pipelines and related materials.

LESLIE-LOCKE, SMARTFAX #7038
4501 Circle 75 Pkwy NW, Suite F6300, Atlanta, GA 30339 (770) 953-6366. Profile: Manufactures heating and ventilation equipment and supplies.

LITHONIA LIGHTING, SMARTFAX #5630
1335 Industrial Blvd, Conyers, GA 30207 (770) 922-9000. Profile: Nation's largest lighting firm, employing 1700 in Atlanta.

PINKERTON AND LAWS, INC., SMARTFAX #7030
1810 Water Place, Suite 220, Atlanta, GA 30339 (770) 956-9000. Profile: Construction firm specializing in retail and commercial services.

PURYEAR & SON'S GRADING CO, SMARTFAX #5598
8834 County Line Rd, Hiram, GA 30141 (770) 943-4929. Profile: Grading F sitework contractor handling underground utilities, roadway and site development.

PYRAMID MASONRY CONTRACTORS, INC., SMARTFAX #7040

2330 Mellon Court, Decatur, GA 30035 (770) 987-4750. Profile: Specialized contractor handling masonry and other related services.

RAINWATER CONSTRUCTION CO., SMARTFAX #7027

2555 Chantilly Drive NE, Atlanta, GA 30324 (404) 636-8615. Profile: A general contracting firm offering building services, supplies and equipment.

RAYTHEON ENGINEERS, SMARTFAX #7041

145 Technology Park, Norcross, GA 30092 (770) 662-2049. Profile: This subsidiary of its' international parent company provides engineering, construction and consulting services.

RUSSELL, H.J. & CO., SMARTFAX #5935

504 Fair Str SW, Atlanta, GA 30313 (404) 330-1000. Profile: Fourth largest minority-owned business in the US, with real estate, property management, construction and communications divisions.

STO CORP, SMARTFAX #5307

PO Box 44609, Atlanta, GA 30336 (404) 346-3666. Profile: Manufactures specialty construction related products.

W.C.C. INC., SMARTFAX #5331

PO Box 317, Kennesaw, GA 30144 (770) 974-0766. Profile: One of the largest plastering contracting companies in the Atlanta area.

WELDING SERVICES, INC., SMARTFAX #7039

2225 Skyland Court, Norcross, GA 30071 (770) 452-0005. Profile: Provides welding repair services for nuclear and fossil fuel power plants.

WINTER CONSTRUCTION CO., SMARTFAX #5983

530 Means Street, Suite 200, Atlanta, GA 30318 (404) 588-3300. Profile: General contractor handling commercial construction.

CHEM-TURF LANDSCAPES/ RUSSELL & CO INC, SMARTFAX #5061

PO Box 920695, Norcross, GA 30092 (770) 446-3552. Profile: Commercial landscape contractor.

HARTRAMPF ENGINEERING, INC., SMARTFAX #8580
180 Allen Rd, Suite 217N, Atlanta, GA 30328 (404) 252-2063. Profile: Full service architectural and engineering firm.

HEERY INTERNATIONAL, SMARTFAX #5133
999 Peachtree S NE, Atlanta, GA 30367 (404) 881-9880. Profile: Architectural, engineering and construction management firm, employing 300 in Atlanta.

LAND DEVELOPMENT TECHNOLOGIES, SMARTFAX #8582
200 Cobb Pkwy N, Suite 417, Marietta, GA 30062 (770) 971-0121. Profile: Land survey company.

LOCKWOOD-GREENE ENGINEERS, INC., SMARTFAX #8579
250 Williams Street, Suite 4000, Atlanta, GA 30303 (404) 818-8585. Profile: Architecture, engineering and construction firm.

ROSSER INTERNATIONAL, INC., SMARTFAX #5870
524 West Peachtree Street NW, Atlanta, GA 30308 (404) 876-3800. Profile: Offers architectural services for government and commercial projects.

WEATHERLY, INC., SMARTFAX #8581
1100 Spring Street NW, Suite 800, Atlanta, GA 30309 (404) 873-5030. Profile: Handles architectural and services related to constructing chemical processing plants.

Advanced Drainage Systems SmartFax #7042
6106 Buford Highway, Suite B, Norcross, GA 30071. (770) 416-1063.

Amarlite Architectural Products SmartFax #7043
3765 Atlanta Industrial Drive NW, Atlanta, GA 30331. (404) 691-5750.

Ames Taping Tool Systems Co. SmartFax #7044
3305 Breckinridge Blvd, Suite 122, Duluth, GA 30136. (770) 381-1212.

Aviation Constructors Inc. SmartFax #7045
2690 Cumberland Pkwy, Suite 200, Atlanta, GA 30339. (770) 431-0800.

Barton Malow Co. SmartFax #7046

1301 Hightower Trail, Suite 205, Atlanta, GA 30202. (770) 552-6300.

Batson-Cook Co. SmartFax #7047
817 Fourth Ave, West Point, GA 31833. (706) 643-2101.

BCD Inc. SmartFax #7048
PO Box 401, Buford, GA 30518. (770) 932-1187.

Beazer Homes Georgia Inc. SmartFax #7049

1927 Lakeside Pkwy,
Suite 602, Tucker, GA
30084. (770) 934-9500.

**Bowen & Bowen
Homebuilders** SmartFax
#7051
430 Fairmount St,
Norcross, GA 30071.
(770) 446-1189.

**Brasfield & Gorrie
General Contract**
SmartFax #7052
5660 New Northside
Drive, Suite 250, Atlanta,
GA 30328. (770) 988-
0996.

Brownlow & Sons Co.
SmartFax #7053
1654 Roswell Rd NE,
Marietta, GA 30062.
(404) 977-8404.

Centex Homes SmartFax
#7054
1150 Northmeadow
Pkwy, Suite 100,
Roswell, GA 30076.
(770) 663-7670.

Centimark Corp.
SmartFax #5053
2150 L Northmont Pkwy,
Duluth, GA 30136. (770)
497-0844.

**Choate Construction
Co.** SmartFax #7055
1640 Powers Fy Rd, Bldg
11, Suite 300, Marietta,
GA 30067. (770) 644-
2170.

Cleveland Group Inc.
SmartFax #7056
2690 Cumberland Pkwy,
Suite 200, Atlanta, GA
30339. (770) 436-0879.

Colony Homes SmartFax
#7057
5134 Highway 92 E,
Woodstock, GA 30188.
(770) 928-0092.

Consolidated Stainless
SmartFax #7058
829 Pickens Industrial
Drive, Marietta, GA
30062. (770) 427-8477.

Cowan Supply SmartFax
#7059
485 Bishop St NW,
Atlanta, GA 30318. (404)
351-6351.

CrafCo SmartFax #7060
160 Belleau Woods
Drive, Newnan, GA
30263. (770) 254-8435.

D.R. Horton SmartFax
#7061
2434 Highway 120, Suite
210, Duluth, GA 30136.
(770) 476-5786.

David Bock Homes L.P.
SmartFax #7062
743 Washington Ave,
Marietta, GA 30060.
(770) 499-1188.

**Denney Construction
Co.** SmartFax #7063

164 West Oak St,
Lawrenceville, GA
30245. (770) 995-5733.

**Dixie Plywood &
Lumber** SmartFax #7064
2803 Pleasant Hill Rd,
Duluth, GA 30136. (770)
497-8331.

**Doors & Building
Components** SmartFax
#7065
4310 Industrial Acces Rd,
Douglasville, GA 30134.
(770) 944-6313.

Dresser Industries
SmartFax #7066
5672 Peachtree Pkwy,
Norcross, GA 30092.
(770) 840-8360.

**Dykes Paving &
Construction Co.**
SmartFax #7067
2775 Jones Mill Rd,
Norcross, GA 30071.
(770) 448-3392.

Economy Forms Corp.
SmartFax #7068
1545 Henrico Rd,
Conley, GA 30027. (404)
243-5400.

**Ellis-Don Construction
Inc.** SmartFax #7069
3100 Medlock Bridge Rd,
Suite 335, Norcross, GA
30071. (770) 409-9985.

ER Snell Contractor
SmartFax #7070
7800 Covington Hwy,
Lithonia, GA 30058.
(770) 482-5861.

**Georgia Fence
Wholesale** SmartFax
#7071
4180 Angellette Drive,
Austell, GA 30001-1006.
(770) 941-2761.

**Glenn Sims Remodeling
Co.** SmartFax #7072
1924 Tucker-Industrial
Rd, Tucker, GA 30084.
(404) 934-9576.

GT Architecture
SmartFax #7073
9344 South Main St,
Jonesboro, GA 30236.
(770) 478-0032.

H.J. Russell & Co.
SmartFax #7074
504 Fair St, Atlanta, GA
30313. (404) 330-1000.

**Halstead New England
Corp.** SmartFax #7075
1326 Witham Drive,
Atlanta, GA 30338. (770)
698-0345.

HammerSmith Inc.
SmartFax #7076
2103 North Decatur Rd,
Suite 101, Decatur, GA
30033. (404) 377-1021.

**Hardin Construction
Group Inc.** SmartFax
#7077
1380 West Paces Fy Rd
NW, Atlanta, GA 30327.
(404) 264-0404.

HCB Contractors
SmartFax #7078
3495 Piedmont Rd NE,
Bldg 10, Suite 510,
Atlanta, GA 30305. (404)
261-2200.

**Hedgewood Properties
Inc.** SmartFax #7079
5930 Post Rd, Cumming,
GA 30130. (770) 889-
3667.

Herman Homes Inc.
SmartFax #7080
333 Main St NW, Suite
100, Suwanee, GA
30174. (770) 271-8227.

Highland Homes Inc.
SmartFax #7081
302 Perimeter Center N,
Suite 400, Atlanta, GA
30346. (770) 698-0519.

**Holder Construction
Co.** SmartFax #7082
3333 Cumberland Cir,
Suite 400, Atlanta, GA
30339. (770) 988-3000.

**Homeland Communities
Inc.** SmartFax #7083
6251 Smithpointe Drive,
Norcross, GA 30084.
(770) 416-0634.

Homestar Industries
SmartFax #5694
12o Interstate N Pkwy E,
Atlanta, GA 30367. (770)
952-9552.

J&P Supply SmartFax
#7084
209 E Franklin Street,
Dalton, GA 30721. (706)
226-6597.

**Kajima Construction
Services Inc.** SmartFax
#7086
2859 Paces Fy Rd, Suite
1500, Atlanta, GA 30339.
(770) 431-6300.

Leslie Contracting Inc.
SmartFax #7087
213 Jeff Davis Place,
Suite 101, Fayetteville,
GA 30214. (770) 460-
7400.

**M.G. Patton
Construction Co.**
SmartFax #7088
5775 Peachtree-
Dunwoody Rd, Suite 400-
D, Atlanta, GA 30342.
(404) 303-1200.

Main Street Homes
SmartFax #7089
PO Box 1658, Kennesaw,
GA 30144. (770) 426-
5545.

**McCar Development
Corp.** SmartFax #7090

2941-D Piedmont Rd, Atlanta, GA 30305. (404) 262-9234.

McDaniel Remodeling Co. SmartFax #7091
1916 Tucker-Industrial Rd, Tucker, GA 30084. (404) 939-1621.

McDevitt Street Bovis SmartFax #7092
7000 Central Pkwy, Suite 1400, Atlanta, GA 30328. (770) 481-9380.

Metric Constructors Inc. SmartFax #7093
1800 Pkwy Place, Suite 810, Marietta, GA 30067. (770) 428-4999.
Mingledorffs SmartFax #7094
6675 Jones Mill Court, Norcross, GA 30092. (770) 446-6311.

Moon Brothers Inc. SmartFax #7095
1662 McLendon Ave NE, Atlanta, GA 30307. (404) 377-6006.

New South Construction Co. SmartFax #7096
1800 Phoenix Blvd, Suite 206, Atlanta, GA 30349. (770) 996-5600.

Paulding Properties Inc. SmartFax #7097
8585 Indian Lake Court, Hiram, GA 30141. (770) 943-0949.

Peachtree Windows & Doors SmartFax #7098
PO Box 720, Gainesville, GA 30503. (770) 534-8070.

Piedmont Residential inc. SmartFax #7099
3023 Maple Drive, Atlanta, GA 30305. (404) 841-9301.

R.J. Griffin & Co. SmartFax #7101
5775 Peachtree-Dunwoody Rd, Suite 400-C, Atlanta, GA 30342. (404) 255-0082.

Rawn Construction Co. SmartFax #7102
3723 Clairmont Rd, Atlanta, GA 30341. (404) 452-1295.

Richport Properties Inc. SmartFax #7103
PO Box 427, Tucker, GA 30085. (770) 934-0710.

Robert Bowden SmartFax #7104
850 White Cir Court, Marietta, GA 30060. (770) 429-9285.

Ruby-Collins SmartFax #7105
4806 Wright Drive, Smyrna, GA 30082. (404) 432-2900.

Ryland Homes SmartFax #7106
1000 Holcomb Woods Pkwy, Roswell, GA 30076. (770) 587-1667.

S.G. Torrey Atlanta Ltd. SmartFax #7107
5400 Highlands Pkwy, Smyrna, GA 30082. (770) 431-8311.

Sawhorse Inc. SmartFax #7108
5600 Roswell Rd, Suite 368, Atlanta, GA 30342. (404) 256-2567.

Shepherd Construction Co., Inc. SmartFax #7109
PO Box 8088, Atlanta, GA 30306. (404) 325-9350.

Southern Energy & Construction SmartFax #7110
1955 Cliff Valley Way, Suite 235, Atlanta, GA 30329. (404) 315-0445.

Southern Traditional Builders SmartFax #7111
635 Holmes St, Atlanta, GA 30318. (404) 355-1332.

Southlife Development Inc. SmartFax #7112

1875 Marietta Highway, Dallas, GA 30132. (770) 443-2444.

Summers & Sons Development Co.
SmartFax #7113
2853 Henderson Mill Rd, Suite 100, Atlanta, GA 30341. (404) 934-2700.

Tampella Power Machinery SmartFax #7114
2300 Windy Ridge Pkwy, Marietta, GA 30067. (770) 984-8871.

The Building Firm Inc.
SmartFax #7115
4 Executive Park Drive, Suite 2203, Atlanta, GA 30329. (404) 636-4313.

The Conlan Co.
SmartFax #7116
1800 Pkwy Place, Suite 520, Marietta, GA 30067. (770) 423-8000.

The Flagler Co.
SmartFax #7117
305 Techwood Drive, Atlanta, GA 30313. (404) 522-3648.

The Home Rebuilders Inc. SmartFax #7118
1629 Monroe Drive, Atlanta, GA 30324. (404) 876-3000.

The Lennon Cos.
SmartFax #7119
5920 Roswell Rd, Suite B107-106, Atlanta, GA 30328. (404) 252-9848.

The Winter Construction Co.
SmartFax #7120
530 Means St NW, Suite 200, Atlanta, GA 30318. (404) 588-3300.

TLC Remodeling Inc.
SmartFax #7121
785-A Myrtle St, Roswell, GA 30075. (404) 642-8825.

Total Supply SmartFax #7122
4620 S Atlanta Rd, Smyrna, GA 30080. (404) 792-1696.

Traton Corp. SmartFax #7123
639 Whitlock Ave, Marietta, GA 30064. (770) 427-9064.

Turner Construction Co. SmartFax #7124
7000 Central Pkwy, Suite 650, Atlanta, GA 30328. (770) 551-2100.

Venture Construction Co. SmartFax #7125
5660 Peachtree Industrial Blvd, Norcross, GA 30071. (770) 441-2404.

Venture Homes Inc.
SmartFax #7126
5755 Dupree Drive, Atlanta, GA 30327. (770) 955-8300.

Waterford Homes
SmartFax #7127
5825 Live Oak Pkwy, Suite 2D, Norcross, GA 30093. (770) 448-2175.

Weeks Construction Services Inc. SmartFax #7128
4497 Park Drive, Norcross, GA 30093. (770) 923-4076.

Weidmann & Associates Inc. SmartFax #7129
110 Georgian Manor Court, Alpharetta, GA 30202. (404) 552-8396.

Wellons SmartFax #7130
8613 Roswell Rd, Atlanta, GA 30350. (770) 993-8015.

Westside Builders Inc.
SmartFax #7131
2985 Cherokee St, Kennesaw, GA 30144. (770) 919-0695.

White Contracting Co.
SmartFax #7132
3922 North Peachtree Rd, Chamblee, GA 30341. (770) 452-8778.

Zumpano Enterprises
SmartFax #7133

7411 Tara Blvd,
Jonesboro, GA 30236.
(770) 471-0666.

**Chapman Coyle &
Associates** SmartFax
#8585
1225 Johnson Fy Rd,
Building 800, Marietta,
GA 30068. (770) 973-
6644.

**Chegwidden Dorsey
Holmes Archit.**
SmartFax #8586
675 Tower Rd, Suite 200,
Marietta, GA 30060.
(770) 423-0016.

**Cooper Carry &
Associates** SmartFax
#8587
3520 Piedmont Rd NE,
Suite 200, Atlanta, GA
30305. (404) 237-2000.

**Diedrich Architects &
Associates** SmartFax
#8588
3399 Peachtree Rd, Suite
820, Atlanta, GA 30326.
(404) 364-9633.

**Eberly & Associates
Inc.** SmartFax #8589
2308 Perimeter Park
Drive, Atlanta, GA
30341. (770) 452-7849.

EDAW Inc. SmartFax
#8590
3475 Lenox Rd, Suite
100, Atlanta, GA 30326.
(404) 365-1110.

EDC Pickering
SmartFax #8591
1372 Peachtree St NE,
Suite 203, Atlanta, GA
30309. (404) 872-3910.

**Franzman/Davis &
Associates Ltd.**
SmartFax #8592
2675 Cumberland Pkwy,
Atlanta, GA 30339. (770)
432-0731.

**Greenberg Farrow
Architecture Inc.**
SmartFax #8593
3927 Peachtree Rd,
Atlanta, GA 30319. (404)
237-5297.

HOH Associates Inc.
SmartFax #8596
1575 Northside Drive,
Bldg 200, Suite 240,
Atlanta, GA 30318. (404)
351-1592.

**Howell Rusk Dodson
Architects** SmartFax
#8597
3355 Lenox Rd NE, Suite
1190, Atlanta, GA 30326.
(404) 266-9631.

**Hughes, Good, O'Leary
and Ryan** SmartFax
#8598
1708 Peachtree St,
Atlanta, GA 30309. (404)
876-7726.

Jova/Daniels/Busby
SmartFax #8599

1380 Peachtree St,
Atlanta, GA 30309. (404)
892-2890.

Leo A. Daly Co.
SmartFax #8600
1201 Peachtree St, Suite
1730, Atlanta, GA 30361.
(404) 874-8333.

**Lockwood Greene
Architects** SmartFax
#8601
250 Williams St, Suite
4000, Atlanta, GA 30303.
(404) 525-0500.

**Lord, Aeck & Sargent
Inc.** SmartFax #8602
1201 Peachtree St, 400
Colony Square, Suite
300, Atlanta, GA 30361.
(404) 872-0330.

**Lynch, Kenneth &
Associates** SmartFax
#8415
56 E. Andrews Dr NW,
Atlanta, GA 30305. (404)
262-3762.

**Nichols Carter Grant
Architects Inc** SmartFax
#8603
1 baltimore place, Suite
401, Atlanta, GA 30308.
(404) 892-4510.

**Niles Bolton Associates
Inc.** SmartFax #8604
3060 Peachtree Rd, Suite
600, Atlanta, GA 30305.
(404) 365-7600.

Nix, Mann and Associates SmartFax #8605
1382 Peachtree St NE, Atlanta, GA 30309. (404) 873-2300.

P.M. Architects Inc.
SmartFax #8606
100 Galleria Pkwy, Suite 1120, Atlanta, GA 30339. (770) 980-0020.

Pieper O'Brien Herr Architects SmartFax #8607
2 Ravinia Drive, Suite 1700, Atlanta, GA 30346. (770) 512-6622.

R.L. Brown & Associates Inc. SmartFax #8608
101 West Ponce De Leon Ave, Suite 670, Decatur, GA 30030. (404) 377-2460.

Reece, Hoopes & Fincher SmartFax #8609
400 Perimeter Center Terrace, Suite 85, Atlanta, GA 30346. (770) 394-8313.

Rick Jack Designs
SmartFax #8610
851 Cedar Street, Carrollton, GA 30117. (770) 832-0004.

Robert & Co. SmartFax #7192

96 Poplar St NW, Atlanta, GA 30335. (404) 577-4000.

Robert H. Lee & Association SmartFax #8612
1901 Powers Fy Rd, Marietta, GA 30067. (770) 859-9868.

Robertson/Loia/Roof
SmartFax #8613
5780 Peachtree-Dunwoody Rd, Suite 195, Atlanta, GA 30342. (404) 257-9790.

Roy Ashley & Associates Inc. SmartFax #8615
1212 Fowler St NW, Atlanta, GA 30318. (404) 874-7546.

Sizemore Floyd Architects SmartFax #8616
1700 Commerce Drive NW, Atlanta, GA 30318. (404) 605-0690.

Smallwood,Reynolds,Stewart,Stewart SmartFax #8617
3565 Piedmont Rd, Bldg 1, Suite 303, Atlanta, GA 30305. (404) 233-5453.

Stang & Newdow Inc. SmartFax #8618
84 Peachtree St, Suite 500, Atlanta, GA 30303. (404) 584-0500.

Thompson,Ventulett,Stainback&Assoc. SmartFax #8620.
2700 Promenade Two, 1230 Peachtree St NE, Atlanta, GA 30309. (404) 888-6600.

Tunnell-Spangler & Associates Inc. SmartFax #8621
134 Peachtree St, Suite 1200, Atlanta, GA 30303. (404) 524-3835.

Wakefield Beasley & Associates SmartFax #8622
7840 Roswell Rd, Suite 400, Atlanta, GA 30350. (770) 396-3792.

Engineering Services

A&C ENERCOM, SMARTFAX #7135
1797 Northeast Expressway, Suite 100, Atlanta, GA 30329 (404) 633-8899. Profile: Engineering consulting firm.

ACCURATE INVENTORY & CALCULATING SVC OF GA, SMARTFAX #5002
2001 Montreal Rd #102, Tucker, GA 30084 (770) 939-6567. Profile: Inventory service employing 20.

ADVANCED SYSTEMS TECHNOLOGY, SMARTFAX #7136
3490 Piedmont Rd NE, Suite 140, Atlanta, GA 30305 (404) 240-2930. Profile: Engineering services company.

ALLISON-SMITH CO., SMARTFAX #7134
PO Box 20215, Atlanta, GA 30325 (404) 351-6430. Profile: Electrical contracting and engineering business.

ASEA, BROWN, BOVERI, INC., SMARTFAX #7139
400 Embassy Rd, Suite 400, Atlanta, GA 30328 (770) 804-2066. Profile: Part of a worldwide engineering firm.

AUSTELL NATURAL GAS SYSTEM, SMARTFAX #7140
2838 Washington St, Austell, GA 30001 (770) 948-1841. Profile: Provides heavy construction services.

BYERS ENGINEERING CO., SMARTFAX #5404
6285 Barfield Rd, Atlanta, GA 30328 (404) 843-1000. Profile: Consulting firm that provides engineering and computer graphic services for major utilities, employing over 900.

GOLDER ASSOCIATES, SMARTFAX #5469
3730 Chamblee Tucker Rd, Atlanta, GA 30341 (770) 496-1893. Profile: Engineering consulting firm, employing almost 100.

HEERY INTERNATIONAL, SMARTFAX #5133

999 Peachtree St NE, Atlanta, GA 30367 (404) 881-9880. Profile: Architectural, engineering and construction management firm, employing 300 in Atlanta.

INGLETT & STUBBS, INC., SMARTFAX #5111
PO Box 93007, Atlanta, GA 30318 (404) 881-1199. Profile: Electrical contracting company.

LAW COMPANIES GROUP, SMARTFAX #5546
1000 Abernathy Rd NE, Atlanta, GA 30328 (770) 396-8000. Profile: Engineering and environmental consulting firm, employing 1000.

LAW ENGINEERING & ENVIRONMENTAL SERVICES INC, SMARTFAX #5166
114 Town Park Drive, Kennesaw, GA 30144 (770) 590-4600. Profile: Provides engineering and environmental services.

MAYES SUDDERTH & ETHEREDGE INC, SMARTFAX #5183
2217 Roswell Rd #C-100, Marietta, GA 30062 (770) 971-5407. Profile: Provides engineering, architectural and related services.

MORELAND ALTOBELLI ASSOC, INC., SMARTFAX #5202
4000 Dekalb Pkwy, Atlanta, GA 30340 (770) 455-9375. Profile: A transportation civil engineering consulting firm.

ROSSER INTERNATIONAL, SMARTFAX #5870
524 W Peachtree St, NW, Atlanta, GA 30308 (404) 876-3800. Profile: One of Atlanta's largest architectural/engineering firms.

SIMONS-EASTERN CONSULTANT/WORLDWIDE ENGINEERS, SMARTFAX #5943
PO Box 1286, Atlanta, GA 30301 (404) 370-3200. Profile: Multi-discipline design and consulting firm, employing 600.

SOUTHERN ELECTRIC INTERNATIONAL, SmartFax #6016

100 Ashford Center N, S 400, Atlanta, GA 30338 (770) 261-4700. Profile: Engineering and consulting firm that builds, owns and operates power plants, employing 100.

SOUTHERN ENGINEERING CO., SmartFax #5251

1800 Peachtree St NW, Atlanta, GA 30367-8301 (404) 352-9200. Profile: Provides services in a variety of electric utility specialties, employing nearly 200.

UNITED ENERGY SERVICES CORP., SmartFax #7137

1110 Northchase Pkwy, Suite 150, Marietta, GA 30067 (770) 951-8989. Profile: Engineering services firm.

Armor Kone Elevator SmartFax #7141 1600 Wilson Way, Smyrna, GA 30082. (770) 438-1194.

Armour Cape & Pond Inc. SmartFax #7142 2635 Century Pkwy, Suite 800, Atlanta, GA 30345. (404) 633-8998.

ATEC Associates Inc. SmartFax #5558 1300 Williams Drive, Marietta, GA 30066-6299. (770) 427-9456.

Atlanta Testing & Engineering SmartFax #7143 11420 Johns Creek Pkwy, DUluth, GA 30136. (770) 476-3555.

Baldwin Paving Co. SmartFax #7146

170 Marr Ave, Marietta, GA 30060. (770) 425-9191.

Batchelor & Kimball NC SmartFax #7147 PO Box 70, Lithonia, GA 30058. (770) 482-2000.

Black & Veatch Waste Science Inc. SmartFax #7148 400 Northridge Rd, Suite 350, Atlanta, GA 30350. (770) 594-2500.

CH2M Hill Inc. SmartFax #7149 115 Perimeter Center Place NE, Suite 700, Atlanta, GA 30346. (770) 604-9095.

Coolray Heating & AC SmartFax #7150 1200 Williams Drive, Suite 1216, Marietta, GA 30066. (770) 421-8400.

Dames & Moore SmartFax #7151 6 Piedmont Center NE, Suite 500, Atlanta, GA 30305. (404) 262-2915.

Dillard Smith Construction Co. SmartFax #7152 548 Lake Mirror Rd, Atlanta, GA 30349. (404) 761-7924.

Duren Grading Contractors SmartFax #7153 1987 Fowler Rd, Decatur, GA 30035. (770) 981-6195.

Emcon SmartFax #7154 1560 Oakbrook Drive, Suite 100, Norcross, GA 30093. (770) 447-4665.

Facility Constructors SmartFax #7155

2233 Lake Park Drive,
Smyrna, GA 30080. (770)
435-0027.

Fayette First Builders
SmartFax #7156
64 Wide Water Drive,
Newnan, GA 30265.
(770) 256-9378.
Fenwal Safety Systems
SmartFax #7157
1360 Chatley Way,
Woodstock, GA 30188.
(770) 591-3394.

**Frank M. Hall
Construction Co.**
SmartFax #7158
1635 Phoenix Blvd, Suite
7, Atlanta, GA 30349.
(770) 991-3900.

Gay Construction Co.
SmartFax #7159
650 14th Street NW,
Atlanta, GA 30318. (404)
873-4941.

**Golder Construction
Service** SmartFax #7161
3751 Venture Drive,
Duluth, GA 30136. (770)
476-9445.

**Greg Pruitt
Construction** SmartFax
#7162
152 Southridge Drive,
Griffin, GA 30223. (770)
228-3306.

Griffin & Co. SmartFax
#7163

5775 Peachtree
Dunwoody Rd NE,
Atlanta, GA 30342. (404)
255-0082.

Harco Technologies
SmartFax #7164
2567 Park Central Blvd,
Decatur, GA 30035.
(770) 981-3150.
**Herman Biles
Construction** SmartFax
#7165
541 S Pine Rd, Griffin,
GA 30223. (770) 228-
2948.

Highland Homes
SmartFax #7081
1395 Prestige Valley
Drive, Roswell, GA
30075. (770) 442-8440.

**Jordan, Jones &
Goulding Inc.** SmartFax
#7168
2000 Clearview Ave NE,
Atlanta, GA 30340. (770)
455-8555.

Lauren Engineers
SmartFax #7169
4317 Park Drive,
Norcross, GA 30093.
(770) 381-9660.

**Lockwood Greene
Engineers Inc.** SmartFax
#7171
250 Williams St, Suite
4000, Atlanta, GA
30303-1036. (404) 525-
0500.

Lowry & Associates
SmartFax #7172
1015 North Street NW,
Conyers, GA 30207.
(770) 483-1774.

**Madison Industries of
GA** SmartFax #7173
1035 Iris Drive SW,
Conyers, GA 30207.
(770) 483-4401.

Mallory & Evans
SmartFax #7174
PO Box 447, Decatur,
GA 30031. (404) 297-
1000.

Marvin Black Co.
SmartFax #7175
PO Box 888506, Atlanta,
GA 30356. (770) 448-
7197.

**McCleskey Construction
Co.** SmartFax #7177
6244 Crooked Creek Rd,
Norcross, GA 30092.
(770) 447-9370.

McDevitt Street Bovis
SmartFax #7092
400 Northridge Rd,
Atlanta, GA 30350. (770)
993-4300.

McKenney's SmartFax
#7179
1056 Moreland Industrial
Blvd, Atlanta, GA 30316.
(404) 622-5000.

**Metro Waterproofing
Co.** SmartFax #7180

PO Box 867, Scottdale, GA 30079. (404) 292-8013.

Newcomb & Boyd SmartFax #7181
1 Northside 75, Atlanta, GA 30318. (404) 352-3930.

Nobles Construction SmartFax #7182
840 N Highway 100, Tallapoosa, GA 30176. (770) 574-5746.

Noland Co. SmartFax #7183
4084 Presidential Pkwy, Atlanta, GA 30340. (770) 458-2111.

Piedmont Olsen Hensley SmartFax #7184
3200 Professional Pkwy NW, Atlanta, GA 30339. (770) 952-8861.

Pittman Construction Co. SmartFax #7186
PO Box 155, Conyers, GA 30207. (770) 922-8660.

Post, Buckley, Schuh & Jernigan Inc SmartFax #7187
1575 Northside Drive, Suite 350, Atlanta, GA 30318. (404) 351-5608.

Power Plant Constructors SmartFax #7188

4048 Big Texas Valley Rd NW, Rome, GA 30165. (706) 295-2498.

Precision Concrete Construction SmartFax #7189
1155 McFarland 400 Drive, Alpharetta, GA 30201. (770) 751-3887.

Premium Roofing Service SmartFax #7190
2838 Washington Street, Avondale Estates, GA 30002-1010. (404) 299-1228.

Restoration Co. SmartFax #7191
3120 Medicalock Bridge Rd, Norcross, GA 30071. (770) 448-7250.

Robert & Co. SmartFax #7192
96 Poplar St, Atlanta, GA 30335. (404) 577-4000.

Sandwell Inc. SmartFax #7194
2690 Cumberland Pkwy, Atlanta, GA 30339. (770) 433-9336.

Signal Control Systems SmartFax #7195
56 Canton Street, Alpharetta, GA 30201. (770) 664-9137.

Simons Engineering Inc. SmartFax #7196

1 West Court Square, Decatur, GA 30030. (404) 370-3200.

Spartan Constructors SmartFax #7197
3412 Pierce Drive NE, Chamblee, GA 30341. (770) 452-8735.

SW&B Construction Corp. SmartFax #7198
2300 Peachford Rd, Suite 2124, Atlanta, GA 30338. (770) 454-7111.

The Facility Group Inc. SmartFax #7199
2233 Lake Park Drive, Smyrna, GA 30080. (770) 437-2700.

United Consulting Group Ltd. SmartFax #1565
808 Park North Blvd, Suite 100, Clarkston, GA 30021. (404) 296-9881.

US General Construction SmartFax #7201
11245 Old Roswell Rd, Alpharetta, GA 30201. (770) 442-3334.

Voltelcom SmartFax #7202
1590 N Robert Rd, Kennesaw, GA 30144. (770) 919-8658.

Williams Enterprises of GA SmartFax #7203

1285 Hawthorne Street,
Smyrna, GA 30080. (770)
436-1596.

**Worthing Southeast
Builders** SmartFax
#5299
1117 Perimeter Center W
NE, Atlanta, GA 30338.
(770) 698-0566.

Legal Services

Alston & Bird SmartFax
#7206
1201 West Peachtree St,
Atlanta, GA 30309-3424.
(404) 881-7000.

**Arnall, Golden &
Gregory** SmartFax #7207
1202 West Peachtree St,
Atlanta, GA 30309-3450.
(404) 873-8500.

**Constangy, Brooks &
Smith** SmartFax #7208
230 Peachtree St NW,
Atlanta, GA 30303-1557.
(404) 525-8622.

**Deming, Parker,
Hoffman, Green &
Campbell, PC** SmartFax
#5666
4851 Jimmy Carter Blvd,
Norcross, GA 30093.
(770) 564-2600.

Drew, Eckl & Farnham
SmartFax #7209
880 West Peachtree St,
Atlanta, GA 30327. (404)
885-1400.

Fisher & Phillips
SmartFax #7210
945 East Paces Fy Rd,
Suite 1500, Atlanta, GA
30326. (404) 231-1400.

Ford & Harrison
SmartFax #7211
1275 Peachtree St NE,
Atlanta, GA 30309. (404)
888-3800.

Freeman & Hawkins
SmartFax #7212
303 Peachtree St NE,
Suite 4000, Atlanta, GA
30308-3243. (404) 614-
7400.

**Glass,
McCullough, Sherrill &
Harold** SmartFax #7213
1409 Peachtree St NE,
Atlanta, GA 30309. (404)
885-1500.

Holland & Knight
SmartFax #7214
1202 Peachtree St NW,
Suite 3100, Atlanta, GA
30309-3400. (404) 817-
8500.

Hunton & Williams
SmartFax #7215
600 Peachtree St NE,
Atlanta, GA 30308-2216.
(404) 888-4000.

Jones & Askew
SmartFax #7216
191 Peachtree St NE,
37th Floor, Atlanta, GA
30303-1769. (404) 818-
3700.

**Jones, Day Reavis &
Pogue** SmartFax #7217
303 Peachtree St NE,
Suite 3500, Atlanta, GA
30308-3242. (404) 581-
8000.

Kilpatrick & Cody
SmartFax #7218
1100 Peachtree St, Suite
2800, Atlanta, GA
30309-4530. (404) 815-
6500.

King & Spalding
SmartFax #7219
191 Peachtree St,
Atlanta, GA 30303-1763.
(404) 572-4600.

Long, Aldridge & Norman SmartFax #7220
303 Peachtree St, Suite 5300, Atlanta, GA 30308. (404) 527-4000.

Long, Weinberg, Ansley & Wheeler SmartFax #7221
999 Peachtree St NE, Suite 2700, Atlanta, GA 30309. (404) 876-2700.

Morris, Manning & Martin LLP SmartFax #7222
3343 Peachtree Rd NE, Suite 1600, Atlanta, GA 30326. (404) 233-7000.

Nelson, Mullins,Riley & Scarborough SmartFax #7223
1201 Peachtree St, Bldg 400, Suite 2200, Atlanta, GA 30361. (404) 817-6000.

Nightrider SmartFax #5528
225 Peachtree StreetSte 501, Atlanta, GA . (770) 589-8100.

Paul, Hastings, Janofsky & Walker SmartFax #7224
600 Peachtree St NE, Atlanta, GA 30208. (404) 815-2400.

Pope, Mcglamry, Kilpatrick & Morrison SmartFax #5948
83 Walton St NW, Atlanta, GA 30303. (404) 523-7706.

Powell, Goldstein, Frazer & Murphy SmartFax #7225
191 Peachtree St, 16th Floor, Atlanta, GA 30303. (404) 572-6600.

Smith, Currie & Hancock SmartFax #7226
233 Peachtree St NE, Suite 2600, Atlanta, GA 30303-1530. (404) 521-3800.

Smith, Gambrell & Russell SmartFax #7227
1230 Peachtree St NE, Suite 3100, Atlanta, GA 30309. (404) 815-3500.

Sutherland, Asbill & Brennan SmartFax #7228
999 Peachtree St NE, Atlanta, GA 30309-3996. (404) 853-8000.

Swift, Currie, McGhee & Hiers SmartFax #7229
1355 Peachtree St NE, Suite 300, Atlanta, GA 30309-3238. (404) 874-8800.

Troutman Sanders LLP SmartFax #7230
600 Peachtree St NE, Atlanta, GA 30308-2216. (404) 885-3000.

Webb,Carrlock,Copeland,Semler,Stair SmartFax #7231
285 Peachtree Center Ave, Suite 2600, Atlanta, GA 30303. (404) 522-8220.

Office Equipment and Supplies

BARCO/CHROMATICS DIVISION, SMARTFAX #5395
2558 Mountain Ind Blvd, Tucker, GA 30084 (770) 493-7000. Profile: Manufacturer of high performance color graphic work stations, employing70.

BARCO/DISPLAY DIVISION, SMARTFAX #6011
1000 Cobb Place Blvd, Kennesaw, GA 30144 (770) 590-7900. Profile: Manufacturer of visualization equipment, employing 140.

CANNON USA AND CO., SMARTFAX #5573
5625 Oakbrook Pkwy, Norcross, GA 30093 (770) 448-1430. Profile: SE region sales and distribution center for office equipment and consumer photographic products, employing 200.

DEKALB OFFICE ENVIRONMENTS, INC., SMARTFAX #5995
1690 Northeast Expressway, Atlanta, GA 30329 (404) 366-3311. Profile: Sells office furniture and design services, employing over 100.

ELECTROLUX CORP., SMARTFAX #5441
2300 Windy Ridge Pkwy/900, Atlanta, GA 30339 (770) 933-1000. Profile: International manufacturer and distributor of vacuum cleaners, employing 180 in Atlanta.

IKON OFFICE SOLUTIONS, INC, SMARTFAX #5105
6971 Peachtree Ind Blvd, Norcross, GA 30092 (770) 448-0770. Profile: Largest distributor of commercial business equipment in the world, employing 650.

IVAN ALLEN, SMARTFAX #5149
221 Peachtree Center Ave, Atlanta, GA 30303 (404) 332-3000. Profile: Office supply, furniture and printing company, employing 400.

RICOH ELECTRONICS, SMARTFAX #6030
1125 Hurricane Shoal Rd, Lawrenceville, GA 30243 (770) 995-5000. Profile: Manufactures toner for copying machines and repackages and distributes thermal paper.

SONITROL OF ATLANTA, SMARTFAX #5250
330 Edgewood Ave NE, Atlanta, GA 30312 (404) 688-7483. Profile: Sells, installs, monitors and maintains commercial security systems.

TELEMED, INC, SMARTFAX #5261
18 Beck St, Atlanta, GA 30318 (404) 355-1555. Profile: Southeast's largest medical answering/paging service.

Apex Supply Co., Inc.
SmartFax #5468
2500 Button Gwinnett
Dr, Atlanta, GA 30340.
(770) 449-7000.

**Artlite Office Supply
Co.** SmartFax #7232
1851 Piedmont Rd NE,
Atlanta, GA 30324. (404)
875-7271.

Atlantic Envelope Co.
SmartFax #5388
1700 Northside Drive,
Atlanta, GA . (404) 351-
5011.

Brown Reporting
SmartFax #7233
501 Broad St, Suite 309,
Rome, GA 30309. (404)
876-8979.

**Corporate Express of
The South Inc.** SmartFax
#7234
8145 Troon Cir, Suite H,
Austell, GA 30001. (770)
941-0155.

Georgia Office Supply
SmartFax #7236
2000 Cobb International
Blvd, Suite A, Kennesaw,
GA 30144. (770) 427-
7361.

MI&M Services
SmartFax #7238
5667 Peachtree-
Dunwoody Rd NE,
Atlanta, GA 30342. (404)
257-8460.

Minton-Jones Co.
SmartFax #7239
6690-D Jones Mill Court,
Norcross, GA 30092.
(770) 449-4787.

Office Depot SmartFax
#7240
2581 Piedmont Rd,
Atlanta, GA 30324. (404)
261-4111.

OfficeMax SmartFax
#7241
5615 Memorial Drive,
Stone Mountain, GA
30084. (404) 508-8260.

OfficeWorx Inc.
SmartFax #7242
8601 Dunwoody Place,
Suite 444, Dunwoody,
GA 30350. (770) 552-
6050.

One Source Supply Inc.
SmartFax #7243
5555 Oakbrook Pkwy,
Sute 240, Norcross, GA
30093. (770) 242-0281.

**Piedmont Janitorial
Service** SmartFax #5988
3525 Piedmont Rd NE,
Altanta, GA 30305. (404)
231-3633.

**Seals & Stamps
Unlimited** SmartFax
#5875
550 Franklin Rd, #F,
Marietta, GA . (770) 514-
1234.

Secrephone SmartFax
#7244
118 North Ave,
Jonesboro, GA 30236.
(770) 471-5414.

**Universal Security
Systems, Inc.** SmartFax
#5931
4289 Memorial Dr, Suite
I, Decatur, GA 30032.
(404) 296-5803.

Transportation

ALLIED HOLDINGS, SMARTFAX #5989
160 Clairmont Ave #600, Decatur, GA 30030 (404) 371-0379. Profile: Second largest car hauler in the US, employing 375 in Atlanta.

AMERICAN COACH LINES INC, SMARTFAX #5011
PO Box 646, Norcross, GA 30091 (770) 449-1806. Profile: Largest charter bus company in Atlanta, employing 130.

ARMSTRONG RELOCATION, SMARTFAX #5021
6950 Business Court, Atlanta, GA 30340 (770) 362-0368. Profile: Largest household goods mover in Atlanta.

AUTOSAVE CAR RENTALS, SMARTFAX #5675
4945 Peachtree Ind Blvd, Chamblee, GA 30341 (770) 451-2951. Profile: Atlanta-based company with two locations in North Carolina and five in Atlanta

DEKALB COUNTY SCHOOLS TRANSPORTATION, SMARTFAX #5443
1380 Montreal Rd, Tucker, GA 30084 (770) 934-3610. Profile: With a staff of over 800, nearly 200 new drivers are hired annually.

ENTERPRISE RENT-A-CAR, SMARTFAX #5086
3109 Maple Drive #218, Atlanta,, GA 30305 (404) 266-2778. Profile: Largest rental car company in the U.S.

GREYHOUND LINES, INC, SMARTFAX #5104
232 Forsyth Street SW, Atlanta, GA 30303 (404) 584-1751. Profile: The only nationwide provider of intercity bus transportations services.

HERTZ CORP., THE, SMARTFAX #5134
1920 Autoport Dr, Smyrna, GA 30320 (404) 209-3205. Profile: A larger rental car service.

JIM PALMER TRUCKING, SMARTFAX #5337
4215 Thurman Rd PO Box 9, Conley, GA 30087 (404) 608-1764. Profile: Long haul, refrigerated truck load carrier, with 35 employees in Atlanta.

JONES MOTOR GROUP, THE, SMARTFAX #5154
2124 Forest Pkwy #B, Morrow, GA 30260 (404) 362-9259. Profile: Provides flatbed and van truckload services.

MARTA (METRO ATLANTA RAPID TRANSIT AUTH), SMARTFAX #5970
2424 Piedmont Rd NE, Atlanta, GA 30324-3330 (404) 848-5544. Profile: Atlanta's Transit Authority, employing over 3,000.

NORFOLK SOUTHERN CORP., SMARTFAX #5974
223 East City Hall Ave, Norfolk, VA 23510 (804) 629-2688. Profile: Railroad and transportation company based in Virginia.

TRANSUS, SMARTFAX #5898
2090 Jonesboro Rd SE, Atlanta, GA 30315 (404) 627-7331. Profile: Common carrier and transportation service, employing 800.

UNITED PARCEL SERVICE, DORAVILLE, SMARTFAX #5984
3951 Pleasantdale Rd #110, Doraville, GA 30340 (770) 246-9230. Profile: Corporate headquarters employing 2100.

UNITED PARKING, INC., SMARTFAX #8675
100 Peachtree Street, Suite 335, Atlanta, GA 30303 (404) 658-9053. Profile: Owns, manages, and offers consulting services for the operation of parking facilities.

Atlanta Forklifts	**Dollar Rent A Car**	**Georgia Crown**
SmartFax #5383	SmartFax #5439	**Distributing Co.**
3111 E Ponce De Leon	4003 Main St, College	SmartFax #5689
Ave, Scottsdale, GA	Park, GA 30337. (404)	255 Villa Nova Drive,
30079. (404) 373-1606.	766-0244.	Atlanta, GA 30336-2523.
		(404) 344-9550.

Utilities

ATLANTA GAS LIGHT CO., SMARTFAX #5384
PO Box 4569, Atlanta, GA 30302 (404) 584-4164. Profile: Public gas utility employing 2000.

GEORGIA POWER CO., SMARTFAX #5465

PO Box 4545, Atlanta, GA 30308 (404) 526-6526. Profile: Largest electric utility in Georgia, employing over 5000.

MEDIAONE, INC., SMARTFAX #8694

2925 Courtyards Dr, Norcross, GA 30071 (770) 631-2424. Profile: Largest cable television provider in Atlanta.

MUNICIPAL ELECTRIC AUTHORITY OF GEORGIA, SMARTFAX #5613

1470 Riveredge Pkwy NW, Atlanta, GA 30328-4640 (770) 952-5445. Profile: Provider of electricity to 48 Georgia cities.

OGLETHORPE POWER, SMARTFAX #5473

2100 E Exchange Place, Tucker, GA 30085-1349 (770) 270-7600. Profile: Nation's largest power generation and transmission cooperative, based in Atlanta.

RIFKIN & ASSOCIATES, SMARTFAX #5231

3075 Breckinridge Bvd #450, Duluth, GA 30136 (770) 806-7060. Profile: Cable TV company serving northern Gwinnett and Roswell.

SOUTHERN CO. SERVICES, SMARTFAX #6022

64 Perimeter Center E, Atlanta, GA 30346 (770) 393-0650. Profile: Provides engineering, information resources and administrative services to electrical utilities throughout the Southeast, employing 1200.

Other

BXI/ATLANTA, SMARTFAX #5048

PO Box 1984, Lilburn, GA 30226 (770) 931-4637. Profile: National barter company that coordinates the trade of products and services between small to medium sized corporations.

ISS CLEANING SERVICES GROUP, SMARTFAX #7911

1445 Marietta Blvd NW, Atalnta, GA 30318 (404) 351-7100. Profile: Large janitorial service.

PARK 'N FLY, INC., SMARTFAX #5210
2060 Mt Paran Rd #207, Atlanta, GA 30327 (404) 264-1000. Profile: Largest office parking company in the U.S.

PINKERTON SECURITY SERVICES, SMARTFAX #5586
2987 Clairmont Rd #220, Atlanta, GA 30329 (404) 634-9770. Profile: Oldest private security service in North America.

THE FORTUNE GROUP, SMARTFAX #7245
Six Concourse Pkwy, Suite 1930, Atlanta, GA 30328 (770) 395-2808. Profile: Produces and markets video-based training systems.

BXI/ATLANTA
SmartFax #5048
PO Box 1984, Lilburn, GA 30226. (770) 931-4637.

ISS CLEANING SERVICES GROUP
SmartFax #7911
1445 Marietta Blvd NW, Atalnta, GA 30318. (404) 351-7100.

PARK 'N FLY, INC.
SmartFax #5210
2060 Mt Paran Rd #207, Atlanta, GA 30327. (404) 264-1000.

THE FORTUNE GROUP SmartFax #7245
Six Concourse Pkwy, Suite 1930, Atlanta, GA 30328. (770) 395-2808.

Consulting

BORG-WARNER PROTECTIVE SERVICES, SMARTFAX #5046
2300 Henderson Ml Rd #121, Atlanta, GA 30345 (770) 492-5080. Profile: Uniformed protective services employing over 80,000 security officers throughout the country.

C-STAFF/BENEFIT ADMIN SERVICES, INC., SMARTFAX #6013
400 Northridge Rd #200, Atlanta, GA 30350-3352 (770) 642-7400. Profile: Employee benefit service provider.

DELOITTE AND TOUCHE MANAGEMENT CONSULTING GRP, SMARTFAX #5436
285 Peachtree Center Av/2000, Atlanta, GA 30303-1234 (404) 220-1000. Profile: Southeast headquarters for D&T's consulting division, employing 135.

FIRST HEALTH SERVICES, SMARTFAX #5455
1927 Lakeside Pkwy,S606, Tucker, GA 30084 (770) 491-6262. Profile: Third party health care administration, employing 125 at three Atlanta offices.

HEWITT ASSOCIATES, SMARTFAX #5135
2100 Riveredge Pkwy, Atlanta, GA 30328 (770) 956-7777. Profile: Atlanta's largest employee benefits and compensation consulting firm, employing 150.

INTERNATIONAL PERSONNEL RESOURCES LTD, SMARTFAX #5145
1655 Phoenix Blvd #4, College Park, GA 30349 (770) 997-1995. Profile: Human resource and benefit administrators.

NORRELL CORP., SMARTFAX #7246
3535 Piedmont Rd NE, Atalnta, GA 30305 (404) 240-3000. Profile: International temporary help provider.

PRICE WATERHOUSE LLP, (CONSULTING DIVISION), SMARTFAX #5592
3200 Windy Hill Rd #900W, Atlanta, GA 30339 (770) 933-9191. Profile: Management consulting firm specializing in large-scale client-server implementation.

TOWERS PERRIN COMPANIES, SMARTFAX #5942

950 E Paces Fy Rd NE, Atlanta, GA 30326-1119 (404) 365-1600. Profile: Fifth largest international consulting firm, employing 300 in Atlanta.

A. Foster Higgins & Co.
SmartFax #7247
191 Peachtree St NE,
Atlanta, GA 30303. (404) 586-1700.

Agape Consulting Froup SmartFax #7248
3145 Tucker-Norcross Rd, Suite 209-212,
Tucker, GA 30084. (770) 414-9723.

Alexander & Alexander Consulting Group
SmartFax #7250
1 Piedmont Center, 3565 Piedmont Rd NE,
Atlanta, GA 30363. (404) 264-3141.

American Cancer Society Inc. SmartFax #7251
1699 Clifton Rd NE,
Atlanta, GA 30329. (404) 320-3333.

Atlanta Pension Funds
SmartFax #7252
68 Mitchell St SW, Suite 1600, Atlanta, GA 30335. (404) 330-6260.

Buck Consultants Inc.
SmartFax #7253

200 Galleria Pkwy NW,
Suite 1200, Atlanta, GA 30339. (770) 955-2488.

Callan Associates
SmartFax #7254
6 Concourse Pkwy, Suite 2900, Atlanta, GA 30328. (770) 804-5585.

DeKalb Employee Retiremtent System
SmartFax #7255
1300 Commerce Drive,
Annex Bldg, Decatur, GA 30030. (770) 371-2296.

Design Benefit Plans, Inc. SmartFax #5446
100 Crescent Center Pkwy #390, Tucker, GA 30084. (770) 414-5657.

EBS/Atlanta SmartFax #7256
3340 Peachtree Rd NE,
Suite 710, Atlanta, GA 30326. (404) 231-5643.

Fulton County Employees' Pension
SmartFax #7257
141 Pryor St, Suite 7001,
Atlanta, GA 30303. (404) 730-7600.

Georgia Division of Investment Svs.
SmartFax #7258

2 Northside 75, Suite 500, Atlanta, GA 30318. (404) 656-2151.

Georgia Firemen's Pension Fund SmartFax #7259
720 Church St, Decatur, GA 30031. (404) 370-5070.

Godwins Booke & Dickenson SmartFax #7260
400 Interstate North Pkwy, Suite 1630,
Atlanta, GA 30339. (770) 952-9009.

Hamilton Dorsey Alston Co. SmartFax #7261
3350 Cumberland Cir,
Suite 100, Atlanta, GA 30339. (770) 850-0050.

Hay Group Inc.
SmartFax #7262
5901-A Peachtree-Dunwoody Rd, Suite 450,
Atlanta, GA 30328. (770) 394-5500.

Hazlehurst & Associates Inc. SmartFax #7263
400 Perimeter Center Terrace, Suite 850,
Atlanta, GA 30346. (770) 395-9880.

Metcalf Rice Fricke & Davis SmartFax #7019
950 East Paces Fy Rd, Atlanta, GA 30326. (404) 264-1700.

Pension Financial Services Inc. SmartFax #7265
2970 Clairmont Rd, Suite 925, Atlanta, GA 30329. (404) 728-0280.

Sedgwick Noble Lowndes SmartFax #7266
3333 Peachtree Rd, Atlanta, GA 30326. (404) 237-8444.

Sellutions, Inc. SmartFax #5876
30 South Park Sq, #202, Marietta, GA 30060. (770) 427-5560.

Southern Co. Services Inc. SmartFax #6022
64 Perimeter Center E, Atlanta, GA 30346. (770) 668-3534.

Taylor & Co. SmartFax #7268
1936 North Druid Hills, Atlanta, GA 30319. (404) 321-5474.

The Benefit Co. SmartFax #7269
3340 Peachtree Rd, Suite 2200, Atlanta, GA 30326. (404) 233-2200.

The Segal Co. SmartFax #7270
1000 Parkwood Cir, Suite 200, Atlanta, GA 30339. (770) 955-4003.

The Wyatt Co. SmartFax #7271
4170 Ashford-Dunwoody Rd NE, Suite 432, Atlanta, GA 30319. (404) 252-4030.

United Food & Commercial Workers SmartFax #7272
1800 Phoenix Blvd, Suite 310, Atlanta, GA 30349. (404) 997-9910.

Waddell, Smith, Magoon, O'Neal&Saul SmartFax #7024
10892 Crabapple Rd, Suite 100, Roswell, GA 30075. (770) 993-6818.

William M. Mercer Inc. SmartFax #7274
3700 Georgia-Pacific Center, Atlanta, GA 30303. (404) 521-2200.

Education

AMS DISTRIBUTORS INC, SMARTFAX #5013
PO Box 457, Roswell, GA 30077 (770) 442-1945. Profile: Produces and distributes job training and regulatory compliance programs - video and print.

APOSTLES LUTHERAN CHILD DEVELOPMENT CENTER, SMARTFAX #5017
6025 Glenridge Dr, Atlanta, GA 30328 (404) 256-3091. Profile: Licensed NAEYC accredited church-run center.

ASHER SCHOOL OF BUSINESS, SMARTFAX #5023
100 Pinnacle Way #110, Norcross, GA 30071 (770) 368-0800. Profile: Trains post-secondary students in software packages, accounting and front office medical skills with 50 instructors.

CHILDREN'S WORLD LEARNING CENTER, SmartFax #5062
1835 Savoy Drive #210, Atlanta, GA 30341 (770) 458-4646. Profile: America's third largest child care provider with over 500 centers in 23 states, and more than 300 employees here in Atlanta.

CREME DE LA CREME, SmartFax #5080
4669 Roswell Rd, Atlanta, GA 30342 (404) 256-4488. Profile: Preschool with three locations in Atlanta.

DEVRY INSTITUTE OF TECHNOLOGY, SmartFax #5930
250 N Arcadia Ave, Decatur, GA 30030 (404) 292-7900. Profile: Offers educational classes in information technology.

EMORY UNIVERSITY, SmartFax #5954
1762 Clifton Rd NE, Atlanta, GA 30322 (404) 727-7611. Profile: Private university with 9000 students, employing 3775 non-faculty personnel and 2800 hospital personnel.

GEORGIA INSTITUTE OF TECHNOLOGY, SmartFax #5462
955 Fowler Street NW, Atlanta, GA 30332 (404) 894-3245. Profile: Third largest university in GA and second largest in Atlanta, with over 12,000 students and 4000 employees.

GEORGIA STATE UNIVERSITY, SmartFax #5466
Univ Plaza, 1 Park Place, Atlanta, GA 30303 (404) 651-2000. Profile: Georgia's second largest and Atlanta's largest university, with more than 20,000 students and 1500 non-faculty employees.

KIDS 'R' KIDS #16, SmartFax #5159
200 Pine Grove Rd, Roswell, GA 30075 (770) 642-1900. Profile: Nursery school and daycare center.

PROFESSIONAL CAREER DEVELOPMENT INSTITUTE, SmartFax #5595
3597 Pkwy Lane #100, Norcross, GA 30092 (770) 729-9296. Profile: Correspondence school.

SIKES SCHOOLS, INC, SMARTFAX #5246

2311-C Henry Clower Blvd, Snellville, GA 30278 (770) 979-3666. Profile: Child care provider with 8 Gwinnett county locations.

Agnes Scott College
SmartFax #7275
11 East College Ave,
Decatur, GA 30030.
(404) 638-6285.

American Child Care Center SmartFax #7276
1144 N Indian Creek Dr,
Clarkston, GA 30021.
(404) 292-9550.

Atlanta Area Technical Institute SmartFax #7278
1560 Stewart Ave,
Atlanta, GA 30310. (404) 756-3700.

Atlanta Christian College SmartFax #7279
2605 Ben Hill Rd,
Atlanta, GA 30334. (404) 761-8861.

Atlanta College of Art SmartFax #7280
1280 Peachtree St NE,
Atlanta, GA 30309. (404) 733-5001.

Atlanta Metropolitan College SmartFax #7281
1630 Stewart Ave SW,
Atlanta, GA 30310. (404) 756-4000.

Atlanta Parent-Child SmartFax #7282

240 James P Brawley Dr,
Atlanta, GA 30314. (404) 880-8085.

Bauder College
SmartFax #7283
3500 Peachtree Rd NE,
Atlanta, GA 30326. (404) 237-7573.

Berlitz Language Center SmartFax #7284
3400 Peachtree Rd NE,
Atlanta, GA 30326. (404) 261-5062.

Berry College SmartFax #7285
Mount Berry Station,
Rome, GA 30149. (706) 232-5374.

Bremen City School District SmartFax #7286
504 Laurel St, Bremen,
GA 30110. (770) 537-5508.

Brenau University SmartFax #7287
1 Centennial Cir,
Gainesville, GA 30501.
(770) 534-6299.

Brookwood High School SmartFax #7288
1255 Dogwood Rd,
Snellville, GA 30278.
(770) 972-7642.

Carroll Technical Institute SmartFax #7289
997 South Highway 16,
Carrollton, GA 30117.
(770) 836-6800.

Carrollton Elementary School SmartFax #7290
401 Stadium Drive,
Carrollton, GA 30117.
(770) 832-2120.

Cass High School SmartFax #7291
738 Grassdale Rd NW,
Cartersville, GA 30120.
(770) 382-0230.

Cedar Shoals High School SmartFax #7292
1300 Cedar Shoals Dr,
Athens, GA 30605. (706) 546-5375.

Chattahoochee High School SmartFax #7293
5230 Taylor Rd,
Alpharetta, GA 30202.
(770) 740-7080.

Chattahoochee Technical Institute SmartFax #7294
980 South Cobb Drive,
Marietta, GA 30060.
(770) 528-4500.

Children's House
SmartFax #7295
2350 Wisteria Dr,
Snellville, GA 30278.
(770) 979-0500.

Children's World
Learning Center,
Lilburn SmartFax #7296
641 Rockbridge Rd,
Lilburn, GA 30247. (770)
279-2016.

Childtime Children's
Centers SmartFax #7298
1988 Scenic Hwy N,
Snellville, GA 30278.
(770) 985-8946.

Clark Atlanta
University SmartFax
#7299
James P Brawley Drive
SW, Atlanta, GA 30314.
(404) 880-8000.

Clarke Central High
School SmartFax #7300
350 S Milledge Ave,
Athens, GA 30605. (706)
357-5200.

Clayton State College
SmartFax #7301
5900 North Lee St,
Morrow, GA 30260.
(770) 961-3400.

Columbia High School
SmartFax #7302
2106 Columbia Dr,
Decatur, GA 30032.
(404) 284-8720.

Columbia Theological
Seminary SmartFax
#7303
301 Columbia Drive,
Decatur, GA 30031.
(404) 378-8821.

Coosa Valley Technical
Institute SmartFax
#7304
112 Hemlock St, Rome,
GA 30161. (706) 235-
1142.

Crawford Long Hosp. of
Emory Univ. SmartFax
#7305
550 Peachtree St NE,
Atlanta, GA 30365. (404)
686-4411.

Creekside High School
SmartFax #7306
7405 Herndon Rd,
Fairburn, GA 30213.
(770) 969-6070.

David H. Kistner Day
Care Center SmartFax
#7307
2466 Buford Hwy,
Duluth, GA 30136. (770)
476-1340.

DeKalb College
SmartFax #7308
3251 Pantersville Rd,
Decatur, GA 30034.
(404) 244-2360.

DeKalb Medical Center
SmartFax #7309

2701 North Decatur Rd,
Decatur, GA 30033.
(770) 501-1000.

DeKalb Technical
Institute SmartFax
#7310
495 North Indian Creek
Drive, Clarkston, GA
30021. (404) 297-9522.

Douglas High School
SmartFax #7312
225 Hightower Rd NW,
Atlanta, GA 30318. (404)
792-5925.

Duluth Middle School
SmartFax #7313
3057 Peachtree Industrial
Blvd, Duluth, GA 30136.
(770) 476-3372.

Dunwoody Medical
Center SmartFax #7314
4575 North Shallowford
Rd, Atlanta, GA 30338.
(770) 454-2000.

Eastside Medical Center
SmartFax #7315
1700 Medical Way,
Snellville, GA 30278.
(770) 979-0200.

Egleston Children's
Hosp./Emory University
SmartFax #7316
1405 Clifton Rd NE,
Atlanta, GA 30322. (404)
325-6101.

124

Emory University Hospital SmartFax #5954
1364 Clifton Rd NE, Atlanta, GA 30322. (404) 727-7021.

Epstein School SmartFax #7319
335 Colewood Way NW, Atlanta, GA 30328. (404) 843-0111.

Fayette County High School SmartFax #7320
205 Lafeyette Dr, Fayetteville, GA 30214. (770) 460-3540.

Five Forks Middle School SmartFax #7321
3250 River Dr, Lawrenceville, GA 30244. (770) 921-1776.

Floyd College SmartFax #7322
PO Box 1864, Rome, GA 30162. (706) 802-5000.

Gainesville College SmartFax #7323
PO Box 1358, Gainesville, GA 30503. (770) 535-6239.

Georgia Academy of Music SmartFax #7325
1424 W Paces Fy Rd NW, Atlanta, GA 30327. (404) 355-3451.

Georgia Baptist College of Nursing SmartFax #7326
300 Boulevard NE, Atlanta, GA 30312. (404) 653-4800.

Georgia Baptist Medical Center SmartFax #7327
300 Boulevard NE, Atlanta, GA 30312. (404) 265-4000.

Grady Memorial Hospital Prof.School SmartFax #7330
80 Butler St SE, Atlanta, GA 30335. (404) 616-3610.

Griffin High School SmartFax #7331
1617 W Poplar St, Griffin, GA 30223. (770) 228-8641.

Griffin Technical Institute SmartFax #7332
501 Varsity Rd, Griffin, GA 30223. (404) 228-7348.

Gwinnett Medical Center SmartFax #7333
1000 Medical Center Blvd, Lawrenceville, GA 30245. (770) 995-4321.

Gwinnett Technical Institute SmartFax #7334
1250 Atkinson Rd, Lawrenceville, GA 30246. (404) 962-7580.

Hapeville Elementary School SmartFax #7336
3440 N Fulton Ave, Atlanta, GA 30354. (404) 669-8220.

Harper High School SmartFax #7337
500 Wendell Ct SW, Atalnta, GA 30336. (404) 699-4511.

Henry General Hospital SmartFax #7338
1133 Eagle's Landing Pkwy, Stockbridge, GA 30281. (770) 389-2200.

Heritage High School SmartFax #7339
2400 Granade Rd SW, Conyers, GA 30207. (770) 483-5428.

Institute of Paper Science & Tech. SmartFax #5958
500 10th St NW, Atlanta, GA 30314. (404) 853-9500.

Interdenominational Theological Center SmartFax #7341
671 Beckwith St SW, Atlanta, GA 30314. (404) 527-7700.

J.F. Kennedy Community Center Daycare SmartFax #7342 225 James P Brawley Dr SW, Atlanta, GA 30314. (404) 330-4133.

Jere Via Day Care Center SmartFax #7343 2253 Fairburn Rd, Douglasville, GA 30135. (770) 949-3717.

Johnson High School SmartFax #7344 3505 Poplar Springs Rd, Gainesville, GA 30507. (770) 536-2394.

Jonesboro High School SmartFax #7345 7728 Mount Zion Blvd, Jonesboro, GA 30236. (770) 473-2855.

Keller Graduate School SmartFax #7346 2 Ravinia Drive, Atlanta, GA 30346. (404) 671-1744.

Kennesaw St. College/Office of Personnel Svcs SmartFax #5551 PO Box 444, Marietta, GA 30061. (770) 423-6031.

Kennesaw State College SmartFax #7347 3455 Frey Lake Rd, Marietta, GA 30061. (404) 423-6300.

La Petite Academy SmartFax #7348 3320 Hwy 124, Lithonia, GA 30058. (770) 972-5626.

LaGrange College SmartFax #7349 601 Broad St, LaGrange, GA 30240. (706) 882-2911.

Lassiter High School SmartFax #7350 2600 Shallowford Rd, Marietta, GA 30066. (770) 591-6819.

Let's Talk About The Family SmartFax #5968 3013 Rainbow Dr, #115, Decatur, GA 30034. (404) 212-0047.

Life College SmartFax #7351 1269 Barclay Cir, Marietta, GA 30060. (404) 424-0554.

Lilburn Middle School SmartFax #7352 4994 Lawrenceville Hwy NW, Lilburn, GA 30247. (770) 921-1776.

Lovett School SmartFax #7353 4075 Paces Fy Rd NW, Atlanta, GA 30327. (404) 262-3032.

Lullwater School SmartFax #5174

705 S Candler St, Decatur, GA 30030. (404) 378-6643.

Marietta High School SmartFax #7354 121 Winn St, Marietta, GA 30064. (770) 428-2631.

Marietta Middle School SmartFax #7355 340 Aviation Rd, Marietta, GA 30060. (770) 422-0311.

McIntosh High School SmartFax #7356 201 Walt Banks Rd, Peachtree City, GA 30269. (770) 631-3232.

Meadowcreek High School SmartFax #7357 4455 Steve Reynolds Blvd, Norcross, GA 30093. (770) 381-9680.

Mercer University SmartFax #7358 3001 Mercer University Drive, Atlanta, GA 30341. (770) 986-3134.

Morehouse College SmartFax #7359 830 Westview Drive SW, Atlanta, GA 30314. (404) 681-2800.

Morehouse School of Medicine SmartFax #7360

720 Westview Drive SW, Atlanta, GA 30310. (404) 752-1500.

Morris Brown College SmartFax #7361 643 Martin Luther King Jr SW, Atlanta, GA 30314. (404) 220-0270.

National Louis University SmartFax #7362 1777 Northeast Expressway, Atlanta, GA 30329. (404) 633-1223.

Newnan High School SmartFax #7363 190 LaGrange St, Newnan, GA 30263. (770) 254-2880.

Newton County High School SmartFax #7364 140 Ram Dr, Covington, GA 30209. (770) 787-2250.

Norcross High School SmartFax #7365 600 Beaver Ruin Rd, Norcross, GA 30071. (770) 448-3674.

North Fulton Regional Hospital SmartFax #7366 3000 Hospital Blvd, Roswell, GA 30076. (770) 751-2500.

North Hall Middle School SmartFax #7367

4956 Rilla Rd, Gainesville, GA 30506. (770) 983-9749.

North Metro Technical Institute SmartFax #7368 5198 Ross Rd, Acworth, GA 30102. (770) 975-4010.

North Springs High School SmartFax #7369 7447 Roswell Rd NE, Atlanta, GA 30328. (770) 551-2490.

Northside Hospital SmartFax #7370 1000 Johnson Fy Rd NE, Atlanta, GA 30342. (404) 851-8700.

Oglethorpe University SmartFax #7371 4484 Peachtree Rd NE, Atlanta, GA 30319. (404) 261-1441.

Parkview Community School SmartFax #7373 998 Cole Rd SW, Lilburn, GA 30247. (770) 921-2874.

Parkway Medical Center SmartFax #7374 1000 Thornton Rd, Lithia Springs, GA 30057. (770) 732-7717.

Paulding County School District SmartFax #7375

522 Hardee St, Dallas, GA 30132. (770) 443-8000.

Pickens Technical Institute SmartFax #7376 100 Pickens Tech Drive, Jasper, GA 30143. (706) 692-3411.

Piedmont Hospital SmartFax #7377 1968 Peachtree Rd NW, Atlanta, GA 30309. (404) 605-5000.

Pope High School SmartFax #7378 3001 Hembree Rd NE, Marietta, GA 30062. (770) 509-6077.

Preston Ridge Montessori School SmartFax #7379 3800 N Point Pkwy, Alpharetta, GA 30202. (770) 751-9510.

Prodigy Child Development Center SmartFax #5920 4506 Roswell Rd, Atlanta, GA 30342. (404) 252-0389.

Promina Cobb Hospital SmartFax #7380 3950 Austell Rd, Austell, GA 30001. (770) 732-4010.

Promina Kennestone Hospital SmartFax #7381
677 Church St, Marietta, GA 30060. (770) 793-5170.

Redan High School SmartFax #7382
5247 Redan Rd, Stone Mountain, GA 30088. (770) 469-1500.

Reinhardt College SmartFax #7383
PO Box 128, Waleska, GA 30183. (770) 720-5600.

Riverdale High School SmartFax #7384
160 Roberts Dr, Riverdale, GA 30274. (770) 473-2905.

Rockdale County High School SmartFax #7385
1174 Bulldog Cir NE, Conyers, GA 30207. (770) 483-8754.

Rockdale Hospital SmartFax #7386
1412 Milstead Ave, Conyers, GA 30207. (770) 918-3000.

Scottish Rite Children's Med. Ctr. SmartFax #7387
1001 Johnson Fy Rd, Atlanta, GA 30342. (404) 256-5252.

Sheltering Arms Daycare Center SmartFax #7388
529 Flint Tr, Jonesboro, GA 30236. (770) 447-1746.

Shepherd Center SmartFax #7389
2020 Peachtree Rd NW, Atlanta, GA 30309. (404) 352-2020.

Shiloh High School SmartFax #7390
4210 Shiloh Rd, Lithonia, GA 30058. (770) 972-8471.

Shiloh Middle School SmartFax #7391
4285 Shiloh Rd, Lithonia, GA 30058. (770) 972-3224.

Shorter College SmartFax #7392
315 Shorter Ave, Rome, GA 30165. (706) 291-2121.

Snellville Middle School SmartFax #7394
3155 Pate Rd, Snellville, GA 30278. (770) 972-1530.

South Cobb Daycare Center SmartFax #7395
5541 Austell Rd, Austell, GA 30001-3532. (770) 941-5000.

South Fulton Medical Center SmartFax #7396
1170 Cleveland Ave, Atlanta, GA 30344. (404) 305-3500.

South Gwinnett High School SmartFax #7397
2288 E Main St, Snellville, GA 30278. (770) 972-4840.

Southern College of Technology SmartFax #7398
1100 South Marietta Pkwy, Marietta, GA 30060. (770) 528-7230.

Southern Regional Medical Center SmartFax #7399
11 Upper Riverdale Rd SW, Riverdale, GA 30274. (770) 991-8000.

Spalding Regional Hospital SmartFax #7400
601 South 8th St, Griffin, GA 30223. (770) 229-6462.

Spelman College SmartFax #7401
305 Spelman Lane SW, Atlanta, GA 30314. (404) 681-3643.

St. Joseph's Hospital of Atlanta SmartFax #7402
5665 Peachtree-Dunwoody Rd, Atlanta, GA 30342. (404) 851-7001.

Tanner Medical Center/Carrollton
SmartFax #7403
705 Dixie St, Carrollton, GA 30117. (770) 836-9580.

The American College
SmartFax #7404
3330 Peachtree Rd, Atlanta, GA 30326. (404) 231-9000.

Towers High School
SmartFax #7405
3919 Brookcrest Cir, Decatur, GA 30032. (404) 289-7166.

University of Georgia
SmartFax #7406
(706) 542-8776.

Washington Evening Community School
SmartFax #7407
45 Whitehouse Drive SW, Atlanta, GA 30314. (404) 752-0733.

West Georgia Medical Center SmartFax #7409
1514 Vernon Rd, LaGrange, GA 30240. (706) 882-1411.

West Hall High School
SmartFax #7410
5500 McEver Rd, Oakwood, GA 30566. (770) 967-9826.

West Paces Medical Center SmartFax #7411
3200 Howell Mill Rd NW, Atlanta, GA 30327. (404) 350-5600.

Hospitals and Medical Services

CHAMBREL AT ROSWELL, SMARTFAX #5055
1000 Applewood Drive, Roswell, GA 30076 (770) 594-4600. Profile: Retirement community.

EMORY UNIVERSITY HOSPITAL, SMARTFAX #5954
1762 Clifton Rd NE, Atlanta, GA 30322 (404) 727-7611. Profile: Private university with 9000 students, employing 3775 non-faculty personnel and 2800 hospital personnel.

GRADY HEALTH SYS/FULTON-DEKALB HOSPITAL AUTH, SMARTFAX #5101
80 Butler Street SE, Atlanta, GA 30335 (404) 616-1900. Profile: Atlanta's largest hospital, employing 6500 total.

HEALTHDYNE TECHNOLOGIES, SMARTFAX #5476

1255 Kennestone Cir NW, Marietta, GA 30066 (770) 499-1212. Profile: Home care subsidiary of Healthdyne, Inc.

HEALTHDYNE, INC., SMARTFAX #5552
1850 Pkwy Place, Marietta, GA 30067 (770) 423-4500. Profile: National corporation that provides home health care services and manufactures medical equipment.

KAISER PERMANENTE, SMARTFAX #5987
3495 Piedmont Rd, Bldg 9, Atlanta, GA 30305 (404) 233-0555. Profile: Nation's largest health maintenance organization (HMO), employing 1300 in Atlanta.

MANN HEALTH SERVICES INC, SMARTFAX #5181
5413 Northland Drive, Atlanta, GA 30342 (404) 257-0097. Profile: Operators of residential elderly care homes.

MEDAPHIS HOSPITAL SERVICES, SMARTFAX #5187
5300 Oakbrook Pkwy, Suite 300, Norcross, GA 30093 (770) 319-3300. Profile: Provides business management services to hospitals.

MENDERS INC, SMARTFAX #5191
1795 Peachtree St, Suite 270, Atlanta, GA 30309 (404) 355-4780. Profile: Provides in-home support services to senior adults.

MOUNT VERNON TOWERS, SMARTFAX #5204
300 Johnson Fy Rd, Atlanta, GA 30328 (404) 255-3534. Profile: A senior living retirement community.

NATIONAL LINEN SERVICE, P'TREE RD., SMARTFAX #5217
1420 Peachtree St NE, Atlanta, GA 30309 (404) 853-6259. Profile: Textile rental division of National Service Industries, a Fortune 500 company, servicing the hospitality industry and health care facilities.

PLASTIC SURGERY USA, SMARTFAX #5589
6021 Sandy Springs Cir, Atlanta, GA 30328-3841 (404) 252-2892. Profile: Combination physician practice, laser and skin care center, and an ambulatory surgery center.

THERA TX INC, SMARTFAX #5266

400 Northridge Rd #400, Atlanta, GA 30350-3353 (770) 518-9449. Profile: Short-term rehabilitation provider with 200+ centers nationwide.

VISITING NURSE HEALTH SYSTEM, SMARTFAX #5306
133 Luckie Stret NW, Atlanta, GA 30303 (404) 527-0754. Profile: In-home health care company.

WESLEY WOOD CENTER, SMARTFAX #5294

1817 Clifton Rd NE, Atlanta, GA 30329 (404) 728-6226. Profile: Provides a range of medical services.

Asbury Harris Epworth Towers SmartFax #7412
3033 Continental Colony Pkwy, Atlanta, GA 30331. (404) 344-9400.

Atherton Place
SmartFax #7413
111 Tower Rd, Marietta, GA 30060. (770) 421-7300.

Atlanta Cardiothoracic Surgical Associates
SmartFax #5927
315 Boulevard NE, #224, Atlanta, GA 30312. (404) 265-3550.

Atlanta Medical Associates SmartFax #7414
100 10th St, Atlanta, GA 30309. (404) 897-1010.

Branan Towers
SmartFax #7415
1200 Glenwood Ave SE, Atlanta, GA 30316. (404) 622-5471.

Calvin Court Apartments SmartFax #7416
479 East Paces Fy Rd, Atlanta, GA 30305. (404) 261-1223.

Campbell-Stone Apartments SmartFax #7417
2911 South Pharr Court NW, Atlanta, GA 30305. (404) 261-4132.

Campbell-Stone North Apartments SmartFax #7418
350 Carpenter Drive NE, Atlanta, GA 30328. (404) 256-2612.

Cardiology of GA
SmartFax #7419
95 Collier Rd, Suite 2075, Atlanta, GA 30309. (404) 355-6562.

Central Home Health Care SmartFax #7420
6666 Powers Fy Rd, Suite 220, Atlanta, GA 30339. (770) 953-8570.

Children's Heart Center
SmartFax #7422
2040 Ridgewood Drive, Atlanta, GA 30322. (404) 248-5111.

Christian City Retirement Homes
SmartFax #7423
7350 Lester Rd, Union City, GA 30291. (770) 964-3301.

Clairmont Oaks
SmartFax #7424
441 Clairmont Ave, Decatur, GA 30030. (404) 378-8887.

Clairmont Place
SmartFax #7425
2100 Clairmont Lake, Decatur, GA 30033. (404) 633-8875.

Clark-Holder Clinic
SmartFax #7426
303 Smith St, LaGrange, GA 30240. (706) 882-8831.

Cobb Home Health
SmartFax #7427
3200 Highlands Pkwy, Suite 300, Smyrna, GA 30082. (770) 319-1455.

Diagnostic Imaging Specialists SmartFax #7428
340 West Ponce De Leon Ave, Decatur, GA 30031. (404) 377-1380.

Dunwoody Medical Services SmartFax #5919
5775 Peachtree-Dun Rd, #B230, Atlanta, GA 30342. (404) 252-9090.

Emory Clinic SmartFax #7429

1365 Clifton Rd, Atlanta, GA 30322. (404) 321-0111.

Emory Egleston Pediatric Care Foundation SmartFax #7430
2032 Ridgewood Drive, Atlanta, GA 30322. (404) 727-1400.

Extended Community Home Health/Atl. SmartFax #7431
4151 Memorial Drive, Suite 223-A, Decatur, GA 30032. (770) 292-3007.

Fayette Medical Clinic SmartFax #7432
101 Yorktown Drive, Fayetteville, GA 30214. (770) 460-3000.

First American Health Care of GA SmartFax #7433
3528 Darien Highway, Brunswick, GA 31521. (912) 264-1940.

Georgia Baptist Home Care Services SmartFax #7434
100 10th St NW, Suite 800, Atlanta, GA 30309. (404) 265-1144.

Georgia Lung Associates, PC SmartFax #5097

1700 Hosp So Drive #202, Austell, GA 30001. (770) 948-6041.

Goldstein, Goldstein & Garber, DDD, PA SmartFax #5924
1218 West Paces Fy Rd, #200, Atlanta, GA 30327. (404) 261-4941.

Harbin Clinic SmartFax #7435
1825 Martha Berry Blvd, Rome, GA 30165. (706) 295-5331.

Healthways Family Medical Centers SmartFax #7436
3500 Piedmont Rd, Fifth Floor, Atlanta, GA 30505. (404) 814-4300.

Housecall Medical Resource Inc. SmartFax #7437
400 Perimeter Center Terrace, Suite 160, Atlanta, GA 30346. (770) 913-1355.

Huntcliff Summit SmartFax #7438
8592 Roswell Rd, Atlanta, GA 30350. (770) 552-3050.

King Springs Village Smyrna SmartFax #7439
404 King Springs Village Pkwy, Smyrna, GA 30082. (770) 432-4444.

King's Bridge Retirement Community SmartFax #7440
3055 Briarcliff Rd, Atlanta, GA 30329. (404) 321-0263.

Lenbrook Square SmartFax #7441
3747 Peachtree Rd NE, Atlanta, GA 30319. (404) 233-3000.

Lenox Summit Apartments SmartFax #7442
2449 East Club Drive, Atlanta, GA 30319. (404) 231-1580.

Lutheran Towers SmartFax #7443
727 Juniper St NE, Atlanta, GA 30308. (404) 873-6087.

Magellan Health Service SmartFax #5409
3414 Peachtree Rd NE, Atlanta, GA . (404) 841-9200.

Medaphis Physician Services Corp. SmartFax #5570
2700 Cumberland Pkwy #300, Atlanta, GA 30339. (770) 319-3300.

Medical College of Ga. Physicians SmartFax #7444

1499 Walton Way, Suite 1400, Augusta, GA 30901. (706) 724-6100.

Metro Home Health Services Inc. SmartFax #7445
2045 Peachtree Rd NE, Suite 100, Atlanta, GA 30309. (404) 350-0484.

Morehouse Medical Associates SmartFax #7446
75 Piedmont Ave, Suite 700, Atlanta, GA 30303. (404) 752-1500.

National Linen Service, Glen Iris Dr. SmartFax #5218
525 Glen Iris Drive, Atlanta, GA 30308. (404) 522-7335.

Northeast GA Health Services Inc SmartFax #5224
743 Spring Street, Gainesville, GA 30501-3899. (770) 535-3500.

Northside Anesthesiology Consultant SmartFax #7448
1000 Johnson Fy Rd, Atlanta, GA 30342. (404) 851-8917.

Northside Hospital Home Health Svs. SmartFax #7449

5825 Glenridge Drive, Bldg 4, Atlanta, GA 30328. (404) 851-6293.

Northwest GA Health Systems SmartFax #5534
677 Church Street, Marietta, GA 30060. (770) 793-7070.

Paces Ferry Apartments SmartFax #7450
374 East Paces Fy NE, Atlanta, GA 30305. (404) 233-4421.

Pain & Health Mgmt Center SmartFax #5539
3855 Pleasant Hill Rd 460, Duluth, GA 30136-8030. (770) 476-8810.

Papp Clinic SmartFax #7451
15 Cavender St, Newnan, GA 30263. (770) 254-6120.

Philips Presbyterian Tower SmartFax #7452
218 East Trinity Place, Decatur, GA 30030. (404) 373-4361.

Physician Specialists In Anesthesia SmartFax #7453
5667 Peachtree-Dunwoody Rd, Suite 240, Atlanta, GA 30342. (404) 257-1415.

Piedmont Anesthesia Associates SmartFax #7454
1984 Peachtree Rd, Suite 515, Atlanta, GA 30309. (404) 351-1745.

Piedmont Medical Care Foundation SmartFax #7455
1968 Peachtree Rd NW, Atlanta, GA 30309. (404) 605-5000.

Promina Northwest Physicians Group SmartFax #7456
850 Kennesaw Ave, Suite C4, Marietta, GA 30064. (770) 427-9564.

Quantum Radiology SmartFax #7457
5775 Peachtree-Dunwoody Rd, Suite 310B, Atlanta, GA 30342. (404) 255-5162.

Radiology Associates In Macon SmartFax #7458
770 Pine St, Suite L10, Macon, GA 31201. (912) 745-7928.

Renaissance On Peachtree SmartFax #7459
3755 Peachtree Rd NE, Atlanta, GA 30319. (404) 237-2323.

Roche Biomedical Laboratories SmartFax #7460

1380 Milstead Ave NE, Conyers, GA 30207. (770) 918-0667.

Southeast Permanente Medical Group SmartFax #7461 3495 Piedmont Rd, Atlanta, GA 30305. (404) 364-7000.

Southeastern Health Services Inc. SmartFax #7462 2839 Paces Fy Rd, Suite 900, Atlanta, GA 30339. (770) 432-5945.

Southside Healtcare Inc. SmartFax #7463 1039 Ridge Ave, Atlanta, GA 30315. (404) 688-1350.

Sparks Inn Retirement Center SmartFax #7464 7290 Lester Rd, Union City, GA 30291. (770) 964-3301.

Staff Builders Home Health SmartFax #5594 1835 Savoy Drive, Suite 205, Atlanta, GA 30341. (770) 457-1245.

The Atrium at Georgetown SmartFax #7466 4355 Georgetown Square Rd, Atlanta, GA 30338. (770) 986-1100.

The Hughston Clinic SmartFax #7467 105 Collier Rd NE, Suite 1030, Atlanta, GA 30309. (404) 352-1053.

Toccoa Clinic SmartFax #7468 800 East Doyle St, Toccoa, GA 30577. (706) 886-3148.

Trinity Towers SmartFax #7469 2611 Springdale Rd SW, Atlanta, GA 30315. (404) 763-4044.

Williamsburg Senior Community SmartFax #7472 1060 North Jamestown Rd, Decatur, GA 30033. (404) 634-1234.

Medical Supply

BARD, C.R. INC - UROLOGICAL DIVISION, SMARTFAX #5396
8195 Industrial Park Blvd, Covington, GA 30209 (770) 784-6100. Profile: Division headquarters facility that manufactures and markets urological medical devices with over 500 employees.

BIOLAB, INCORPORATED SmartFax #5519
PO Box 1489, Decatur, GA 30031-1489. (404) 378-1761.

HEALTH IMAGES, INC., SMARTFAX #5131
8601 Dunwoody Pl Bldg200, Atlanta, GA 30350 (770) 587-5084. Profile: Design and manufacture MRI equipment for use in medical imaging centers.

IMMUCOR, INC, SMARTFAX #5106

PO Box 5625, Norcross, GA 30091-5625 (770) 441-2051. Profile: Produces diagnostic (blood bank) reagents, employing 100.

INBRAND CORP., SMARTFAX #5108
1169 Canton Rd, Marietta, GA 30066 (770) 422-3036. Profile: Manufactures and markets disposable incontinence items, employing 325.

INFORMS INC, SMARTFAX #5144
141 W Wieuca Rd #100b, Atlanta, GA 30342 (404) 303-1400. Profile: Designs and markets forms to dentists nationwide.

INTERNATIONAL SAFETY INSTRUMENTS INC, SMARTFAX #5146
922 Hurricane Shoals Rd, Lawreceville, GA 30243 (770) 962-2552. Profile: Manufacturers of breathing apparatus, employing 70.

LIFTCON ELECTRONIC DIVISION, SMARTFAX #5169
4220 #ve Reynolds Bl #6, Norcross, GA (770) 923-8755. Profile: Sells and services laboratory equipment.

MEDEX INC, SMARTFAX #5190
11360 Technology Cir, Duluth, GA 30155 (770) 623-9809. Profile: Medical manufacturing.

OHMEDA, INC. - MEDICAL ENGINEERING SYSTEMS, SMARTFAX #6006
2850 Colonnades, Box 4225, Norcross, GA 30071 (770) 448-6684. Profile: Manufactures and sells hospital medical gas delivery systems.

Recreation/Sports

ATLANTA MOTOR SPEEDWAY, SMARTFAX #7475
1550 Highways 19&41, Hampton, GA 30228 (770) 946-4211. Profile: NASCAR's third fastest race track.

BASS PRO SHOPS SPORTMAN'S WAREHOUSE, SMARTFAX #5040
3825 Shackleford Rd, Duluth, GA 30136 (770) 931-1550. Profile: Recreational sporting goods company, with 230 employees.

MIZUNO CORP OF AMERICA, SMARTFAX #5197

1 Jack Curran Way, Norcross, GA 30071 (770) 840-4747. Profile: Manufacturer and distributor of sports equipment and athletic wear.

MOUNTASIA ENTERTAINMENT INTERNATIONAL, INC., SMARTFAX #7474

5895 Windward Pkwy, Suite 220, Alpharetta, GA 30202 (770) 442-6640. Profile: Family entertainment center company.

SIX FLAGS OVER GEORGIA, SMARTFAX #7473

7561 Six Flags Pkwy SW, Austell, GA 30001 (770) 948-9290. Profile: Atlanta's largest theme park with more than 100 rides, shows and other attractions.

SOFTBALL COUNTRY CLUB SPORTSPLEX, SMARTFAX #5248

3500 North Decatur Rd, Scottdale, GA 30079 (404) 299-3588. Profile: Private nine-field softball complex.

SPORTS LIFE, INC, SMARTFAX #5256

294 Interstate North Cir, Suite 100, Atlanta, GA 30342 (770) 984-0031. Profile: Workout facility.

Athletic Club Northeast
SmartFax #7476
1515 Sheridan Rd NE, Atlanta, GA 30324. (404) 325-2700.

Australian Body Works
SmartFax #7477
5956 Roswell Rd, Atlanta, GA 30328. (404) 255-8889.

Bally's Holiday Fitness Center SmartFax #7478
6780 Roswell Rd NW, Atlanta, GA 30328. (770) 392-1861.

Buckhead Towne Club
SmartFax #7479
2900 South Pharr Court NW, Atlanta, GA 30305. (404) 262-3455.

Cecil B. Day Wellness Center SmartFax #7480
1445 Mount Vernon Rd, Atlanta, GA 30338. (770) 393-9355.

City Athletic Club
SmartFax #7481
1 CNN Center, Suite 211, Atlanta, GA 30303. (404) 659-4097.

Concourse Athletic Club SmartFax #7482
8 Concourse Pkwy, Atlanta, GA 30328. (770) 698-2000.

Corporate Sports Executive Health Club
SmartFax #7483
6400 Highlands Pkwy, Smyrna, GA 30082. (770) 432-0100.

Discovery Zone
SmartFax #7484
4400 Roswell Rd, Marietta, GA 30062. (770) 565-5699.

Douglasville Health & Athletic Club SmartFax #7485
8741 Hospital Drive, Douglasville, GA 30117. (770) 949-7507.

East Hampton Community Center SmartFax #7486
2051 W Flat Shoals Terrace, Decatur, GA 30034. (404) 212-9539.

Falcon Sports & Fitness Complex SmartFax #7487
I-85 at Suwanee Rd, Suwanee, GA 30174. (770) 945-8977.

Fitness International Inc. SmartFax #7488
2410 Wisteria Drive, Snellville, GA 30278. (770) 979-2111.

Fitness Today SmartFax #7489
4800 Lawrenceville Highway, Lilburn, GA 30247. (770) 925-1599.

New Life Fitness Cartersville Inc. SmartFax #7490
695 Henderson Drive, Cartersville, GA 30120. (770) 382-3333.

Northside Athletic Club SmartFax #7491

1160 Moores Mill Rd, Atlanta, GA 30327. (404) 352-1919.

Peachtree Center Athletic Club SmartFax #7492
227 Courtland St, Ninth Floor, Atlanta, GA 30303. (404) 523-3833.

Piedmont Hospital Health & Fitness SmartFax #7493
2001 Peachtree Rd NE, Atlanta, GA 30309. (770) 499-9458.

Promina Health Place SmartFax #7494
65 South Medical Drive, Marietta, GA 30060. (770) 793-7300.

Raquet Club of The South SmartFax #7495
6200 Peachtree Corners Cir, Norcross, GA 30092. (770) 449-6060.

River Ridge Tennis & Swim Club SmartFax #7496
Driver Cir Court, Alpharetta, GA 30201. (770) 594-1821.

Saint Ives Country Club SmartFax #7497
10245 Medlock Bridge Rd, Duluth, GA 30136. (770) 497-9432.

Southern Athletic Club SmartFax #7498
754 Beaver Ruin Rd, Lilburn, GA 30247. (770) 923-5400.

The Sporting Club at Windy Hill SmartFax #7500
135 Interstate North Pkwy NW, Atlanta, GA 30339. (770) 953-1100.

The Vinings Club SmartFax #7501
2859 Paces Fy Rd, Atlanta, GA 30339. (770) 431-9166.

The Wellness Ctr/DeKalb Med. Center SmartFax #7502
2701 North Decatur Rd, Decatur, GA 30033. (404) 501-2222.

White Water Park SmartFax #7503
250 Cobb Pkwy N, Marietta, GA 30062. (770) 424-9283.

Workout America SmartFax #7504
122 Proctor Square, Duluth, GA 30136. (770) 623-9373.

YMCA of Metropolitan Atlanta SmartFax #7505
100 Edgewood Ave, Suite 902, Atlanta, GA 30341. (404) 588-9622.

YWCA of Greater
Atlanta SmartFax #7506
100 Edgewood Ave, Suite
806, Atlanta, GA 30303.
(404) 527-7575.

Other

ARC SECURITY, SMARTFAX #7508
417 North Central Ave, Atlanta, GA 30354 (404) 768-3311. Profile: Offers security and investigation services.

FLORAL HILLS MEMORY GARDENS, SMARTFAX #5127
3000 Lawrenceville Hwy, Tucker, GA 30084 (770) 939-3424. Profile: Over 3600 locations, employing 100 in Atlanta.

GREAT EXPECTATIONS, SMARTFAX #5102
320 Interstate Pkwy #110, Atlanta, GA 30339 (770) 956-9223. Profile: Video dating service.

HEART TO HEART, SMARTFAX #5132
550 Interstate N Pkw #205, Atlanta, GA 30339 (770) 980-1607. Profile: Dating service.

WELLS FARGO GUARD SERVICES, SMARTFAX #7509
6060 McDonough Drive, Suite O, Norcross, GA 30093 (770) 441-1050. Profile: Provides protective and detective services.

Allied Security
SmartFax #7510
6825 Jimmy Carter Blvd,
Norcross, GA 30071.
(770) 441-2200.

Barton Protective
Services SmartFax #7511
5 Piedmont Center NE,
Suite 110, Atlanta, GA
30305. (404) 266-1038.

Cheatham Hill
Memorial Park
SmartFax #5057
1861 Dallas Rd,
Marietta, GA 30064.
(770) 424-1111.

Confidential Security
Agency SmartFax #7512
362 W Peachtree St NW,
Atlanta, GA 30308. (404)
586-0777.

Digital Pathways
SmartFax #7513
210 Interstate North
Pkwy NW, Atlanta, GA
30339. (770) 980-6648.

Jenny Craig Personal
Weight Management
SmartFax #5153
4015 Holcomb Bridge Rd
#320, Norcross, GA
30092. (770) 447-0121.

Multisoft Incorporated
SmartFax #5520
11660 Alpharetta Hwy
#110, Roswell, GA
30076. (770) 475-8400.

Optimage SmartFax
#5329
4763 Jamerson Forest
Cir, Marietta, GA 30066.
(770) 924-9807.

**Petsmart Veterinary
Services of GA, Inc.**
SmartFax #5977
6370 N Point Pkwy,
Alpharetta, GA . (602)
944-7070X6807.

Rentz Security Services
SmartFax #7514
1627 Peachtree Street
NE, Suite 104, Atlanta,
GA 30309. (404) 875-
8401.

Stanley Smith Security
SmartFax #7515
3286 Buckeye Rd,
Atlanta, GA 30341. (770)
451-4745.

FINANCIAL

Banks, etc.

BANKER'S BANK, SMARTFAX #5394
3715 Northside Pkwy NW, #80, Atlanta, GA 30327 (404) 848-2900. Profile: Correspondence bank, serving smaller community banks, employing 80+.

FEDERAL HOME LOAN BANK OF ATLANTA, SMARTFAX #5449
1475 Peachtree Street NE, Atlanta, GA 30309 (404) 999-8000. Profile: $18 billion reserve credit bank.

FEDERAL HOME LOAN MORTGAGE CORP., SMARTFAX #6025
2300 Windy Rdg Pkwy 200 N, Atlanta, GA 30339 (770) 857-8800. Profile: SE region office for government sponsored enterprise.

FEDERAL NAT'L MORTGAGE ASS'N (FANNIE MAE), SMARTFAX #5946
950 E Paces Fy Rd/1900, Atlanta, GA 30326-1161 (404) 398-6000. Profile: Secondary mortgage company, employing 230 in Atlanta.

FEDERAL RESERVE BANK OF ATLANTA, SMARTFAX #5947
104 Marietta St, NW, Marietta, GA 30303-2713 (404) 521-8500. Profile: Head office for the Sixth District of the Federal Reserve System, employing 1030 in Atlanta.

FIRST NORTH AMERICAN NATIONAL BANK, SMARTFAX #5125
1800 Pkwy Place #500, Marietta, GA 30067 (770) 423-7958. Profile: Financial institution that supplies Circuit City's credit card.

FIRST UNION NATIONAL BANK OF GEORGIA, SMARTFAX #5685
999 Peachtree St, Atlanta, GA 30303 (404) 827-7119. Profile: Second largest bank in Georgia and subsidiary of one of the largest bank holding companies in the SE, employing 2000 in Atlanta branches.

HOMEBANC MORTGAGE CORP., SMARTFAX #5137
5775 Glenridge Bldg E-500, Atlanta, GA 30328 (404) 303-4113. Profile: Has been the #1 mortgage lender in Atlanta since 1992.

NATIONSBANK, CORPORATE RECRUITING, SMARTFAX #5219

100 N Tryon Street, Charlotte, NC 28255 (704) 607-6554. Profile: Headquarters for NationsBank Corporation.

NATIONSBANK, GEORGIA, SmartFax #5973
PO Box 4899, Atlanta, GA 30302-4899 (404) 607-6157. Profile: Full service financial institution.

PRUDENTIAL BANK, SmartFax #5600
2 Concourse Pkwy, S 500, Atlanta, GA 30328-6107 (770) 551-6700. Profile: Issues and services credit cards, home equity loans and other consumer financial needs.

SOUTH TRUST BANK OF GA, N.A., SmartFax #5311
2000 River Edge Pkwy, Atlanta, GA 30328 (770) 951-4011. Profile: Operates 115 branches in Georgia.

TRUST CO. BANK, SmartFax #5899
PO Box 4418, Atlanta, GA 30302 (404) 588-7199. Profile: One of the three largest banks in Georgia in assets, employing 5000.

WACHOVIA BANK OF GEORGIA, SmartFax #5488
191 Peachtree Street, Atlanta, GA 30303 (404) 332-5000. Profile: Third largest bank in Georgia, employing 5400 total in GA.

Albany Government Employee Federal Credit SmartFax #7516 200 Loftus Drive, Albany, GA 31705. (912) 883-5701.

Allied Bank of GA SmartFax #7517 PO Box 1020, Thomson, GA 30824. (706) 556-3451.

Alpha Mortgage Bankers SmartFax #5593

1745 Old Spring House Lane 417, Atlanta, GA 30338. (770) 451-8550.

Amsouth Bank of GA SmartFax #7518 400 North Fifth Ave, Rome, GA 30162. (706) 236-3956.

Associated Credit Union SmartFax #7519 2250 North Druid Hills Rd NE, Suite 144, Atlanta, GA 30329. (404) 321-4100.

AT&T Small Business Lending Corp. SmartFax #7520 500 Chastain Center Blvd, Suite 555, Kennesaw, GA 30144. (770) 514-4420.

Athens First Bank and Trust Co. SmartFax #7521 124 East Hancock Ave, Athens, GA 30613. (706) 357-7000.

Atlanta Mortgage Services SmartFax #7522

142

3340 Peachtree Rd NE, Suite 1000, Atlanta, GA 30326. (404) 240-7440.

Atlanta Postal Credit Union SmartFax #7523
3900 Crown Rd, Atlanta, GA 30380. (404) 768-4126.

Bank Atlanta SmartFax #7524
1221 Clairmont Rd, Decatur, GA 30030. (770) 320-3300.

Bank of Canton SmartFax #7525
231 Main St, Box 649, Canton, GA 30114. (706) 479-1931.

Bank of Covington SmartFax #7526
1134 Clark St, Box 1098, Covington, GA 30209. (770) 786-3441.

Bank of Coweta SmartFax #7527
110 Jefferson St, Newnan, GA 30263. (770) 253-1340.

Bank of North Georgia SmartFax #7529
1184 Alpharetta St, Roswell, GA 30075. (770) 594-6462.

Bank South Mortgage Inc. SmartFax #7531

32 Perimeter Center E, Suite 200, Atlanta, GA 30346. (404) 705-1130.

Bankers First Savings Bank, FSB SmartFax #7533
PO Box 1332, Augusta, GA 30903. (706) 849-3200.

Barnett Bank of Southwest Georgia SmartFax #7535
PO Box 1497, Columbus, GA 31993. (706) 571-7800.

Bibb Teachers Federal Credit Union SmartFax #7536
4810 Mercer University Drive, Macon, GA 31210. (912) 471-9946.

Brand Banking Co. SmartFax #7537
106 Crogan St, Box 1110, Lawrenceville, GA 30246. (770) 963-9225.

Carrollton Federal Bank, FSB SmartFax #7538
110 Dixie St, Carrollton, GA 30117. (706) 834-1071.

CDC Federal Credit Union SmartFax #7539
1947 Briarwood Court, Atlanta, GA 30329. (404) 325-3270.

Central & Southern Bank of GA SmartFax #7540
150 West Green St, Milledgeville, GA 31061. (912) 452-5541.

Charter Federal Savings & Loan SmartFax #7541
600 Third Ave, West Point, GA 31833. (706) 645-1391.

Citizens Bank & Trust Co./West Ga SmartFax #7542
115 College St, Carrollton, GA 30117. (706) 836-6900.

Citizens Mortgage Corp. SmartFax #7543
900 Circle 75 Pkwy, Suite 1500, Atlanta, GA 30339. (770) 952-8933.

Cobb America Bank & Trust Co. SmartFax #7544
1200 Johnson Fy Rd, Marietta, GA 30068. (770) 977-8585.

Columbus Bank & Trust Co. SmartFax #7545
1148 Broadway, Columbus, GA 31902. (706) 649-2311.

Commercial Bank SmartFax #7546
101 South Crawford St, Box 710, Thomasville,

GA 31799. (912) 226-3535.

Commercial Bank of GA SmartFax #7547
500 Northridge Rd, Atlanta, GA 30350. (770) 992-1800.

Community Federal Savings Bank SmartFax #7548
385 Battlefield Pkwy, Fort Oglethorpe, GA 30742. (706) 866-4924.

Delta Employees Credit Union SmartFax #7549
PO Box 20541, Atlanta, GA 30320. (404) 715-4748.

Dunwoody Mortgage Co. SmartFax #7550
1100 Ashwood Pkwy, Suite 350, Atlanta, GA 30338. (770) 396-4300.

Entrust SmartFax #7551
2000 RiverEdge Pkwy, Suite 880, Atlanta, GA 30328. (770) 980-4700.

Etowah Bank SmartFax #7552
140 West Main St, Box 649, Canton, GA 30114. (770) 479-8761.

Farmers & Merchants Bank SmartFax #7553
125 West Jackson St, Box 31040, Dublin, GA 31040. (912) 272-3100.

Federal Employees Credit Union SmartFax #6003
6789 Peachtree Ind Blvd, Atlanta, GA 30360. (770) 448-8200.

Fidelity Federal Savings Bank SmartFax #7555
500 East Walnut Ave, Dalton, GA 30720. (706) 226-2600.

Fidelity National Bank SmartFax #7556
160 Clairemont Rd, Decatur, GA 30030. (770) 371-5500.

First Bulloch Bank and Trust Co. SmartFax #7557
40 North Main St, Box 878, Statesboro, GA 30458. (912) 764-6611.

First Colony Bank SmartFax #7558
300 South Main St, Alpharetta, GA 30201. (770) 751-3100.

First Federal Savings & Loan Assoc. SmartFax #7559
PO Box 888, Valdosta, GA 31603. (912) 244-0164.

First Financial Bank SmartFax #7560

2030 Powers Fy Rd NW, Suite 325, Atlanta, GA 30339. (770) 916-0711.

First Georgia Bank SmartFax #7561
4510 Altama Ave, Brunswick, GA 31520. (912) 267-0100.

First Liberty Bank SmartFax #7562
201 Second St, Macon, GA 31297. (706) 743-0911.

First National Bank of Northwest Ga SmartFax #7563
PO Box 12169, Calhoun, GA 30703. (706) 629-4531.

First National Bank of Paulding County SmartFax #7564
160 Confederate Ave, Dallas, GA 30132. (770) 445-2742.

First National Bank-Cherokee SmartFax #7565
6395 East Alabama Rd, Woodstock, GA 30188. (770) 591-9000.

First Railroad Community Federal Credit SmartFax #7567
505 Haines Ave, Waycross, GA 31501. (912) 283-4711.

First State Bank and Trust Co. SmartFax #7569
PO Box 28, Stockbridge, GA 30281. (770) 474-7293.

Five Star Federal Credit Union SmartFax #7571
Highway 370, Cedar Springs, GA 31732. (912) 372-4586.

General Electric Employee Credit Union SmartFax #7572
2010 Redmond Cir, Rome, GA 30165. (706) 235-8551.

Georgia Bank and Trust Co. SmartFax #7573
3530 Wheeler Rd, Augusta, GA 30909. (706) 739-6990.

Georgia Federal Credit Union SmartFax #7574
652 North Indian Creek Drive, Clarkston, GA 30021. (404) 292-6868.

Georgia Telco Credit Union SmartFax #7575
1155 Peachtree St, Suite 400, Atlanta, GA 30309. (404) 874-0777.

Georgia-Pacific Federal Credit Un. SmartFax #7576

1401 West Ninth St, Brunswick, GA 31521. (912) 264-2973.

Great Western Mortgage SmartFax #7577
861 Holcomb Bridge Rd, Suite 200, Roswell, GA 30076. (770) 998-2182.

Griffin Federal Savings Bank SmartFax #7578
160 Bastille Way, Fayetteville, GA 30214. (770) 460-4207.

Gwinnett Federal Bank, FSB SmartFax #7579
750 Perry St, Lawrenceville, GA 30245. (770) 995-6000.

Habersham Bank SmartFax #7580
Washington Street, Box 5, Clarkesville, GA 30523. (706) 778-1000.

Hardwick Bank and Trust Co. SmartFax #7581
Hardwick Square, Dalton, GA 30722. (706) 278-3030.

Home Federal Savings Bank SmartFax #7582
307 East Second Ave, Rome, GA 30161. (706) 291-4500.

HomeSouth Mortgage Corp. SmartFax #7584

1669 Phoenix Pkwy, Suite 109, Atlanta, GA 30349. (770) 997-9009.

IT Corp. of America SmartFax #5697
3399 Peachtree Rd #595, Atlanta, GA . (404) 842-0241.

Lockheed-Georgia Employee Federal Credit Union SmartFax #7585
430 Commerce Park Drive, Marietta, GA 30061. (770) 424-0060.

Maco Educators Federal Credit Union SmartFax #7586
69 South Ave, Marietta, GA 30060. (770) 422-8100.

Main Street Savings Bank SmartFax #7587
940 Main St NW, Conyers, GA 30207. (770) 483-4721.

Metro Bank SmartFax #7590
6637 Roswell Rd, Atlanta, GA 30328. (404) 255-8550.

Milton National Bank SmartFax #7591
11650 Alpharetta Highway, Roswell, GA 30076. (770) 664-1990.

Mountain National Bank SmartFax #7593

5100 LaVista Rd, Tucker, GA 30084. (770) 491-8808.

Mt. Vernon Federal Savings Bank SmartFax #7594
4800 Ashford-Dunwoody Rd, Atlanta, GA 30338. (770) 396-3966.

Mutual Savings Credit Union SmartFax #7595
1219 Caroline St NE, Atlanta, GA 30307. (404) 584-4368.

National Mortgage Investments Co. SmartFax #7596
1815 North Expressway, Griffin, GA 30223. (770) 946-9873.

NationsBanc Mortgage SmartFax #7597
2059 Northlake Pkwy, Tucker, GA 30084. (770) 491-4127.

Newnan Savings Bank, FSB SmartFax #7599
19 Jefferson St, Newnan, GA 30263. (706) 253-5017.

Newton Federal Savings & Loan Assoc SmartFax #7600
PO Box 1037, Covington, GA 30209. (770) 786-7088.

North American Mortgage Co. SmartFax #7601
1100 Johnson Fy Rd NE, Suite 140, Atlanta, GA 30342. (404) 843-3446.

Northwest Georgia Bank SmartFax #7602
US 151, Robin Rd, Ringgold, GA 30736. (706) 965-3000.

Peachtree Federal Credit Union SmartFax #7603
1375 Peachtree St NE, Suite 181, Atlanta, GA 30367. (404) 892-2720.

Pinnacle Credit Union SmartFax #7604
536 North Ave, Atlanta, GA 30308. (404) 888-1648.

Powerco Federal Credit Union SmartFax #7605
333 Piedmont Ave, Atlanta, GA 30302. (404) 526-3750.

Premier Lending Corp. SmartFax #7606
2759 Delk Rd, Suite 201, Marietta, GA 30067. (770) 952-0606.

Prudential Bank and Trust Co. SmartFax #7607
1 Ravinia Drive, Suite 1000, Atlanta, GA 30346. (770) 551-6700.

Prudential Savings Bank, FSB SmartFax #7608
200 West Main St, Cartersville, GA 30120. (770) 382-4171.

Red Disk Credit Union aka Coca Cola SmartFax #7609
1 Coca Cola Plaza, Atlanta, GA 30313. (404) 515-2566.

Robins Federal Credit Union SmartFax #7610
803 Watson Blvd, Warner Robins, GA 31088. (912) 923-3773.

Sea Island Bank SmartFax #7611
2 East Main St, Box 568, Statesboro, GA 30458. (912) 489-8661.

Security Bank and Trust Co. SmartFax #7612
PO Box 1912, Albany, GA 31703. (912) 430-7000.

Security State Bank SmartFax #7613
1600 Marietta Highway, Canton, GA 30114. (770) 479-2111.

South State Mortgage Inc. SmartFax #7614
990 Hammond Drive, Suite 350, Atlanta, GA 30328. (770) 551-2400.

Southeastern Bank
SmartFax #7615
PO Box 455, Darien, GA
31305. (912) 437-4141.

Southern Crescent Bank
SmartFax #7616
1585 Southlake Pkwy,
Morrow, GA 30260.
(770) 968-6868.

**SouthTrust Bank of
Georgia NA** SmartFax
#7618
2000 RiverEdge Pkwy,
Atlanta, GA 30328. (770)
951-4000.

**Southwest Georgia
Bank** SmartFax #7619
PO Box 849, Moultrie,
GA 31776. (912) 985-
1120.

**State Employees Credit
Union** SmartFax #7620
130 Memorial Drive,
Atlanta, GA 30303. (404)
656-3748.

Summitt National Bank
SmartFax #7621
4360 Chamblee-
Dunwoody Rd, Atlanta,
GA 30341. (770) 454-
0400.

**Sumter Bank and Trust
Co.** SmartFax #7622
201 East Lamar St, Box
767, Americus, GA
31709. (912) 924-0301.

Sun America Mortgage
SmartFax #7623
5775-A Glenridge Drive,
Suite 100, Atlanta, GA
30328. (404) 252-0192.

**Sunshine Mortgage
Corp.** SmartFax #5978
2401 Lake Park Dr,
Smyrna, GA 30080. (770)
437-4100.

**The Bank of Gwinnett
County** SmartFax #7625
150 South Perry St SW,
Lawrenceville, GA
30245.

The Bank of Newnan
SmartFax #7626
40 Bullsboro Drive,
Newnan, GA 30263.
(770) 253-8080.

**The Business
Development Corp.**
SmartFax #7627
4000 Cumberland Pkwy,
Suite 1200-A, Atlanta,
GA 30339. (770) 434-
0273.

**The First National Bank
of Gainesville** SmartFax
#7628
111 Green St SE,
Gainesville, GA 30503.
(770) 525-5500.

The First State Bank
SmartFax #7629
4806 North Henry Blvd,
Stockbridge, GA 30281.
(770) 474-7293.

**The Money Store
Investment Corp.**
SmartFax #7630
2970 Clairmont Rd NE,
Suite 560, Atlanta, GA
30329. (404) 636-4075.

**The Southern Federal
Credit Union** SmartFax
#7631
430 East Lanier Ave,
Fayetteville, GA 30214.
(770) 719-1111.

**Thomas County Federal
Savings & Loan**
SmartFax #7632
131 South Dawson St,
Thomasville, GA 31792.
(912) 226-3221.

**TIC Federal Credit
Union** SmartFax #7633
2786 Eckel St, Fort
Benning, GA 31995.
(770) 682-0830.

**Tucker Federal Savings
& Loan Assoc** SmartFax
#7637
2355 Main St, Tucker,
GA 30084. (770) 938-
1222.

**Union Camp Savannah
Federal Credit Union**
SmartFax #7638
1085 West Lathrop Ave,
Savannah, GA 31402.
(912) 236-4400.

Union County Bank
SmartFax #7639

Highway 76, Blairsville
Bypass, Box 398,
Blairsville, GA 30512.
(706) 745-5571.

Unity Mortgage Corp.
SmartFax #7640
6600 Peachtree-
Dunwoody Rd, Bldg 600,
Suite 600, Atlanta, GA
30328. (770) 604-4000.

**Vidalia Federal Savings
& Loan Asso** SmartFax
#7641
PO Box 666, Vidalia, GA
30474. (912) 537-8805.

Wachovia Mortgage
SmartFax #7644
3333 Cumberland Cir,
Suite 320, Atlanta, GA
30339. (770) 618-1800.

Financial Services

ALLMERICA FINANCIAL, SMARTFAX #6002
1455 Lincoln Pkwy #310, Atlanta, GA 30346 (770) 353-6600. Profile: Sales and
customer service operations, employing 400+ in Atlanta.

BUYPASS THE SYSTEM, SMARTFAX #5629
360 Interstate Pkwy,S 400, Atlanta, GA 30339 (770) 953-2664. Profile: Point-of-sale
check and debit card processor, employing 300.

EQUIFAX INFORMATION SERVICES CENTER, SMARTFAX #5445
3200 Windy Hill Rd, S 500, Marietta, GA 30339 (770) 612-3000. Profile: Credit
reporting office employing 700.

EQUIFAX, INC., SMARTFAX #5963
1600 Peachtree St, Atlanta, GA 30309 (404) 885-8000. Profile: Nation's largest
computer-based information gathering company, employing 3000 in Atlanta.

FEDERAL DEPOSIT INSURANCE CORP., SMARTFAX #5955
1201 W Peachtree S NE,1600, Atlanta, GA 30309-3449 (404) 817-2500. Profile:
Regional office covering seven states.

FINANCIAL SERVICE CORP., SMARTFAX #5119
2300 Windyridge Pkwy S1100, Atlanta, GA 30339 (770) 916-6500. Profile:
Distributes financial products and services through its two major subsidiaries.

FIRST ALLIANCE FINANCIAL PROCESSING SERVICES, SMARTFAX #5121
1530 Dunwoody Village Pkwy, #120, Atlanta, GA 30338 (770) 391-9014. Profile: Sells credit card processing systems.

FIRST DATA CORP., SMARTFAX #5123
5660 New Northside Dr, Atlanta, GA 30328 (770) 857-0001. Profile: Provider of information and transaction processing services.

FISERV, INC., SMARTFAX #5126
1475 Peachtree St NE #600, Atlanta, GA 30309 (404) 873-2851. Profile: Provides data processing services to financial institutions, employing 210.

GE CAPITAL-RETAILER FINANCIAL SERVICES, SMARTFAX #5091
5665 New N'side Drive #400, Atlanta, GA 30328 (770) 988-2107. Profile: Supplier of private label credit cards.

HARLAND, JOHN H. CO., SMARTFAX #5321
PO Box 105250, Atlanta, GA 30348 (800) 732-3690. Profile: Leading provider of value-added products and services to the financial services industry.

J.P. ATKINSON & ASSOCIATES, INC., SMARTFAX #5915
5775 Peachtree-Dun Rd, C-355, Atlanta, GA 30342 (404) 250-3340. Profile: Financial services company.

MASTER CREDIT SYSTEMS, SMARTFAX #6012
2520 Shallowford Rd #-H, Marietta, GA 30066 (770) 591-4030. Profile: Contingency fee based collection agency.

MEDAPHIS CORP, SMARTFAX #5186
2700 Cumberland Pkwy #300, Atlanta, GA 30339 (770) 319-3300. Profile: Provides billing and collection services to the health care industry.

ROBINSON-HUMPHREY CO., SMARTFAX #5928
3333 Peachtree Rd, 7th Fl, Atlanta, GA 30326 (404) 266-6656. Profile: Full-service financial services firm selling institutional and individual investment opportunities.

WADDELL & REED INC, SmartFax #5289

1785 The Exchange #300, Atlanta, GA 30339 (770) 980-0742. Profile: National financial services company.

Noble Wealth Inc
SmartFax #5222
3125 Presidential Pk
#115, Atlanta, GA 30340.
(770) 457-3038.

South Star Mortgage
SmartFax #5253
990 Hammond Drive
#350, Atlanta, GA 30328.
(770) 551-2400.

Insurance/Insurance Services

AETNA, SmartFax #5354

3587 Pkwy Lane, Bldg 4, Norcross, GA 30092 (770) 242-8787. Profile: Full lines insurance provider, employing 240.

ALLSTATE INSURANCE, SmartFax #5358

7000 Central Pkwy #700, Atlanta, GA 30328 (770) 551-0686. Profile: Regional office providing support for sales staff of this P&C insurance company.

AMERICAN SECURITY GROUP, SmartFax #5926

POBox 50355, Atlanta, GA 30302 (404) 261-9000. Profile: Dutch-owned credit insurance company, employing 775 here in Atlanta.

BLUE CROSS / BLUE SHIELD OF GEORGIA, SmartFax #5401

3350 Peachtree Rd NE, Atlanta, GA 30326 (404) 842-8001. Profile: Nation's largest health care insurer employing over 900 in Atlanta.

CANADA LIFE ASSURANCE CO., SmartFax #5049

6201 Powers Fy Rd NE, Atlanta, GA 30339 (770) 953-1959. Profile: North American corporate headquarters for international life insurance company, employing 375 in Atlanta.

CONFEDERATION LIFE INSURANCE CO., SmartFax #5614

PO Box 105103, Atlanta, GA 30348
770) 953-5100. Profile: Canadian life and health insurance company, with the US headquarters employing 900 here in Atlanta.

COTTON STATES INSURANCE GROUP, SmartFax #5527

PO Box 105303, Atlanta, GA 30348 (770) 391-8600. Profile: P&C and life insurance company, employing 320 in Atlanta.

CRAWFORD AND CO., SMARTFAX #5421
PO Box 5047, Atlanta, GA 30302 (404) 256-0830. Profile: Provides insurance and risk management industries with claims-related services in 40 countries. Corporate HQ in Atlanta employs over 900.

CREDITOR RESOURCES, INC., SMARTFAX #6000
1100 Johnson Fy Rd, Suite 300, Atlanta, GA 30342 (404) 257-8200. Profile: Credit life and disability insurance administrator, employing 230.

GAY & TAYLOR, INC, SMARTFAX #5526
6 Concourse Pkwy, S 2000, Atlanta, GA 30328 (770) 390-1184. Profile: Insurance services firm, employing 186.

LIFE OF GEORGIA / SOUTHLAND LIFE, SMARTFAX #5504
5780 Powers Fy Rd NW, Atlanta, GA 30327-4390 (770) 980-5710. Profile: Life and health insurance company, employing 1000.

MAG MUTUAL INSURANCE CO., SMARTFAX #5510
PO Box 52979, Atlanta, GA 30355 (404) 842-5600. Profile: Professional liability insurer to physicians and hospitals.

METROPOLITAN LIFE INS CO/INVESTMENT INFO DIV., SMARTFAX #5514
303 Perimeter Center N/S 500, Atlanta, GA 30346 (770) 804-4600. Profile: One of five departments that provide data processing and accounting/finance reporting support to the Corporate Investment Division.

NATIONAL SERVICE INDUSTRIES, SMARTFAX #5971
1420 Peachtree St NE, Atlanta, GA 30309 (404) 853-1000 OR 1282. Profile: Corporate headquarters for this Fortune 500 corporation.

OFFICE OF THRIFT SUPERVISION, SMARTFAX #5964
PO Box 105217, Atlanta, GA 30348 (404) 888-0771. Profile: Federal agency that regulates the savings and loan industry.

PRIMERICA FINANCIAL SERVICES, SMARTFAX #6010

3120 Breckinridge Blvd, Duluth, GA 30199-0001 (770) 381-1000. Profile: Provides term life insurance and mutual funds.

PRUDENTIAL INSURANCE & FINANCIAL SERVICES, SMARTFAX #5664
2302 Parklake Drive NE, #150, Atlanta, GA 30345 (770) 934-3218 EXT. 308. Profile: Regional claims office handling six SE states.

SAFECO INSURANCE COMPANIES, SMARTFAX #5240
PO Box A, Stone Mountain, GA 30083 (770) 469-1117. Profile: Full-lines insurance company employing 320 in Atlanta.

STATE FARM INSURANCE COMPANIES, SMARTFAX #5543
11350 John Creek Pkwy, Duluth, GA 30198-0001 (770) 418-5000. Profile: Office that consolidates all support operations for policy holder in Georgia, employing 1800.

THE TRAVELERS COMPANIES, SMARTFAX #5650
PO Box 4416, Atlanta, GA 30374-0087 (770) 393-7500. Profile: Insurance company handling all lines, employing 500 in Atlanta.

UNITED FAMILY LIFE INSURANCE, SMARTFAX #5281
PO Box 2204, Atlanta, GA 30301 (404) 588-9400. Profile: Life insurance company, employing 220.

WAUSAU INSURANCE COMPANIES, SMARTFAX #5933
PO Box 105067, Atlanta, GA 30348-5067 (404) 633-1451. Profile: Sixth largest US commercial property and casualty insurance company.

WESTCHESTER SPECIALTY GROUP, SMARTFAX #5530
6 Concourse Pkwy So #2700, Atlanta, GA 30328-5346 (770) 393-9955. Profile: Commercial specialty insurance company, employing 200.

WINDSOR GROUP, SMARTFAX #5334
PO Box 105091, Atlanta, GA 30348 (770) 951-5599. Profile: Non-standard auto insurance and insurance services company, employing 400.

Aetna Health Plan of GA SmartFax #7645
3500 Piedmont Rd, Suite 300, Atlanta, GA 30305. (404) 814-4300.
Aetna Insurance Co. SmartFax #7646

3500 Piedmont Rd, Suite 430, Atlanta, GA 30305. (404) 814-4600.

AIG Life Insurance Co. SmartFax #7647 PO Box 720594, Atlanta, GA 30358. (770) 671-2000.

Amer. General Life & Accident Ins. SmartFax #7649 1279 Kennestone Cir, Marietta, GA 30066. (770) 590-1737.

Atlanta Casualty Co. SmartFax #7650 PO Box 105435, Atlanta, GA 30348. (770) 447-8930.

Auto-Owners Insurance Co. SmartFax #7651 PO Box 2687, Norcross, GA 30091. (770) 825-0775.
Beech Street SmartFax #7652 500 Northridge Rd, Suite 800, Atlanta, GA 30350. (770) 518-5300.

BlueChoice Healthcare Plan SmartFax #7654 3350 Peachtree Rd NE, Atlanta, GA 30326. (404) 842-8400.

Cigna HealthCare of GA SmartFax #7655 1349 West Peachtree St NE, Suite 1300, Atlanta,

GA 30309. (404) 881-9779.

Circle of Care SmartFax #7656 PO Box 790, Columbus, GA 31902. (706) 660-6148.

CNA/Private Healthcare Systems SmartFax #7657 2302 Parklake Drive NE, Atlanta, GA 30345. (770) 491-5397.

Complete Health of GA SmartFax #7658 2970 Clairmont Rd, Suite 300, Atlanta, GA 30329. (404) 982-8838.

Continental Casualty Co. SmartFax #7659 PO Box 3200, Atlanta, GA 30302. (770) 491-5100.

Employers Insurance of Wausau Mut. SmartFax #7661 2987 Clairmont Rd, Atlanta, GA 30329. (404) 633-1451.
Equitable Variable Life Insurance SmartFax #7662 1000 Monarch Plaza, Atlanta, GA 30326. (404) 266-1200.

Federal Insurance Co. SmartFax #7663

3535 Piedmont Rd, Bldg 14, Suite 600, Atlanta, GA 30305. (404) 266-4000.

Federated Mutual Insurance SmartFax #5118 5887 Glenridge Drive NE, Atlanta, GA 30328. (404) 257-1511.

Fidelity Acceptance Corp. SmartFax #5683 11060 Alpharetta Hwy #158, Roswell, GA 30076. (770) 518-5588.

Fireman's Fund Insurance Co SmartFax #5120 302 Perimeter Center Nort, Atlanta, GA 30346. (770) 399-7195.

First Health SmartFax #7664 115 Perimeter Center Place, Suite 150, Atlanta, GA 30346. (770) 390-9990.
Georgia Farm Bureau Mutual Ins. Co. SmartFax #7665 PO Box 187, Roswell, GA 30076. (770) 442-5755.

Glen Falls Insurance Co. SmartFax #7666 3700 Crestwood Pkwy, Duluth, GA 30136. (770) 279-3200.

Government Employees Insurance Co. SmartFax #7667
5455 Buford Highway, Suite B124, Atlanta, GA 30340. (404) 986-8010.

Guardian Life Insurance Co. of America SmartFax #7668
4170 Ashford-Dunwoody Rd, Atlanta, GA 30319. (404) 255-0003.

Gulf Life Insurance Co. SmartFax #7669
1279 Kennestone Cir, Marietta, GA 30066. (770) 590-1737.

Hartford Life Insurance Co. SmartFax #7670
4170 Ashford-Dunwoody Rd, Atlanta, GA 30319. (404) 256-1155.

Hazlehurst & Associates, Inc. SmartFax #6009
400 Perimeter Center Tr#850, Atlanta, GA 30346. (770) 395-9880.

HealthStar Managed Care SmartFax #7671
4 Concourse Pkwy, Suite 215, Atlanta, GA 30328. (770) 396-1009.

Healthy Results SmartFax #7672

5300 Oakbrook Pkwy, Suite 220, Norcross, GA 30093. (770) 806-8014.

Independent Life & Accident Ins. Co SmartFax #7673
1450 West Peachtree St, Atlanta, GA 30309. (404) 892-6573.

Insurance House, The SmartFax #5982
PO Box 28155, Atlanta, GA 30358-0155. (770) 952-0080.

Jackson National Life Insurance Co. SmartFax #7674
1000 Circle 75 Pkwy, Atlanta, GA 30339. (770) 956-8311.

John Hancock Mutual Life Ins. Co. SmartFax #7675
200 Hannover Park Rd, Atlanta, GA 30350. (770) 641-5700.

Kaiser Found. Health Plan of GA Inc SmartFax #7676
3495 Piedmont Rd NE, Atlanta, GA 30305. (404) 364-7000.

Liberty Mutual Insurance Co. SmartFax #7677
200 Galleria Pkwy, Suite 550, Atlanta, GA 30339. (770) 955-0003.

Liberty National Life Insurance Co, Stone Mtn SmartFax #5503
2300 W Park Pl Blvd, #124, Stone Mountain, GA 30087. (770) 498-7158.

Liberty National Life Insurance Co., Marietta SmartFax #5548
PO Drawer E, Marietta, GA 30061. (770) 427-4616.

Life Insurance Co. of GA SmartFax #5168
Ste 101 1301 Hightower Tr, Dunwoody, GA 30350. (770) 642-1321.

Massachusetts Mutual Life Ins. Co. SmartFax #7681
1100 Abernathy Rd, Atlanta, GA 30328. (770) 399-7773.

Master Health Plan SmartFax #7682
3652 J Dewey Gray Cir, Augusta, GA 30909. (706) 863-5955.

Medical Control Inc. SmartFax #7683
13 West Park Square, Suite D, Marietta, GA 30060. (770) 499-9466.

MedPlan SmartFax #7684

PO Box 1900, Dalton, GA 30722. (706) 272-6000.

MetLife HealthCare Network of GA SmartFax #7685
1130 Northchase Pkwy, Suite 250, Marietta, GA 30067. (770) 980-0740.

Metropolitan Life Insurance Co. SmartFax #7686
1707 Blair Bridge Rd, Suite 100, Austell, GA 30001. (770) 739-0171.

Murdock-Taylor SmartFax #5911
3350 Peachtree Rd, #1050, Atlanta, GA 30326. (404) 237-2233.

National Life Insurance Co. SmartFax #7687
10 Piedmont Center, Suite 700, Atlanta, GA 30305. (404) 231-0100.

National Union Fire Ins. Co./Pitts. SmartFax #7688
5 Concourse Pkwy, Atlanta, GA 30358. (770) 671-2000.

Nationwide Mutual Fire Insurance SmartFax #7689
PO Box 6923, Alpharetta, GA 30239. (770) 667-6600.

New York Life Insurance Co. SmartFax #7690
1927 Lakeside Pkwy, Tucker, GA 30084. (770) 938-0080.

Northwestern Mutual Life Insurance SmartFax #7691
1360 Peachtree St, Atlanta, GA 30309. (404) 885-6500.

Pacific Mutual Life Insurance Co. SmartFax #7692
115 Perimeter Center Place, Atlanta, GA 30346. (770) 399-7744.

PCA Health Plans of GA Inc. SmartFax #7693
1349 West Peachtree St, Atlanta, GA 30309. (404) 815-7160.

Preferred Care Georgia SmartFax #7694
3350 Peachtree Rd NE, Atlanta, GA 30326. (404) 842-8000.

Preferred Plan of GA SmartFax #7695
3150 Holcomb Bridge Rd, Suite 210, Norcross, GA 30071. (770) 840-1162.

Primerica Life Insurance Co. SmartFax #7696

3120 Breckenridge Blvd, Duluth, GA 30199. (770) 381-1000.

Private Healthcare Systems SmartFax #7697
1000 Abernathy Rd, Suite 940, Atlanta, GA 30328. (770) 394-1084.

Provident Health Care Plan of GA SmartFax #7698
400 Interstate North Pkwy, Suite 200, Atlanta, GA 30339. (770) 858-1900.

Provident Life & Accident Ins. Co. SmartFax #7699
1100 Abernathy Rd, Atlanta, GA 30328. (770) 551-4600.

Provident Preferred Network SmartFax #7700
1300 Parkwood Cir, Suite 400, Atlanta, GA 30339. (770) 858-1900.

Prudential Healthcare Plan of GA SmartFax #7701
2839 Paces Fy Rd, Suite 1000, Atlanta, GA 30339. (770) 955-8010.

Prudential Property And Casualty Claims SmartFax #5574

3150 Holcomb Bridge
Rd, Norcross, GA 30071.
(770) 441-6100.

PruNetwork SmartFax
#7703
2839 Paces Fy Rd, Suite
1000, Atlanta, GA 30339.
(770) 955-8010.

**Quality Healthcare
Partnership** SmartFax
#7704
1340 14th St, Columbus,
GA 31901. (706) 323-
1777.

Sentry Insurance
SmartFax #5243
3500 Pkwy Lane #300,
Norcross, GA 30092.
(770) 368-3754.

**Southcare/Principal
PPO** SmartFax #7706
3715 Northside Pkwy,
Suite 300, Atlanta, GA
30327. (404) 231-9911.

**Southern Farm Bureau
Life Ins. Co.** SmartFax
#7707
1131 West Ave, Conyers,
GA 30207. (770) 922-
3566.

**Southern General
Insurance Co.** SmartFax
#7708
1904 Leland Drive SE,
Marietta, GA 30367.
(770) 952-0552.

**St. Paul Fire &
Casualty Insurance**
SmartFax #7709
100 Crescent Centre
Pkwy, Suite 1000,
Tucker, GA 30084. (770)
934-4350.

U.S. Healthcare
SmartFax #7712
115 Perimeter Center
Place, Suite 930, Atlanta,
GA 30346. (770) 481-
0100.

**United HealthCare of
GA** SmartFax #7713
2970 Clairmont Rd, Suite
300, Atlanta, GA 30329.
(404) 982-8800.

**United Services
Automobile Assoc.**
SmartFax #7714
104 Interstate North
Pkwy E, Atlanta, GA
30339. (770) 955-4106.

Western-Southern Life
SmartFax #6024
3200 Professional Pkwy
220, Atlanta, GA 30339.
(770) 850-8266.

Stockbrokers

TRAMMEL CROW CO., SMARTFAX #5268

3101 Towercreek Pkwy #400, Atlanta, GA 30339 (770) 644-2200. Profile: Diverse management, brokerage, corporate service, development and investment company.

A.G. Edwards & Sons
SmartFax #7715
3399 Peachtree Rd NE,
Suite 1160, Atlanta, GA
30326. (404) 237-2210.

**Atlanta Research &
Trading, Inc.** SmartFax
#5917
300 W Wieuca, #101,
Atlanta, GA 30342. (404)
255-4188.

**Bank South Investment
Services Inc.** SmartFax
#7716
3350 Cumberland Cir,
Atlanta, GA 30339. (770)
989-6181.

Bear Stearns & Co.
SmartFax #7717
50 East Paces Fy Rd,
Suite 2300, Atlanta, GA
30326. (404) 842-4000.

Charles Schwab & Co.
SmartFax #7718
3399 Peachtree Rd,
Atlanta, GA 30326. (770)
393-7360.

Chatfield Dean & Co.
SmartFax #7719

3350 Peachtree Rd, Suite
1450, Atlanta, GA 30326.
(404) 231-0549.

Dean Witter SmartFax
#7720
3414 Peachtree Rd, Suite
628, Atlanta, GA 30326.
(404) 266-4822.

Interstate/Johnson Lane
SmartFax #7721
945 East Paces Fy Rd,
Atlanta, GA 30339. (404)
240-5000.

J.C. Bradford & Co.
SmartFax #7722
5 Concourse Pkwy,
Atlanta, GA 30328. (770)
394-4500.

**Josephthal, Lyon and
Ross Inc.** SmartFax
#7723
11 Piedmont Center,
Suite 800, Atlanta, GA
30305. (404) 240-1000.

Merrill Lynch SmartFax
#7724
3500 Piedmont Rd NE,
Suite 600, Atlanta, GA
30305. (404) 231-2400.

Morgan Keegan & Co.
SmartFax #7725
3060 Peachtree Rd, Suite
1600, Atlanta, GA 30305.
(404) 240-6700.

**Olde Discount
Stockbrokers** SmartFax
#7726
127 Peachtree St NE,
Suite 100, Atlanta, GA
30303. (800) 222-0622.

Oppenheimer & Co.
SmartFax #7727
3414 Piedmont Rd NE,
Atlanta, GA 30326. (404)
262-5300.

Paine Webber SmartFax
#7728
3399 Peachtree Rd NE,
Atlanta, GA 30326. (404)
262-3550.

**Prudential Securities
Inc.** SmartFax #7729
14 Piedmont Center,
Suite 200, Atlanta, GA
30305. (404) 842-9000.

RAF Financial SmartFax
#7730

3399 Peachtree Rd, Suite 1450, Atlanta, GA 30326. (404) 814-0288.

Raymond James & Associates Inc. SmartFax #7731
100 Galleria Pkwy, Suite 1760, Atlanta, GA 30339. (770) 952-1345.

Robert W. Baird & Co.
SmartFax #7732
400 Interstate North Pkwy, Suite 1700, Atlanta, GA 30339. (770) 612-4690.

Smith Barney Inc.
SmartFax #7733
3399 Peachtree Rd NE, Suite 1800, Atlanta, GA 30326. (404) 266-0090.

The Robinson-Humphrey Co. SmartFax #7734
3333 Peachtree Rd NE, Atlanta, GA 30326. (404) 266-6000.

Real Estate - Commercial

COLLIER CAUBLE & CO, SMARTFAX #5070
1355 Peachtree Street #500, Atlanta, GA 30309 (404) 888-9000. Profile: Commercial real estate firm.

COMPASS MANAGEMENT AND LEASING, SMARTFAX #5416
3414 Peachtree Rd NE, Suite 850, Atlanta, GA 30326 (404) 240-2121. Profile: Subsidiary of Equitable Real Estate.

COMPASS RETAIL INC, SMARTFAX #5074
5775 Peachtree Dunwy Rd #D200, Atlanta, GA 30342 (404) 303-6100. Profile: Regional mall management subsidiary of Equitable Real Estate.

COUSINS PROPERTIES, SMARTFAX #5612
2500 Windy Ridge Pkwy, Suite 1600, Atlanta, GA 30339 (770) 955-2200. Profile: Atlanta-based real estate developer and manager.

DOMINION COMPANIES, THE, SMARTFAX #5340
3190 N E Express Way #410, Atlanta, GA 30341 (770) 455-6233. Profile: Property management and development firm.

EQUITABLE REAL ESTATE INVEST. MANAGEMENT, SMARTFAX #5925

1150 Lake Hearn Drive NE, Atlanta, GA 30342-1522 (404) 239-5121. Profile: Manages $38 billion in real estate assets throughout the US and Japan, employing 300 in Atlanta.

EURAMEX MANAGEMENT INC, SMARTFAX #5090
1010 Huntcliff #2210, Atlanta, GA 30350 (770) 518-2401. Profile: Commercial property development and management company.

KOGER EQUITY INC, SMARTFAX #5160
2601 Flowers Rd S #110, Atlanta, GA 30341 (770) 458-7231. Profile: Commercial real estate management company.

LAING PROPERTIES INC, SMARTFAX #5163
5901-B Peachtree D'wdy, #555, Atlanta, GA 30328 (770) 551-3400. Profile: Provides management services to commercial and industrial properties, as well as senior housing facilities.

Anderson Properties
SmartFax #7735
855 Mount Vernon Highway, Suite 200, Atlanta, GA 30067. (404) 252-0100.

Apartment Realty Advisors Inc. SmartFax #7736
4000 Cumberland Pkwy, Suite 300A, Atlanta, GA 30339. (770) 438-6710.

Axiom Real Estate Management Inc.
SmartFax #7738
225 Peachtree St, Suite 600, Atlanta, GA 30303. (404) 522-5477.

Ben Carter Properties
SmartFax #7739

950 East Paces Fy Rd, Suite 975, Atlanta, GA 30326. (404) 364-3222.

Benton Advisory Group Ltd. SmartFax #7740
1640 Powers Fy Rd, Suite 300, Atlanta, GA 30067. (770) 951-2220.

Branch Realty Management Inc.
SmartFax #7741
400 Colony Square, Suite 400, Atlanta, GA 30361. (404) 892-0500.

Brannen/Goddard Co.
SmartFax #7742
3101 Towercreek Pkwy, Suite 250, Atlanta, GA 30339. (770) 980-4000.

Brown Realty Advisors
SmartFax #7743

419 East Crossville Rd, Suite 103, Roswell, GA 30075. (770) 594-1915.

Bryant & Associates
SmartFax #7744
3350 Peachtree Rd, Suite 1250, Atlanta, GA 30326. (404) 262-2828.

Bullock, Terrell & Mannelly Inc. SmartFax #7745
400 Perimeter Center Terrace, Suite 145, Atlanta, GA 30346. (770) 391-1900.

Carter SmartFax #7746
1275 Peachtree St, Atlanta, GA 30367. (404) 888-3000.

159

Carter Oncor International SmartFax #7747
1275 Peachtree St NE, Atlanta, GA 30367. (404) 888-3000.

CB Commercial Real Estate Group Inc SmartFax #7748
100 Galleria Pkwy, Suite 550, Atlanta, GA 30339. (770) 951-7874.

Childers Associates SmartFax #7749
321 14th St NW, Atlanta, GA 30318. (404) 876-5100.

Childress Klein Properties SmartFax #7750
300 Galleria Pkwy, Suite 600, Atlanta, GA 30339. (770) 859-1200.

CNM Management Associates SmartFax #7751
3350 Cumberland Cir, Suite 1500, Atlanta, GA 30339. (770) 612-1700.

Country Club of Roswell SmartFax #5079
2500 Club Springs Dr, Roswell, GA 30076. (770) 475-7800.

Curry & Associates SmartFax #7755
4320 Roswell Rd NE, Atlanta, GA 30342. (404) 252-3750.

Cushman & Wakefield SmartFax #7756
1201 West Peachtree St, Atlanta, GA 30309. (404) 875-1000.

Dabney & Associates SmartFax #7757
1150 Lake Hearn Drive NE, Suite 200, Atlanta, GA 30342. (404) 250-3286.

Dargan Whitington & Maddox Inc. SmartFax #7758
4000 Cumberland Pkwy, Bldg 1892, Atlanta, GA 30339. (770) 438-7002.

Faison Atlanta Inc. SmartFax #7760
5 Concourse Pkwy, Suite 2000, Atlanta, GA 30328. (770) 698-2200.

Graham & Co. SmartFax #7761
3384 Peachtree Rd, Atlanta, GA 30326. (404) 842-9906.

Grubb & Ellis Co. SmartFax #7762
225 Peachtree St, Suite 600, Atlanta, GA 30303. (404) 522-5477.

Harbor Management, Inc. SmartFax #5472
3190 Northeast Expressway, Atlanta, GA 30341. (770) 454-7325.

Hines Interests L.P. SmartFax #7763
2 Ravinia Drive, Suite 1100, Atlanta, GA 30346. (770) 392-7200.

Hodges Ward Elliott Inc. SmartFax #7764
3399 Peachtree Rd NE, Suite 1200, Atlanta, GA 30326. (404) 233-6000.

Insignia Commercial Group SmartFax #7765
3343 Peachtree Rd, Suite 400, Atlanta, GA 30326. (404) 266-7200.

Joseph L. Walker & Associates SmartFax #7766
1389 Peachtree St NE, Suite 130, Atlanta, GA 30309. (404) 873-5533.

Julian LeCraw & Co. SmartFax #7767
1575 Northside Drive, Suite 200, Atlanta, GA 30318. (404) 352-2800.

Kearney Co. SmartFax #5157
1928 Montreal Rd, Tucker, GA 30084. (770) 723-6219.

Kirkland & Co. SmartFax #7768

1475 Peachtree St, Suite 200, Atlanta, GA 30309. (404) 892-1011.

Koll SmartFax #7769
3399 Peachtree Rd, Suite 1900, Atlanta, GA 30326. (404) 842-1200.

Landauer Associates Inc. SmartFax #7770
233 Peachtree St, Suite 1900, Atlanta, GA 30303. (404) 659-4040.

LaVista Associates Inc.
SmartFax #7771
3201 Peachtree Corners Cir, Norcross, GA 30092. (770) 448-6400.

LDA Inc. SmartFax #7772
91 West Wieuca Rd, Atlanta, GA 30342. (404) 256-0690.

Lincoln Property Co.
SmartFax #7773
3405 Piedmont Rd, Atlanta, GA 30305. (404) 266-7600.

M.D. Hodges Enterprises Inc.
SmartFax #7774
300 Great Southwest Pkwy, Atlanta, GA 30336. (404) 691-4007.

Maxwell Properties Inc.
SmartFax #7775
1000 Holcomb Woods Pkwy, Suite 322,

Roswell, GA 30076. (770) 594-8846.

McColgan & Co.
SmartFax #7776
PO Box 451189, Atlanta, GA 30345. (404) 329-9571.

MK Management Co.
SmartFax #7777
1011 Collier Rd, Atlanta, GA 30318. (404) 355-6000.

Peterson Properties
SmartFax #7778
2849 Paces Fy Rd, Suite 700, Atlanta, GA 30339. (770) 319-2700.

Prentiss Properties Ltd.
SmartFax #7779
1201 West Peachtree St, Suite 3600, Atlanta, GA 30309. (404) 892-1616.

Pritchett Ball & Wise Inc. SmartFax #7780
1389 Peachtree St, Suite 300, Atlanta, GA 30309. (404) 874-4499.

Richard Bowers & Co.
SmartFax #7781
3475 Lenox Rd, Suite 800, Atlanta, GA 30326. (404) 816-1600.

Schultz, Carr, Bissette & Associate SmartFax #7782

1795 Peachtree St, Suite 200, Atlanta, GA 30309. (404) 897-1866.

Selig Enterprises Inc.
SmartFax #7783
1100 Spring St, Suite 550, Atlanta, GA 30309. (404) 876-5511.

Singleton & Co.
SmartFax #7784
1506 Brookridge Drive, Woodstock, GA 30188. (770) 924-8421.

Taylor & Mathis
SmartFax #7785
115 Perimeter Place, Suite 200, Atlanta, GA 30346. (770) 394-0222.

The Galbreath Co.
SmartFax #7786
4200 Northside Pkwy NW, Bldg 12, Atlanta, GA 30327. (404) 233-1700.

The Myrick Co.
SmartFax #7787
6025 the Corners Pkwy, Suite 100, Norcross, GA 30092. (770) 449-5622.

The Shopping Center Group SmartFax #7788
6520 Powers Fy Rd, Suite 250, Atlanta, GA 30339. (770) 955-2434.

The Stripling Shaw Stripling Group
SmartFax #7789

5960 Crooked Creek Rd, Suite 20, Norcross, GA 30092. (770) 449-1600.

The Westminister Group Inc. SmartFax #7790
400 Northcreek, Suite 550, Atlanta, GA 30327. (404) 261-6500.

Trammell Crow Co. SmartFax #5268
3101 Tower Creek Pkwy, Suite 400, Atlanta, GA 30339. (770) 644-2200.

U.S. Realty Consultants Inc. SmartFax #7792
3391 Peachtree Rd, Suite 290, Atlanta, GA 30326. (404) 239-0736.

Upton Associates SmartFax #7793
1930 North Druid Hills Rd, Suite 100, Atlanta, GA 30319. (404) 329-9735.

Valuation Counselors Group Inc. SmartFax #7794
340 Interstate North Pkwy, Suite 440, Atlanta, GA 30339. (770) 955-0088.

Valuation Group Inc. SmartFax #7795
3851 Holcomb Bridge Rd, Suite 400, Norcross, GA 30092. (770) 447-8713.

Weeks Corp. SmartFax #7796
4497 Park Drive, Norcross, GA 30093. (770) 923-4076.

Weibel & Associates Inc. SmartFax #7797
8275 Dunwoody Place, Atlanta, GA 30350. (770) 594-8770.

Wheeler/Kolb Management Co. SmartFax #7798
3525 Mall Blvd, Suite 5-AA, Duluth, GA 30136. (770) 476-4801.

White & Associates SmartFax #7799
2200 Century Pkwy, Suite 800, Atlanta, GA 30345. (404) 321-6555.

Wilson & Nolan Southeast Inc. SmartFax #7800
3495 Piedmont Rd NE, Ninth Floor, Atlanta, GA 30305. (404) 231-2272.

Wilson, Hull & Neal SmartFax #7801
1600 Northside Drive NW, Suite 100, Atlanta, GA 30318. (404) 352-1882.

Real Estate - Residential

MORRIS & RAPER REALTORS, SMARTFAX #5203
990 Hammond Drive #710, Atlanta, GA 30328 (770) 671-0088. Profile: Specializes in new homes sales and marketing.

PROMOVE AMERICA INC, SMARTFAX #5998
3620 Piedmont Rd, Atlanta, GA 30305 (404) 842-0042. Profile: Apartment locating service.

S A L E S, INC, SMARTFAX #5239
PO Box 29646, Atlanta, GA 30359 (770) 723-0036. Profile: National apartment leasing firm.

Buckhead Brokers
SmartFax #7802
5395 Roswell Rd,
Atlanta, GA 30342. (404)
252-7030.

Coldwell Banker
SmartFax #7803
400 Northridge Rd, Suite
1100, Atlanta, GA 30350.
(770) 642-3600.

**Electronic Realty
Associates** SmartFax
#7804
950 East Paces Fy Rd,
Suite 2180, Atlanta, GA
30326. (404) 365-0606.

Greenhouse Apartments
SmartFax #5103
11251 Alpharetta
Highway, Roswell, GA
30076. (770) 442-1773.

Harry Norman Realtors
SmartFax #7805
5229 Roswell Rd NE,
Atlanta, GA 30342. (404)
255-7505.

**Jenny Pruitt &
Associates** SmartFax
#7806
990 Hammond Drive,
Suite 1035, Atlanta, GA
30328. (770) 394-5400.

Metro Brokers SmartFax
#7807
750 Hammond Drive,
Bldg 1, Atlanta, GA
30328. (404) 843-2500.

Northside Realty
SmartFax #7809
6065 Roswell Rd, Suite
600, Atlanta, GA 30328.
(404) 252-3393.

Re/Max of Georgia
SmartFax #7810
7000 Central Pkwy NE,
Suite 316, Atlanta, GA
30328. (770) 393-1137.

**The Prudential Atlanta
Realty** SmartFax #7811
1000 Abernathy Rd, Suite
600, Atlanta, GA 30328.
(770) 399-3000.

Other

Fleet Finance, Inc. SmartFax #5686
211 Perimeter Center Pkwy, Atlanta, GA . (770) 392-2400.

Vimpah Corp. SmartFax #5287
6660 Mableton Pkwy, Mableton, GA 30059. (770) 944-6144.

WMA Securities SmartFax #5601
1848 Independence Square, Atlanta, GA 30338. (770) 396-9919.

HOSPITALITY/TRAVEL

Airlines

ATLANTIC SOUTHEAST AIRLINES, SMARTFAX #5389
100 Hartsfield Cir Pkwy, #800, Atlanta, GA 30354 (404) 766-1400. Profile: Feeder airline for Delta, employing 2000 nationwide and growing.

DELTA AIR LINES, SMARTFAX #7815
(404) 765-5000. Profile: Atlanta's largest airline.

American Airlines
SmartFax #7812
(800) 433-7300.

Continental Airlines
SmartFax #7814
(770) 436-3300.

Northwest Airlines, Inc.
SmartFax #5951
1000 Inner Loop Rd,
Atlanta, GA 30337. (404) 530-3941.

Trans World Airlines
SmartFax #7818
(404) 522-5738.

United Airlines
SmartFax #7819
(800) 241-6522.

USAir SmartFax #7820
(800) 428-4322.

ValuJet Airlines
SmartFax #7821
(770) 994-8258.

Hotels/Motels

ATLANTA AIRPORT HILTON & TOWERS, SMARTFAX #5028
1031 Virginia Ave, Atlanta, GA 30236 (404) 767-9000. Profile: 4-Star property.

ATLANTA MARIOTT MARQUIS, SMARTFAX #5386
265 Peachtree Center Ave, Atlanta, GA 30303 (404) 521-0000. Profile: Atlanta's largest hotel with 1671 rooms and 69 suites.

CROWNE PLAZA RAVINIA, SMARTFAX #5081
4355 Ashford-Dunwoody Rd, Atlanta, GA 30346 (770) 395-7700. Profile: 500-room hotel in North Perimeter area, employing nearly 400.

FOUR POINTS HOTEL / ATLANTA NW, SMARTFAX #5124
1775 Pkwy Place, Marietta, GA 30067 (770) 428-4400. Profile: 218-room corporate hotel.

HOLIDAY INN WORLDWIDE, SMARTFAX #5479

3 Ravinia Drive Nd, #2000, Atlanta, GA 30346 (404) 604-2000. Profile: World's largest single-brand hotel chain, headquartered in Atlanta, employing 1000 here.

MARQUE OF ATLANTA, THE, SMARTFAX #5176

111 Perimeter Center West, Atlanta, GA 30319 (770) 396-6800. Profile: Near perimeter with over 150 full suites.

RITZ CARLTON HOTELS, SMARTFAX #5508

3414 Peachtree Rd NE, Atlanta, GA 30326 (404) 237-5500. Profile: Luxury hotel chain with 2 locations in Atlanta.

SUMMERFIELD SUITES HOTEL-ATLANTA PERIMETER, SMARTFAX #5259

760 Mt Vernon Highway, Atlanta, GA 30328 (404) 250-0110. Profile: 122-suite extended stay hotel.

Atlanta Marriott/Norcross SmartFax #5030
475 Technology Pkwy, Norcross, GA 30092. (770) 263-8558.

Atlanta Renaissance Hotel-Airport SmartFax #7825
4736 Best Rd, Atlanta, GA 30337. (404) 762-7676.

Atlanta Renaissance Hotel-Downtown SmartFax #7826
590 West Peachtree St NW, Atlanta, GA 30308. (404) 881-6000.
Doubletree Hotel at Concourse SmartFax #7828

7 Concourse Pkwy, Atlanta, GA 30328. (770) 395-3900.

Embassy Suites Hotel - Buckhead SmartFax #5463
3285 Peachtree Rd NE, Atlanta, GA 30305. (404) 261-7733.

Hilton Hotels (Atlanta Hilton and Towers) SmartFax #5344
255 Courtland Street, Atlanta, GA 30303. (404) 659-2000.
Holiday Inn Atlanta Central SmartFax #7829
418 Armour Drive, Atlanta, GA 30324. (404) 873-4661.

Hotel Nikko Atlanta SmartFax #7830
3300 Peachtree Rd, Atlanta, GA 30305. (404) 365-8100.

Howard Johnsons, Cumberland SmartFax #5568
2700 Curtis Drive, Smyrna, GA 30080. (770) 435-4990.

Hyatt Regency Atlanta SmartFax #7831
265 Peachtree St, Atlanta, GA 30337. (404) 577-1234.

J.W. Marriott SmartFax #5338
3300 Lenox Rd, Atlanta, GA 30326. (404) 262-3344.

166

Marriott Perimeter Center SmartFax #7833
246 Perimeter Center Pkwy, Atlanta, GA 30346. (770) 394-6500.

Radisson Hotel Atlanta SmartFax #5991
165 Courtland Street, Atlanta, GA 30303. (404) 559-6500.

Ramada Hotel-Downtown Atlanta SmartFax #7835
175 Piedmont Ave NE, Atlanta, GA 30303. (404) 559-2727.

Renaissance Atlanta Hotel @ Airport SmartFax #5869
4736 Best Rd, College Park, GA . (404) 762-7676.

Residence Inn Perimeter West SmartFax #5230
5096 Barfield Rd, Atlanta, GA 30328. (404) 252-5066.

Sheraton Atlanta Airport SmartFax #7836
1325 Virginia Ave, Atlanta, GA 30344. (404) 768-6660.

Sheraton Colony Square Hotel SmartFax #7837
188 14th St NE, Atlanta, GA 30361. (404) 892-5000.

Sheraton Gateway Hotel SmartFax #7838
1900 Sullivan Rd, Atlanta, GA 30337. (770) 997-1100.

Stouffer Concourse Hotel SmartFax #7839
1 Hartsfield Centre Pkwy, Atlanta, GA 30354. (404) 209-9999.

Stouffer Waverly Hotel SmartFax #7840
2450 Galleria Pkwy, Atlanta, GA 30339. (770) 953-4500.

Swissotel Atlanta SmartFax #5512
3391 Peachtree Rd NE, Atlanta, GA 30326. (404) 365-6313.

The Omni Hotel at CNN Center SmartFax #7841
100 CNN Center, Atlanta, GA 30335. (404) 659-0000.

The Ritz-Carlton Atlanta SmartFax #7842
181 Peachtree St, Atlanta, GA 30303. (404) 659-0400.

The Ritz-Carlton Buckhead SmartFax #7843
3434 Peachtree Rd NE, Atlanta, GA 30326. (404) 237-2700.

Westin Peachtree Plaza SmartFax #7844
210 Peachtree St NW, Atlanta, GA 30343. (404) 659-1400.

Food Service

AMERICA'S FAVORITE CHICKEN CO., SMARTFAX #5016
6 Concourse Pkwy #1700, Atlanta, GA 30328 (770) 391-9500. Profile: Parent company of Popeye's and Church's Fried Chicken restaurant with 50 units in Atlanta, employing 300.

APPLE SOUTH, INC., SMARTFAX #5372
Hancock At Washington Street, Madison, GA 30650 706) 342-4552. Profile: Largest franchisee of Applebee's restaurants, employing 100 at headquarters, plus store personnel.

BLACKEYED PEA RESTAURANTS, SMARTFAX #5045
PO Box 862037, Marietta, GA 30062 (770) 565-1183. Profile: Restaurant with locations in 17 states across the US.

CHECKERS DRIVE-IN RESTAURANTS OF N.A., SMARTFAX #5622
24 Perimeter Pk Dr, #102, Atlanta, GA 30366 (770) 986-9799. Profile: Regional office for fast food chain with over 300 units.

CHICK-FIL-A, SMARTFAX #5411
5200 Buffington Rd, Atlanta, GA 30349 4047658127. Profile: Corporate headquarters for 563-unit fast food chain, with a staff of 200.

DOBBS INTERNATIONAL SERVICES, SMARTFAX #5438
PO Box 45485, Atlanta, GA 30320 (404) 530-6300. Profile: Provides airline catering services at Atlanta airport, employing 1300 in Atlanta.

HOOTERS OF AMERICA INC, SMARTFAX #5138
1815 The Exchange, Atlanta, GA 30080 (770) 951-2040. Profile: One of the fastest growing restaurant chains in the US.

HOUSTON'S RESTAURANTS, SMARTFAX #5140
8 Piedmont Center, #720, Atlanta, GA 30305 (404) 231-0161. Profile: Atlanta-based chain of full-service restaurants.

LONG JOHN SILVER'S INC, SMARTFAX #5173

1000 Parkwood Cir #400, Atlanta, GA 30339 (770) 953-6967. Profile: 1500 unit chain with 30 company owned restaurants in Atlanta, employing over 700 here.

MCDONALD'S CORP., SMARTFAX #6015
5901 Peachtree D'wdy Rd #500, Atlanta, GA 30328 (770) 399-5067. Profile: Regional office for McDonald's Corporation.

PEASANT RESTAURANTS, INC., SMARTFAX #5962
489 Peachtree St NE, Atlanta, GA 30308 (404) 872-1400. Profile: Encompasses eight white tablecloth and eleven casual dining establishments in Atlanta.

PIZZA HUT, GEORGIA MARKET OFFICE, SMARTFAX #5625
7094 Peachtree Ind Blvd, Norcross, GA 30071 (770) 903-1140. Profile: Third largest fast food chain in the world.

PRESIDENT INTERNATIONAL, SMARTFAX #5603
41 Perimeter Center East, Atlanta, GA 30346 (770) 673-8600. Profile: Baker of Famous Amos cookies and 60% of all Girl Scout Cookies, among other brands.

PROOF OF THE PUDDING, SMARTFAX #5967
2033 Monroe Dr, Atlanta, GA 30324 (404) 898-1743. Profile: Full service, off-site catering company.

TACO BELL CORP., SMARTFAX #5323
1395 Marietta Pkwy #108, Marietta, GA 30067 . Profile: A division of PepsiCo.

US FOODSERVICE OF ATLANTA, SMARTFAX #5275
4280 Stacks Rd, College Park, GA 30349 (404) 766-9601. Profile: Foodservice distribution to restaurants, hotels, schools and hospitals.

WAFFLE HOUSE INC, SMARTFAX #5290
PO Box 6450, Norcross, GA 30091 (770) 729-5209. Profile: Atlanta-based operator of restaurants, employing 175 in headquarters plus stores.

WENDY'S OLD FASHIONED HAMBURGERS, SMARTFAX #5555
375 Franklin Rd So, #400, Marietta, GA 30067 (770) 425-9778. Profile: Fourth-largest fast food chain in the world, Wendy's operates 64 units in Atlanta.

A BoKay By JoAnn
SmartFax #7845
4339 Hugh Howell Rd,
Atlanta, GA 30084. (770)
908-3869.

Affairs To Remember
SmartFax #7846
680 Ponce De Leon Ave,
Atlanta, GA 30308. (404)
872-7859.

Atlanta Catering Co.
SmartFax #7847
4048 Flowers Rd, Suite
200, Atlanta, GA 30360.
(770) 455-3663.

Atlanta Fish Market
SmartFax #7848
265 Pharr Rd, Atlanta,
GA 30305. (404) 262-
3165.

**Atlanta Marriott
Marquis** SmartFax
#5386
265 Peachtree Center
Ave, Atlanta, GA 30303.
(404) 586-6067.

Bagel Break SmartFax
#5537
17 Dunwoody Park, #107,
Atlanta, GA 30338. (770)
396-3349.

**Bagel Palace Deli &
Bakery** SmartFax #5042
2769 N Druid Hills Rd,
Atlanta, GA 30329. (404)
315-9016.

Bone's Restaurant
SmartFax #7850
3130 Piedmont Rd,
Atlanta, GA 30305. (404)
237-2663.

**Brickery Grill & Bar,
The** SmartFax #5956
6125 Roswell Rd,
Atlanta, GA 30328. (404)
843-8002.

Buckhead Diner
SmartFax #7851
3073 Piedmont Rd,
Atlanta, GA 30305. (404)
262-3336.

Carole Parks Catering
SmartFax #7852
494 Plaster Ave, Atlanta,
GA 30309. (404) 872-
1999.

Cartel Restaurants, Inc.
SmartFax #5052
235 E Paces Fy Rd,
Atlanta, GA 30305. (404)
237-2972.

Chequers Bar & Grill
SmartFax #7853
236 Perimeter Center
Pkwy, Atlanta, GA
30302. (770) 391-9383.

**Cherokee Town &
Country Club** SmartFax
#5941
155 W Paces Fy Rd, N,
Atlanta, GA 30363. (404)
365-1200.

Chops SmartFax #7854

70 West Paces Fy Rd,
Atlanta, GA 30305. (404)
262-2675.

Crowne Plaza-Ravinia
SmartFax #5081
4355 Ashford-Dunwoody
Rd, Atlanta, GA 30346.
(770) 392-9864.

**Dailey's Restaurant and
Bar** SmartFax #7856
17 International Blvd,
Atlanta, GA 30303. (404)
681-3303.

**Doubletree Hotel-
Concourse/Atlanta**
SmartFax #7828
7 Concourse Pkwy,
Atlanta, GA 30328. (770)
395-3900.

Events SmartFax #7858
2247 Sewell Mill Rd,
Marietta, GA 30062.
(404) 579-3733.

Hooters of Underground
SmartFax #7859
50 Alabama St, Suite
804, Atlanta, GA 30303.
(404) 688-0062.

Hotel Nikko SmartFax
#7830
3300 Peachtree Rd NE,
Atlanta, GA 30305. (404)
365-8100.

**Houlihan's at Park
Place** SmartFax #7861

4505 Ashford-Dunwoody Rd, Atlanta, GA 30346. (770) 394-8921.

Houston's SmartFax #5140
3321 Lenox Rd, Atlanta, GA 30326. (404) 237-7534.

Johnny Rockets SmartFax #5916
5640 Glen Errol Rd, Atlanta, GA 30327. (404) 798-1430 (252-7298).

Kudzu Cafe SmartFax #7863
3215 Peachtree Rd, Atlanta, GA 30305. (404) 262-0661.

Kurt's SmartFax #5162
4225 River Green Pkwy, Duluth, GA 30136. (770) 623-4128.

Magic Moments SmartFax #7864
539 South Peachtree St, Norcross, GA 30071. (770) 263-7669.

Mick's at Bennett St. SmartFax #7865
2110 Peachtree Rd, Atlanta, GA 30303. (404) 525-2825.

OK Cafe SmartFax #7866

1284 West Paces Fy Rd, Atlanta, GA 30327. (404) 233-2888.

Omni Hotel SmartFax #7867
100 CNN Center, Atlanta, GA 30335. (404) 659-0000.

Peasant Uptown SmartFax #7868
3500 Peachtree Rd NE, Atlanta, GA 30326. (404) 261-6341.

Plaza Catering SmartFax #7869
210 Peachtree St NW, Atlanta, GA 30303. (404) 659-1400.

Ray's On The River SmartFax #7871
6700 Powers Fy Rd, Atlanta, GA 30339. (404) 955-1187.

Rio Bravo Cantina SmartFax #7872
3172 Roswell Rd, Atlanta, GA 30305. (404) 262-7431.

RTM Georgia, Inc SmartFax #5236
14 Perimeter Center E #1430, Atlanta, GA 30346. (770) 671-1179.

Ruth's Chris Steak House SmartFax #7873

5788 Roswell Rd, Atlanta, GA 30328. (404) 255-0035.

Sheraton Colony Square Hotel SmartFax #7837
188 14th St, Atlanta, GA 30308. (404) 892-6000.

Steak 'N' Shake Restaurants SmartFax #5258
5600 Roswell Rd East #240, Atlanta, GA 30342. (404) 843-9463.

Steak And Ale SmartFax #5889
3780 Apple Way, Marietta, GA . (770) 509-6987.

Stouffer Renaissance Waverly Hotel SmartFax #7875
2450 Galleria Pkwy, Atlanta, GA 30339. (770) 953-4500.

Swissotel SmartFax #5512
3391 Peachtree Rd NE, Atlanta, GA 30326. (404) 365-0065.

Tanner's Catering SmartFax #7877
2662 Holcomb Bridge, Suite 320, Alpharetta, GA 30202. (770) 518-1444.

The Cheesecake Factory SmartFax #7878

3024 Peachtree Rd NW, Atlanta, GA 30305. (404) 816-2555.

The Pavillion SmartFax #7879
4800 Olde Towne Pkwy, Marietta, GA 30068. (770) 578-1110.

The Ritz-Carlton, Atlanta SmartFax #7842
181 Peachtree St NE, Atlanta, GA 30303. (404) 659-0400.

The Tavern at Phipps
SmartFax #7881
3500 Peachtree Rd, Atlanta, GA 30326. (404) 814-9640.

The Varsity SmartFax #7882
61 North Ave NW, Atlanta, GA 30308. (404) 881-1707.

The Westin Peachtree Plaza SmartFax #7883
210 Peachtree St NW, Atlanta, GA 30303. (404) 659-1400.

Three Dollar Cafe
SmartFax #7884
3002 Peachtree Rd, Atlanta, GA 30319. (404) 266-8667.

Williamson Brothers Bar-B-Q SmartFax #7885
403 Sycomore, Marietta, GA 30062. (770) 971-7748.

Travel Agencies

TRAVELWAYS, INC., SMARTFAX #5322
2531 Briarcliff Rd, #115, Atlanta, GA 30323 (404) 320-1139. Profile: Full-service travel agency.

UNIGLOBE TECHNOLOGY TRAVEL INC, SMARTFAX #5276
655 Engineering Drive #350, Norcross, GA 30092 (770) 448-1777. Profile: International travel agency.

Age of Travel Inc.
SmartFax #7886
3500 Piedmont Rd, Suite 110, Atlanta, GA 30305. (404) 266-2900.

American Express Travel Related Svs
SmartFax #7887
200 Pinnacle Way, Norcross, GA 30071. (770) 368-5500.

Boehm Travel Co.
SmartFax #7888
1400 Indian Trail Rd, Norcross, GA 30093. (770) 931-5500.

BTI Americas Inc.
SmartFax #7889
3379 Peachtree Rd NE, Suite 850, Atlanta, GA 30326. (404) 264-8800.

Business Travel
SmartFax #7890
5555 Oakbrook Pkwy, Suite 650, Norcross, GA 30093. (770) 409-7462.

Business Travel Consultants SmartFax #7891
1775 the Exchange, Suite 330, Atlanta, GA 30339. (770) 952-8181.

Carlson Wagonlit Travel SmartFax #7892
30 Perimeter Center E, Suite 220, Atlanta, GA 30346. (770) 396-7628.

Century Travel Inc.
SmartFax #7893
1100 Abernathy Rd, Suite 334, Atlanta, GA 30328. (770) 394-6606.

Everest Travel Inc.
SmartFax #7894
3350 Peachtree Rd NE, Atlanta, GA 30326. (404) 231-5222.

Executive Travel Inc./First Travel
SmartFax #7895
1150 Lake Hearn Drive, Atlanta, GA 30342. (404) 303-2966.

Georgia International Travel Inc. SmartFax #7896
2859 Paces Fy Rd, Suite 445, Atlanta, GA 30339. (404) 851-9166.

KC Travel SmartFax #5493
3490 Shallowford Rd, Atlanta, GA 30341. (770) 457-1988.

Maritz Travel Co.
SmartFax #7897
200 Ashford Center, Suite 250, Atlanta, GA 30338. (770) 901-5070.

Midtown Travel Consultants Inc.
SmartFax #7898
1830 Piedmont Rd, Suite F, Atlanta, GA 30324. (404) 872-8308.

Park-N-Ticket Travel
SmartFax #7899
3945 Conley St, College Park, GA 30337. (404) 669-3800.

Peachtree Travel Management Inc.
SmartFax #7900
2 Concourse Pkwy, Suite 250, Atlanta, GA 30342. (770) 901-8750.

Ray Sorrell Travel Co.
SmartFax #7901
6400 Powers Fy Rd, Suite 132, Atlanta, GA 30339. (770) 952-1689.

Rosenbluth International SmartFax #7902
1475 Peachtree St, Suite 1110, Atlanta, GA 30323. (404) 873-7800.

Sprayberry Travel
SmartFax #7903
2440 Sandy Plains Rd, Marietta, GA 30066. (770) 977-0283.

Teplis Travel Service
SmartFax #7904
5885 Glenridge Drive, Suite 250, Atlanta, GA 30328. (404) 843-7460.

The Travel Desk Inc.
SmartFax #7905
1117 Perimeter Center W, Suite 500E, Atlanta, GA 30338. (770) 392-3333.

The Travel Source
SmartFax #7906
2550 Heritage Court, Suite 202, Atlanta, GA 30339. (770) 980-9500.

Travel Inc. SmartFax #7907
3680 North Peachtree Rd, Atlanta, GA 30341. (770) 455-6575.

Uniglobe Travel Southeast Inc. SmartFax #7908
400 Interstate North Pkwy, Suite 530, Atlanta, GA 30339. (770) 955-2224.

Williamsburg Travel Management Co.
SmartFax #7909
210 Interstate North Pkwy, Suite 110, Atlanta, GA 30339. (770) 952-0430.

WorldTravel Partners
SmartFax #7910
1055 Lenox Park Blvd, Suite 420, Atlanta, GA 30319. (404) 841-6600.

Other

FENNELL PROMOTIONS INC, SMARTFAX #5122
6640 Powers Fy Rd S175, Atlanta, GA 30339 (770) 612-0507. Profile: Retailer of travel packages.

WORLD TECHNOLOGY SYSTEMS, SMARTFAX #5298
2400 Herodian Way 1 #330, Smyrna, GA 30080 (770) 989-5900. Profile: Outsource reservations center, employing 400.

WORLDSPAN TRAVEL AGENCY INFORMATION SERVICES, SMARTFAX #5602
300 Galleria Pkwy, Atlanta, GA 30339 (770) 563-7400. Profile: World's largest travel reservations system, employing 2000.

MARKETING

Advertising/Marketing

ARTHUR J. GALLAGHER & CO -ATLANTA, SMARTFAX #5022
2970 Brandywine Rd #200, Atlanta, GA 30341 (770) 455-3337. Profile: International sales and marketing company.

B B D O SOUTH, SMARTFAX #5392
3414 Peachtree Rd NE, Suite 1600, Atlanta, GA 30326 (404) 231-1700. Profile: Largest advertising agency in the Southeast, employing 160 in Atlanta.

BELLSOUTH ADVERTISING & PUBLISHING CORP., SMARTFAX #5398
2295 Park Lake Drive #490, Atlanta, GA 30345 (770) 491-1900. Profile: Responsible for sales and information included in the Yellow Pages, employing over 1100.

CADMUS COMMUNICATIONS CORP., SMARTFAX #5303
2300 Defoor Hills Rd, Atlanta, GA 30318 (404) 355-7220. Profile: Full service marketing and graphic communications company.

COMMUNICATIONS 21, INC., SMARTFAX #5072
550 Pharr Rd #201, Atlanta, GA 30305 (404) 814-1330. Profile: Marketing public relations firm.

COMPASS MARKETING RESEARCH, SMARTFAX #5339
3725 Davinci Court #100, Norcross, GA 30092 (770) 448-0754. Profile: Marketing research firm.

INTERSERV SERVICES CORP., SMARTFAX #5147
4892 N Royal Atlanta Dr, Tucker, GA 30084 (770) 621-5500. Profile: Business-to-business marketing services company, employing 300.

J. WALTER THOMPSON, SMARTFAX #5152
950 E Paces Fy Rd NE, Atlanta, GA 30326 (404) 365-7300. Profile: One of the oldest advertising agencies in the world, employing over 100 in the Atlanta office.

KRANE PRODUCTS INC, SMARTFAX #5655

6820 Roswell Rd #1A, Atlanta, GA 30328 (770) 399-5399. Profile: Telemarketing company expanding its sales office in Sandy Springs.

NEWSLETTERS PLUS, SMARTFAX #5221
100 Crescent Ct Pk, #1200, Tucker, GA 30084 (770) 414-2800. Profile: Full services sales communications company serving the publication and direct mail needs of its' Fortune 500 clients.

OGILVY & MATHER, SMARTFAX #5536
1360 Peachtree St NE, Atlanta, GA 30309 (404) 888-5100. Profile: One of Atlanta's largest advertising agencies.

QUICK TEST INCORPORATED, SMARTFAX #5319
4205 Roswell Rd, Atlanta, GA 30342 (404) 843-3807. Profile: Market research company.

TREASURE CHEST ADVERTISING CO., SMARTFAX #5309
3440 Browns Mill Rd, Atlanta, GA 30354 (404) 761-2100. Profile: Commercial web offset printer.

Aberdeen Marketing Inc. SmartFax #7912 2030 Powers Fy Rd, Suite 120, Atlanta, GA 30339. (770) 544-1850.

Ad Tranz SmartFax #5353 POBox 20846, Atlanta, GA 30320. (404) 530-6872.

Adair Greene Inc. SmartFax #7913 1575 Northside Drive NW, Atlanta, GA 30318. (404) 351-8424.

Adovation Inc. SmartFax #7914

3103 East Shadowlawn Ave, Atlanta, GA 30305. (404) 365-9993.

American Eagle Advertising SmartFax #5363 5144 Peachtree Rd, Atlanta, GA 30341. (770) 454-0889.

Austin Kelley Advertising Inc. SmartFax #7915 5901 Peachtree-Dunwoody RdNE, Suite 200-C, Atlanta, GA 30328. (770) 396-6666.

Aydlotte & Cartwright Inc. SmartFax #7916

6 Concourse Pkwy, Suite 2800, Atlanta, GA 30328. (770) 551-5000.

Basinger & Associates Inc. SmartFax #7917 115 Perimeter Center Place, Suite 945, Atlanta, GA 30346. (770) 396-7808.

BBDO South SmartFax #7918 3414 Peachtree Rd, Suite 1600, Atlanta, GA 30326. (404) 231-1700.

Bennett Kuhn Varner Inc. SmartFax #7919 3 Piedmont Center, Suite 300, Atlanta, GA 30305. (404) 233-0332.

Bigelow & Eigel Inc.
SmartFax #7920
2880 Dresden Drive,
Suite 100, Atlanta, GA
30341. (770) 451-4581.

Bockel & Co. SmartFax
#7921
3379 Peachtree Rd NE,
Suite 925, Atlanta, GA
30326. (404) 814-0500.

**Bressler & Loftis
Advertising** SmartFax
#7922
3400 Peachtree Rd, Suite
1025, Atlanta, GA 30326.
(404) 848-9990.

**Broadus & Associates
Inc.** SmartFax #7923
3400 Peachtree Rd NE,
Atlanta, GA 30326. (404)
237-1503.

**Buffington/Rizzo
Advertising & Des.**
SmartFax #7924
4 Piedmont Center, Suite
210, Atlanta, GA 30305.
(404) 364-9700.

Campaign Inc. SmartFax
#7925
659 Mimosa Blvd,
Roswell, GA 30075.
(770) 640-8806.

**Carroll/White
Advertising** SmartFax
#7926
4170 Ashford-Dunwoody
Rd, Suite 520, Atlanta,

GA 30319. (404) 843-
1293.

**Clarion Marketing &
Communications**
SmartFax #7927
5 Concourse Pkwy, Suite
650, Atlanta, GA 30328.
(770) 395-3877.

**Clockwork Advertising
Inc.** SmartFax #7928
352 Glendale Ave NE,
Atlanta, GA 30307. (404)
378-1055.

**Cole Henderson Drake
Inc.** SmartFax #7929
400 Colony Square, Suite
500, Atlanta, GA 30361.
(404) 892-4500.

Connell & Associates
SmartFax #7930
1200 Johnson Fy Rd NE,
Suite 345, Marietta, GA
30068. (770) 549-1131.

Coston Warner
SmartFax #7931
2675 Paces Fy Rd, Suite
490, Atlanta, GA 30339.
(770) 433-8344.

Cowan & Joseph
SmartFax #7932
2 Concourse Pkwy, Suite
700, Atlanta, GA 30328.
(404) 392-7777.
**Crescent
Communications**
SmartFax #7933

1200 Ashwood Pkwy,
Suite 400, Atlanta, GA
30338. (770) 698-8650.

Crumbley & Associates
SmartFax #7934
600 West Peachtree St,
Suite 2300, Atlanta, GA
30308. (404) 892-2300.

CSI Advertising Inc.
SmartFax #7935
3925 Peachtree Rd NE,
Atlanta, GA 30319. (404)
262-7424.

**Daniel Dodson
Inc./National Promo.**
SmartFax #7936
3405 Piedmont Rd, Suite
550, Atlanta, GA 30305.
(404) 266-9258.

Davis Advertising Inc.
SmartFax #7937
1600 Holcomb Bridge
Rd, Suite 3520, Roswell,
GA 30076. (770) 552-
2678.

Donino & Partners Inc.
SmartFax #7938
7000 Central Pkwy, Suite
1350, Atlanta, GA 30328.
(770) 668-5700.

**DuCharme
Communications Inc.**
SmartFax #7939
400 Northridge Rd, Suite
510, Atlanta, GA 30350.
(770) 594-0110.
Ender Partners
SmartFax #7940

2900 Pharr Court S, Atlanta, GA 30305. (404) 814-0300.

Fishback Stultz Ltd.
SmartFax #7941
8 Perimeter Center East, Suite 8015, Atlanta, GA 30346. (770) 551-8522.

Fitzgerald & Co.
SmartFax #7942
3060 Peachtree Rd NW, Suite 500, Atlanta, GA 30305. (404) 262-8900.

Freebairn & Co.
SmartFax #7943
3343 Peachtree Rd, Suite 1220, Atlanta, GA 30326. (404) 237-9945.

Fricks Advertising Inc.
SmartFax #7944
1100 Abernathy Rd, Suite 1725, Atlanta, GA 30328. (770) 396-6206.

Gordon Bailey & Associates Inc. SmartFax #7945
11445 Johns Creek Pkwy, Atlanta, GA 30355. (404) 296-2777.

Hanevold Advertising & Public Rel. SmartFax #7946
550 Pharr Rd, Suite 646, Atlanta, GA 30305. (404) 233-0656.

Henderson Advertising
SmartFax #7947

3060 Peachtree Rd NW, Suite 1020, Atlanta, GA 30305. (404) 240-4060.

Hood & Associates
SmartFax #7948
400 Colony Square, Suite 1020, Atlanta, GA 30361. (404) 872-2299.

Ivory Communications
SmartFax #7949
887 West Marietta St, Suite 1110, Atlanta, GA 30309. (404) 888-9494.

King & Associates
SmartFax #7951
500 Sugar Mill Rd, Suite 205A, Atlanta, GA 30350. (770) 992-8969.

Kleber & Associates Advertising Inc
SmartFax #7952
555 Sun Valley Drive, Suite N-2, Roswell, GA 30076. (770) 518-1000.

Lambis & Eisenberg Advertising SmartFax #7953
4840 Roswell Rd, Suite B-210, Atlanta, GA 30342. (404) 255-4840.

Larry Smith & Associates Inc. SmartFax #7954
3300 Northeast Expressway, Suite 400, Atlanta, GA 30341. (770) 458-0808.
MailStar Direct
SmartFax #7955

1302 Star Drive, Atlanta, GA 30319. (404) 239-9110.

Marketing Resources
SmartFax #7956
3050 Presidential Drive, Suite 111, Atlanta, GA 30340. (770) 457-6105.

McCann-Erickson Atlanta SmartFax #7957
615 Peachtree St, Atlanta, GA 30365. (404) 881-3100.

Meisner Direct Inc.
SmartFax #7958
800 Old Roswell Lakes Pkwy, Suite 350, Roswell, GA 30076. (770) 640-1722.

Metaphor Inc. SmartFax #7959
1360 Peachtree St, Suite 1110, Atlanta, GA 30309. (404) 888-9494.

Michael Parver Associates SmartFax #7960
1800 Peachtree St NW, Suite 333, Atlanta, GA 30309. (404) 355-5580.

Nolen & Associates Inc.
SmartFax #7961
550 Pharr Rd NE, Suite 700, Atlanta, GA 30305. (404) 365-8340.

Pollak Levitt Chaiet
SmartFax #7963

3565 Piedmont Rd, Suite 505, Atlanta, GA 30305. (404) 261-1566.

Pratt & Buehl SmartFax #7964
3390 Peachtree Rd NE, Suite 500, Atlanta, GA 30326. (404) 231-2311.

Pringle Dixon Pringle SmartFax #7965
303 Peachtree St NE, Suite 3150, Atlanta, GA 30328. (404) 688-6720.

Pritchett & Hull Assoc SmartFax #5662
3440 Oakcliff Rd NE S-110, Atlanta, GA 30340. (770) 451-0602.

Rich/Gardner Advertising SmartFax #7966
211 Perimeter Center Pkwy, Suite 760, Atlanta, GA 30346. (770) 392-0340.

Richard Heiman Advertising Inc. SmartFax #7967
3340 Peachtree Rd, Suite 1750, Atlanta, GA 30326. (404) 261-7777.

Sawyer Riley Compton SmartFax #7968
1100 Abernathy Rd, Suite 800, Atlanta, GA 30328. (770) 393-9849.

Sharp Advertising Inc. SmartFax #7969

100 Colony Square, Suite 424, Atlanta, GA 30306. (404) 875-7967.

T.G. Madison Inc. SmartFax #7970
3340 Peachtree Rd NE, Suite 2850, Atlanta, GA 30326. (404) 262-2623.

Target Marke Team Inc. SmartFax #7971
3350 Peachtree Rd NE, Suite 1700, Atlanta, GA 30326. (404) 848-2700.

Tausche Martin Lonsdorf SmartFax #7972
18 International Blvd, Atlanta, GA 30303. (404) 221-1188.

The Ad Shop SmartFax #7973
2000 Powers Fy, Suite 2-2, Marietta, GA 30067. (770) 956-7779.

The Ad Team Inc. SmartFax #7974
5825 Glenridge Drive, Suite 105, Atlanta, GA 30328. (404) 250-0088.

The Botsford Group SmartFax #7975
3060 Peachtree Rd, Suite 510, Atlanta, GA 30305. (404) 262-8915.

The Criterion Group Inc. SmartFax #7976

12 Piedmont Center, Suite 100, Atlanta, GA 30305. (404) 237-8618.

The Denmark Group SmartFax #7977
5180 Roswell Rd NW, Suite 204, Atlanta, GA 30342. (404) 256-3681.

The Donovan Group SmartFax #7978
8053 Willow Tree Way, Alpharetta, GA 30202. (770) 564-1255.

The Kilgannon Group Inc. SmartFax #7979
1708 Peachtree St, Suite 303, Atlanta, GA 30309. (404) 876-2800.

The Morrison Agency SmartFax #7980
950 East Paces Fy Rd, Suite 1575, Atlanta, GA 30326. (404) 233-3405.

The Puckett Group SmartFax #7981
2970 Clairmont Rd, Atlanta, GA 30329. (404) 248-1500.

Tucker & Associates Inc. SmartFax #7982
80 West Wieuca Rd, Suite 301, Atlanta, GA 30342. (404) 252-6497.

Tucker Wayne / Luckie & Co. SmartFax #5938

1100 Peachtree Street
NE, Atlanta, GA 30309.
(404) 347-8700.

**Turner & Turner
Communications**
SmartFax #7984
1168 14th Place, Atlanta,
GA 30309. (404) 892-
9718.

**Van Winkle &
Associates Inc.** SmartFax
#7985
1819 Peachtree St,
Atlanta, GA 30309. (404)
355-0126.

**Vargas Flores &
Amigos** SmartFax #7986
1776 Peachtree St, Suite
420N, Atlanta, GA
30309. (404) 873-4943.

Visions USA Inc.
SmartFax #7987
57 Forsyth St NW, Suite
1000, Atlanta, GA 30303.
(404) 880-0002.

**Warren Clark &
Graham Inc.** SmartFax
#7988
230 Peachtree St, Suite
1700, Atlanta, GA 30303.
(404) 221-0700.

**Wemmers
Communications Inc.**
SmartFax #7989
1050 Crown Pointe Pkwy,
Suite 450, Atlanta, GA
30329. (404) 399-9508.

WHM&G Advertising
SmartFax #7990
3340 Peachtree Rd, Suite
2250, Atlanta, GA 30326.
(404) 814-1410.

Whole Brain Solutions
SmartFax #7991
887 West Marietta St,
Studio M-207, Atlanta,
GA 30318. (404) 874-
2214.

Wood & Associates
SmartFax #7992
2970 Peachtree Rd, Suite
615, Atlanta, GA 30301.
(404) 261-0052.

Media

ATLANTA JOURNAL-CONSTITUTION, SMARTFAX #5385
72 Marietta Street NW, Atlanta, GA 30303 (404) 526-5151. Profile: Largest
newspaper in the Southeast, employing 7300.

COX ENTERPRISES, SMARTFAX #5420
1400 Lake Hearn Drive, Atlanta, GA 30319 (404) 843-5000. Profile: Atlanta-based
parent of the AJC and Cox Cable, the third largest US TV cable provider.

GENESIS ENTERTAINMENT, SMARTFAX #7993
415 Serrant Court, Alpharetta, GA 30202 (770) 563-9607. Profile: Syndicates and
produces TV shows across the U.S.

LANDMARK COMMUNICATIONS, INC., SMARTFAX #6019
2600 Cumberland Pkwy, Atlanta, GA 30339 (770) 434-6800. Profile: Owner of The
Weather Channel and The Travel Channel, employing 340 in Atlanta.

MEDIAONE, INC, SMARTFAX #5189

2925 Courtyards Dr, Norcross, GA 30071 (770) 613-2424. Profile: Provider of integrated communications, entertainment and information services.

TBS - CABLE NEWS NETWORK, SMARTFAX #5980

PO Box 105366,1 Cnn Center, Atlanta, GA 30348-5366 (404) 827-1500. Profile: Operates a 24-hour cable news gathering organization, employing 1600 in Atlanta.

TBS - CORPORATE HEADQUARTERS, SMARTFAX #5895

1 Cnn Center, Box 105366, Atlanta, GA 30348-5366 (404) 827-1700. Profile: TBS employs 2200 in Atlanta.

TNT & WTBS, SMARTFAX #5897

1050 Techwood Drive NW, Atlanta, GA 30318 (404) 827-1700. Profile: TNT is the entertainment cable operation and WTBS is SuperStation Channel 17; combined employment in Atlanta is 450.

VSC COMMUNICATIONS INC, SMARTFAX #5285

2700 NE Expressway #A-700, Atlanta, GA 30345 (404) 325-6929. Profile: UPN affiliate television broadcaster.

WGUN/AM RADIO, SMARTFAX #5295

2901 Mountain Ind Blvd, Tucker, GA 30084 (770) 491-1010. Profile: Christian AM radio station.

WSB-TV CHANNEL 2, SMARTFAX #5906

1601 W Peachtree Rd NW, Atlanta, GA 30309 (404) 897-7000. Profile: Subsidiary of Cox Enterprises, operating Channel 2 (ABC) and employing 200.

American Sound & Video SmartFax #7994 2225 Faulkner Rd NE, Atlanta, GA 30324. (404) 633-4577.

GCTV (GA TV & Communications) SmartFax #5477

PO Box 1549, Decatur, GA 30031. (404) 299-4999.

Marietta Daily Journal SmartFax #5182 PO Box 449, Marietta, GA 30064. (770) 428-9411.

Peach State Cablevision SmartFax #7995 482 Highway 74 N, Peachtree City, GA 30269. (770) 487-5011.

PR Newswire SmartFax #7996

34 Peachtree Street NW,
Suite 2530, Atalnta, GA
30303. (404) 523-2323.

**Television Production
Service** SmartFax #5264
3514 Chamblee
Dunwoody Rd, Atlanta,
GA 30341. (770) 452-
8700.

Public Relations

A. BROWN OLMSTEAD ASSOCIATES, SᴍᴀʀᴛFᴀx #5348
127 Peachtree Street #200, Atlanta, GA 30303 (404) 659-0919. Profile: One of five
largest Atlanta Public Relations firms. Offers 25 internships (unsalaried) annually.

COHN & WOLFE/ATLANTA, SᴍᴀʀᴛFᴀx #5992
225 Peachtree StreetNe/S2300, Atlanta, GA 30303 (404) 688-5900. Profile:
Corporate headquarters for the largest PR firm in the SE, and the 13th largest in the
US.

**Alba Communications
Associates Inc.** SmartFax
#7997
1850 Pkwy Place,
Marietta, GA 30067.
(770) 425-5600.

**Alexander
Communications**
SmartFax #7998
400 Colony Square, Suite
980, Atlanta, GA 30361.
(404) 897-2300.

**Anderson
Communications**
SmartFax #7999

2245 Godby Rd, Atlanta,
GA 30349. (404) 766-
8000.

**Baron, McDonald &
Wells** SmartFax #8000
6292 Lawrenceville
Highway, Suite C,
Tucker, GA 30084. (770)
492-0373.

**Basinger & Associates
Inc.** SmartFax #7917
115 Perimeter Center
Place, Suite 945, Atlanta,
GA 30346. (770) 396-
7808.

Bates Associates
SmartFax #8002
161 Spring St, Suite 716,
Atlanta, GA 30303. (404)
588-1707.

Communications 21 Inc.
SmartFax #8003
550 Pharr Rd, Suite 201,
Atlanta, GA 30305. (404)
814-1330.

Cookerly & Co.
SmartFax #8004
5 Piedmont Center, Suite
400, Atlanta, GA 30305.
(404) 816-2037.

Copithorne & Bellows Public Relat. SmartFax #8005
1050 Crown Pointe Pkwy, Suite 340, Atlanta, GA 30338. (770) 392-8611.

Cornerstone Communications Group SmartFax #8006
1360 Peachtree St NE, Suite 950, Atlanta, GA 30309. (404) 249-8833.

Corporate Image Group Inc. SmartFax #8007
5775 Peachtree-Dunwoody Rd, Suite 210, Atlanta, GA 30342. (404) 256-5954.

Crumbley & Associates SmartFax #7934
600 West Peachtree St, Suite 2300, Atlanta, GA 30308. (404) 892-2300.

Custer Gamwell Communications Inc. SmartFax #8009
47 Perimeter Center East NE, Suite 460, Atlanta, GA 30346. (770) 396-3996.

Dowling, Langley & Associates SmartFax #8010
1360 Peachtree St NE, Suite 360, Atlanta, GA 30309. (404) 892-0100.

DuCharme Communications Inc. SmartFax #7939

400 Northridge Rd, Suite 510, Atlanta, GA 30350. (770) 594-0110.

Duffey Communications SmartFax #8012
11 Piedmont Center, Suite 600, Atlanta, GA 30305. (404) 266-2600.

Edelman Public Relations Worldwide SmartFax #8013
3343 Peachtree Rd, Suite 200, Atlanta, GA 30326. (404) 237-1952.

ELG Creative Services SmartFax #8014
1100 Circle 75 Pkwy, Suite 800, Atlanta, GA 30339. (770) 984-2293.

First Class Inc. SmartFax #8015
225 West Peachtree Rd, Suite 1440, Atlanta, GA 30326. (404) 521-9607.

Fleishman-Hillard International Com SmartFax #8016
233 Peachtree St NE, Atlanta, GA 30303. (404) 659-4446.

Freebairn & Co. SmartFax #7943
3343 Peachtree Rd, Suite 1220, Atlanta, GA 30326. (404) 237-9945.

GCI/Atlanta SmartFax #8018

1355 Peachtree St NE, Suite 590, Atlanta, GA 30309. (404) 873-5330.

Golin/Harris Communications SmartFax #8019
127 Peachtree St NE, Atlanta, GA 30303. (404) 659-0919.

Hayslett Sorrell & Lane SmartFax #8020
5784 Lake Forrest Drive, Suite 265, Atlanta, GA 30328. (404) 303-1755.

HHH Public Relations SmartFax #8021
161 Spring St, Suite 728, Atlanta, GA 30303. (404) 577-8729.

Hill and Knowlton Inc. SmartFax #8022
1360 Peachtree St, Suite 610, Atlanta, GA 30309. (404) 249-8550.

Hollingsworth, Colborne & Associates SmartFax #8023
57 Forsyth St, Suite 1050, Atlanta, GA 30303. (404) 577-3856.

Jackson Spalding Ledlie SmartFax #8024
1201 Peachtree St, Suite 1905, Atlanta, GA 30361. (404) 874-8389.

John Day & Co. SmartFax #8025

1360 Peachtree St NE, Suite 260, Atlanta, GA 30309. (404) 815-8400.

Judy Harmon & Associates SmartFax #8026
2067 Amberwood Way, Atlanta, GA 30345. (404) 728-0219.

Julie Davis Associates SmartFax #8027
1 Buckhead Plaza, Suite 520, Atlanta, GA 30305. (404) 231-0660.

Ketchum Public Relations Worldwide SmartFax #8028
999 Peachtree St, Suite 1850, Atlanta, GA 30309. (404) 877-1800.

Knapp Inc.&The Knapp/Fletcher Comm. SmartFax #8029
50 Hurt Plaza, Atlanta, GA 30303. (404) 688-1777.

Kudzu Communications SmartFax #8030
321 Pharr Rd, Suite 300, Atlanta, GA 30305. (404) 848-9661.

Landmark Communications SmartFax #8031
3814 Satellite Blvd, Suite 200, Duluth, GA 30136. (770) 813-1000.

Lewin HealthCare Communications SmartFax #8032
750 Hammond Drive, Suite 300, Atlanta, GA 30328. (404) 256-6322.

Maizie Hale Public Relations SmartFax #8033
2964 Peachtree Rd NW, Suite 530, Atlanta, GA 30305. (404) 261-7080.

Manning Selvage & Lee SmartFax #8034
1201 West Peachtree St, Suite 4800, Atlanta, GA 30309. (404) 875-1444.

Mathon & Associates SmartFax #8035
1885 Moores Mill Rd, Atlanta, GA 30318. (404) 352-8015.

Matlock & Associates Inc. SmartFax #8036
1360 Peachtree St NE, Suite 220, Atlanta, GA 30309. (404) 872-3200.

Melissa Libby & Associates SmartFax #8037
6 Piedmont Center, Suite 230, Atlanta, GA 30305. (404) 816-3068.

Michael Parver Associates SmartFax #7960

1800 Peachtree St NE, Suite 333, Atlanta, GA 30309. (404) 355-5580.

Mike Wilson Public Relations Inc. SmartFax #8039
3400 Peachtree Rd, Suite 1239, Atlanta, GA 30326. (404) 365-9000.

MMI Public Relations SmartFax #8040
18 the Fairway, Suite 200, Woodstock, GA 30188. (770) 663-1374.

Molloy Communications SmartFax #8041
1519 Oakmoor Place, Marietta, GA 30062. (770) 565-1231.

Newsmakers SmartFax #8042
1100 Abernathy Rd, Suite 1725, Atlanta, GA 30328. (770) 901-9664.

Pamela A. Keene Public Relations SmartFax #8043
2401 Lake Park Drive, Suite 262, Smyrna, GA 30080. (770) 333-0123.

PD Communications SmartFax #8044
108 North Avondale Rd, Suite A, Avondale Estates, GA 30002. (404) 294-9333.

Primedia Inc. SmartFax #8045
600 West Peachtree St, Suite 1600, Atlanta, GA 30303. (404) 892-2287.

Pringle Dixon Pringle SmartFax #7965
303 Peachtree St NE, Suite 333, Atlanta, GA 30309. (404) 688-6720.

Rountree Group Inc. SmartFax #8047
6065 Roswell Rd, Suite 400, Atlanta, GA 30328. (404) 252-7577.

Roy Communications SmartFax #8048
1987 Wellbourne Drive, Atlanta, GA 30324. (404) 874-7119.

RP Communications Inc. SmartFax #8049
220 Drummen Court NE, Atlanta, GA 30328. (770) 392-0007.

Sawyer Riley Compton Inc. SmartFax #7968
1100 Abernathy Rd, Suite 800, Atlanta, GA 30328. (770) 393-9849.

The DeMoss Group Inc. SmartFax #8051
3473 Satellite Blvd, Suite 211, Duluth, GA 30136. (770) 813-0000.

The Gove Network SmartFax #8052

1776 Peachtree St, Suite 618, Atlanta, GA 30309. (404) 892-3655.

The Headline Group SmartFax #8053
3490 Piedmont Rd, Suite 1504, Atlanta, GA 30305. (404) 262-3000.

The Leatherbury Group Inc. SmartFax #8054
452-B East Paces Fy Rd, Atlanta, GA 30305. (404) 364-0035.

The Maxwell Co. SmartFax #8055
1777 Northeast Expressway, Suite 110, Atlanta, GA 30329. (404) 633-1220.

The Morrison Agency Public Relations SmartFax #7980
950 East Paces Fy Rd, Atlanta, GA 30326. (404) 233-3405.

The Randolph Partnership SmartFax #8057
1201 Peachtree St, Suite 406, Atlanta, GA 30361. (404) 892-4505.

Tortorici & Co. SmartFax #8058
3390 Peachtree Rd, Suite 1738, Atlanta, GA 30326. (404) 365-9393.

Treco-Jones Public Relations SmartFax #8059
1800 Century Blvd, Suite 1225, Atlanta, GA 30345. (404) 320-7269.

Wemmers Communications Inc. SmartFax #7989
1050 Crown Pointe Pkwy, Suite 450, Atlanta, GA 30338. (770) 399-9508.

William Mills Agency SmartFax #8061
3091 East Shawdowlawn Ave, Atlanta, GA 30305. (404) 261-4900.

Printing/Publishing

ADVERTISING TECHNOLOGIES INC, SMARTFAX #5667
2880 Dresden Drive #100, Atlanta, GA 30341 (770) 216-2800. Profile: Full service 24-hour a day graphic design company, employing 50.

AMERICAN SIGNATURE, SMARTFAX #5366
3101 McCall Drive NE, Atlanta, GA 30340 (770) 451-4511. Profile: Commercial printer, handling mostly mail-order catalogs and magazines, employing 475.

ARGUS, INC., SMARTFAX #5616
6151 Powers Fy Rd NW, Atlanta, GA 30339 (770) 955-2500. Profile: Publisher of 50 trade magazines, trade shows and direct mail operations, employing 220.

ATLANTA PRINTING & DESIGN, SMARTFAX #5031
2447 Cobb Pkwy, Smyrna, GA 30080 (770) 952-3991. Profile: Full-service graphic design studio and printer.

ATLANTA WEB PRINTER INC, SMARTFAX #5034
1585 Rdhaven Drive, Stone Mountain, GA 30083 (770) 621-8888. Profile: Provides web offset printing and related graphic services.

BROWN & BIGELOW INC, SMARTFAX #5047
PO Box 7445, Marietta, GA 30065 (770) 591-9917. Profile: Specializes in custom advertising and marketing materials; world's largest customer calendar manufacturer.

CURTIS 1000, SMARTFAX #5423
PO Box 105683, Atlanta, GA 30348 (770) 951-1000. Profile: Subsidiary of American Business Products, employing 250 in Atlanta.

DITTLER BROTHERS, INC., SMARTFAX #5437
1375 Seabord Indust Blvd, Atlanta, GA 30318 (404) 355-3423. Profile: Printer that produces promotional games, ticket jackets and other specialty finishing.

ENTERPRISE SALES SOLUTIONS, SMARTFAX #5087
1165 N'chase Pkwy #300, Marietta, GA 30067 (770) 859-1980. Profile: Publishes trade magazines and sponsors conferences nationwide.

GRAPHIC INDUSTRIES, SMARTFAX #5470

2155 Monroe Drive, Atlanta, GA 30324 (404) 874-3327. Profile: Atlanta-based printing conglomerate, with 18 printing companies, including five in Atlanta.

HEIDELBERG U.S.A., SMARTFAX #5545

1000 Gutenberg Drive, Kennesaw, GA 30144 (770) 419-6500. Profile: Subsidiary of German manufacturer of printing presses, repaired and serviced in Atlanta.

HUMANICS LTD, SMARTFAX #5142

1482 Mecaslin Sq, Atlanta, GA 30309 (404) 874-2176. Profile: Publisher of parenting books and trade paperbacks.

IMPACT PUBLISHING INC, SMARTFAX #5148

1145 Rottenwood Drive #240, Marietta, GA 30067 (770) 425-3777. Profile: Publishing company producing card deck direct mail packs.

PEACHTREE PUBLISHERS LTD, SMARTFAX #5961

494 Armour Cir NE, Atlanta, GA 30324 (404) 876-8761. Profile: A general trade book publishing company.

SCIENTIFIC GAMES, SMARTFAX #5647

1500 Blue Grass Lake Pkwy, Alpharetta, GA 30201 (770) 664-3700. Profile: World's largest printer of lottery tickets.

SHORE-VARRONE, INC, SMARTFAX #5245

6255 Barfield Rd, #200, Atlanta, GA 30328 (404) 252-4436. Profile: Trade magazine publishing company.

STEVENS GRAPHICS, SMARTFAX #5890

713 Abernathy Blvd SW, Atlanta, GA 30310 (404) 753-1121. Profile: Second largest printer in Atlanta.

WALK THRU THE BIBLE MINISTRIES INC, SMARTFAX #5291

4201 North Peachtree Rd, Atlanta, GA 30341 (770) 454-9313. Profile: Christian educational, training and publishing organization with nearly 70 employees.

Active Parenting Publishers SmartFax #5004

810-B Franklin Court, Marietta, GA 30067. (770) 429-0565.

Atlanta Offset SmartFax #8062

120 James Aldredge Blvd, Atlanta, GA 30336. (404) 699-6200.

Braceland SmartFax #8063
5800 Tulane Drive SW, Atlanta, GA 30336. (404) 696-7900.

Cadmus Marketing Services SmartFax #8064
2300 DeFoor Hills Rd NW, Atlanta, GA 30318. (404) 355-7220.

Color Graphics Inc.
SmartFax #8065
4540 Frederick Drive SW, Atlanta, GA 30336. (404) 696-1515.
Corporate Printers Inc.
SmartFax #8066
2195 Pendley Rd, Cumming, GA 30130. (770) 688-6652.

Darby Printing Co.
SmartFax #5113
6215 Purdue Drive, Atlanta, GA 30336. (404) 344-2665.

Executive Printing Inc.
SmartFax #8069
830 Kennesaw Ave, Marietta, GA 30060. (770) 428-1554.

First Image SmartFax #8070

4388 Shackleford Rd, Norcross, GA 30093. (770) 806-2500.

Geographics Inc.
SmartFax #8071
3450 Brown's Mill Rd, Atlanta, GA 30354. (404) 768-5805.

Graphic Communications Corp.
SmartFax #8072
394 North Clayton St, Lawrenceville, GA 30245. (770) 963-1870.

GTE Directories Sales Corp. SmartFax #5093
2100 E Exchange Pl #520, Tucker, GA 30084. (770) 934-8480.

Harris Specialty Lithographers Inc.
SmartFax #8073
1519 Stone Ridge Drive, Stone Mountain, GA 30083. (770) 938-7650.

IPD Printing & Distributing Inc.
SmartFax #8074
5800 Peachtree Rd, Atlanta, GA 30341. (770) 458-6351.

Label America SmartFax #8075
5430 East Ponce De Leon Ave, Stone Mountain, GA 30083. (770) 934-8040.

Magic Graphics Printing Services, Inc.
SmartFax #5180
3561 Hanover Drive, Buford, GA 30519. (770) 271-0110.

Moore Copies Inc.
SmartFax #8076
3343 Peachtree Rd NE, Atlanta, GA 30326. (404) 231-1380.

Network Publications Inc. SmartFax #8077
2 Pamplin Drive, Lawrenceville, GA 30245. (770) 962-7220.

Night Magazine
SmartFax #5934
2936 N Druid Hills Rd #E, Atlanta, GA . (404) 321-0062.

Phoenix Communications Inc.
SmartFax #8078
5664 New Peachtree Rd, Atlanta, GA 30341. (770) 457-1301.

Seiz Printing Inc.
SmartFax #8080
4525 Acworth Industrial Drive, Acworth, GA 30101. (770) 917-7000.
Southern Signatures Inc. SmartFax #8081
201 Armour Drive NE, Atlanta, GA 30324. (404) 872-4411.

The Tucker Group
SmartFax #8084
3500 McCall Place,
Atlanta, GA 30340. (770)
454-1580.

Val Pak SmartFax #5286
5825 Glendridge Drive
#280, Atlanta, GA 30328.
(404) 256-9587.

Voxcom Inc. SmartFax
#8085
100 Clover Green,
Peachtree City, GA
30269. (404) 487-7575.

Walton Press Inc.
SmartFax #8086
402 Mayfield Drive,
Monroe, GA 30655.
(770) 267-2596.

Williams Printing Co.
SmartFax #8087
1240 Spring St NE,
Atlanta, GA 30309. (404)
875-6611.

Retail

A & P SUPERMARKETS, SMARTFAX #5997
1200 White Street SW, Atlanta, GA 30310 (404) 758-4544. Profile: 55 grocery
supermarkets in Atlanta, hires experienced store management.

AARON'S RENTAL PURCHASE, SMARTFAX #5001
309 E Paces Fy Rd, Atlanta, GA 30305 (404) 237-4016. Profile: Home office of
largest furniture rental and sales company in US, employing 100+ in corporate office,
plus store managers and staff.

AMERICAN FROZEN FOODS, SMARTFAX #6027
1899 Power Fy Rd #410, Atlanta, GA 30339 (770) 951-8391. Profile: Sales company
that offers frozen foods directly to the consumer.

ATHLETE'S FOOT, THE, SMARTFAX #5027
1950 Vaughn Rd, Kennesaw, GA 30144 (770) 514-4500. Profile: Corporate
headquarters for specialty footwear retailer, employing 250.

BELLES & BEAUS BRIDAL & FORMALWEAR, SMARTFAX #5043
150 Highway 314, Fayetteville, GA 30214 (770) 461-4818. Profile: Comprehensive
bridal service retail location.

BLOCKBUSTER MUSIC, SMARTFAX #5400
1351 Dividen Dr, #K, Marietta, GA 30067 (770) 858-5500. Profile: Retailer of
records, tapes and videos, operating 60+ stores in Atlanta, with the headquarters staff
of 250, plus store personnel.

BLOCKBUSTER VIDEO, SMARTFAX #5559
2900 South Cobb Drive, Smyrna, GA 30080 (770) 431-0132. Profile: Nation's largest retailer of video rentals and supplies.

BUTLER GROUP, INC (D/B/A BUTLER SHOES), SMARTFAX #5619
1600 Terrell Mill Rd, Marietta, GA 30067 (770) 955-6400. Profile: Specialty retail chain with 230 stores nationwide, employing 100 at the headquarters here in Atlanta.

CIRCLE K STORES INC, SMARTFAX #5065
4275 Shackelford Rd #200, Norcross, GA 30093 (770) 717-7295. Profile: Largest convenience store chain in Atlanta.

ECKERD DRUGS, SMARTFAX #6001
36 Herring Rd, Newnan, GA 30265 (770) 254-4401. Profile: Operates 120 retail stores in Atlanta, with 1500 employees here.

FEDERATED SYSTEMS GROUP, SMARTFAX #5999
6801 Governors Lake Pkwy, Norcross, GA 30071 (770) 246-5000. Profile: Information processing division of Federated department stores.

H KESSLER & CO., SMARTFAX #5310
87 Peachtree StreetSW, Atlanta, GA 30303 (404) 523-0531. Profile: Operates department stores in the metro Atlanta area, employing 200.

HAVERTY FURNITURE CO., SMARTFAX #5959
866 W Peachtree S NW, Atlanta, GA 30308 (404) 881-1911. Profile: Corporate headquarters for retail furniture chain operating 13 stores in Atlanta, with 350 employees in Atlanta.

J.C. PENNEY CATALOG DISTRIBUTION CENTER, SMARTFAX #5507
5500 South Expressway, Forest Park, GA 30050 (404) 361-7700. Profile: One of six national distribution centers, employing 1700.

KROGER SUPERMARKETS, SMARTFAX #5499
2175 Parklake Drive NE, Atlanta, GA 30345 (770) 496-7400. Profile: Largest supermarket chain in Atlanta, operating 70+ stores in this area, employing 15,000.

KUPPENHEIMER MEN'S CLOTHIERS, SMARTFAX #6017
2775 Northwoods Pkwy, Norcross, GA 30071 (770) 449-5877. Profile: Distributes and retails men's clothing.

MEDIA DISTRIBUTING INC, SMARTFAX #5188
17 Dunwoody Pk #125, Atlanta, GA 30338 (770) 804-0890. Profile: Sells magazine subscriptions.

MICRO CENTER, SMARTFAX #5194
1221 Powers Fy Rd, Marietta, GA 30067 (770) 859-1540. Profile: Retailer of computer hardware, software and other related merchandise.

MILLER/ZELL INC, SMARTFAX #5196
4715 Frederick Dr, Atlanta, GA 30336 (404) 696-9330. Profile: Purchases and provides store fixtures, furniture, interior design products, print graphics and more.

MOBILE PAINT MFG CO/WALLPAPER ATLANTA, SMARTFAX #5199
PO Box 2327, Norcross, GA 30091 (770) 449-5180. Profile: One of the 10 largest regional paint manufacturers with 15 retail stores.

NATIONAL VISION ASSOCIATES, SMARTFAX #5972
296 Graceson Hwy, Lawrenceville, GA 30245 (770) 822-3600. Profile: Optical retail chain with over 250 stores, mostly in Wal-Mart stores.

REMCO AMERICA, INC, SMARTFAX #5229
5211-B Buford Highway, Doraville, GA 30340 (770) 458-4940. Profile: A nationwide furniture retailer offering rent-to-own financing to the consumer.

SAM FLAX, SMARTFAX #5241
1460 Northside Drive, Atlanta, GA 30318 (404) 352-7200. Profile: Large graphic and art supply company.

SMITH, W. H. U.S.A., SMARTFAX #5880
3200 Windy Hill Rd, Suite 1500, Atlanta, GA 30339 (770) 952-0705. Profile: British conglomerate with 300+ retail stores in airports and hotels, employing 125 in Atlanta.

SPIEGEL, SMARTFAX #5659

6050 Oakbrook Pkwy, Norcross, GA 30093 (770) 441-1288. Profile: Telephone catalog ordering center, employing 560 in Atlanta.

SPORT SHOE, THE, SMARTFAX #5255
1770 Corporate Drive, Norcross, GA 30093 (770) 279-7494. Profile: Retail company with 22 locations.

SPORTSTOWN, SMARTFAX #5611
680 Engineering Drive So #50, Norcross, GA 30092 (770) 246-5300. Profile: Retailer of sporting goods with five stores in Atlanta, employing 600.

STAR ATHLETICS, SMARTFAX #5345
PO Box 33097, Decatur, GA 30033 (404) 634-6449. Profile: Provides souvenirs items for high schools nationwide.

SUPER DISCOUNT MARKETS, INC D/B/A CUB FOODS, SMARTFAX #5634
420 Thornton Rd, #103, Lithia Springs, GA 30057 (770) 732-6800. Profile: Corporate headquarters for franchise operator of 13 Georgia supermarkets, employing 1900.

TOYS "R" US, SMARTFAX #5267
3710 Atlanta Ind Pkwy, Atlanta, GA 30331 (404) 696-5100. Profile: World's largest retailer of children's products, employing 500 in Atlanta.

UPTON'S DEPARTMENT STORES, SMARTFAX #5656
6251 Crooked Creek Rd, Norcross, GA 30092 (770) 662-2500. Profile: Privately-held apparel chain with 13 stores in Atlanta, employing 180 at corporate office.

WINN DIXIE SUPERMARKETS, SMARTFAX #5494
5400 Fulton Ind Blvd, Atlanta, GA 30336 (404) 346-2400. Profile: Largest supermarket chain in the SE, operating 68 stores in Atlanta.

WOLF CAMERA AND VIDEO, SMARTFAX #5905
1706 Chantilly Dri NE, Atlanta, GA 30324 (404) 633-9000. Profile: Largest camera retailer in the SE, employing 550 in Atlanta.

Americana Furniture Showroom SmartFax #5369
3401 Lawrenceville Hwy, Tucker, GA 30084. (770) 939-4595.

Brookstone SmartFax #5678
1038 North Point Cir, Alpharetta, GA 30202. (770) 442-8851.

CD Connection SmartFax #5660
PO Box 921206, Norcross, GA 30092. (770) 446-1332.

Chapter 11 The Discount Bookstore Inc SmartFax #5056
6305 Roswell Rd, Atlanta, GA 30328. (404) 252-4478.

Duron Paints & Wallcoverings SmartFax #5682
1415 Constitution Rd, Atlanta, GA 30316. (404) 241-7722.

Federated Department Stores SmartFax #5452
223 Perimeter Center Pkwy, Atlanta, GA 30346. (770) 913-5176.

Gingiss Formalwear SmartFax #5914
2732 Candler Rd, Decatur, GA 30034. (404) 244-1560.

HiFi Buys SmartFax #8223
3135 Peachtree Rd, Atlanta, GA 30305. (404) 261-4434.

Macy's SmartFax #8236
180 Peachtree St, Atlanta, GA 30326. (404) 231-8908.

Parisian Town Center SmartFax #5209
400 Ernest Barret Pkwy, Kennesaw, GA 30144. (770) 514-5310.

Peachtree Peddlers Flea Market SmartFax #5212
155 Mill Rd, Mcdonough, GA 30253. (770) 914-2269.

Retail Design Strategies SmartFax #5524
690 Dalrymple Rd, Atlanta, GA 30328. (770) 390-0088.

Sam's SmartFax #8257
150 Cobb Pkwy, Marietta, GA 30062. (770) 424-0903.

Table Decor SmartFax #5092
PO Box 71872, Marietta, GA 30007-1872. (770) 432-1156.

Thorn, Inc. D/B/A Remco SmartFax #5658
2780 Bert Adams Rd #201, Atlanta, GA 30339. (770) 436-9520.

Other

1-800-Database SmartFax #5346
3100 Medlock Bridge Rd, Norcross, GA 30071. (770) 246-1700.

Non-Profit

Arts/Museums

ALTERNATE ROOTS INC, SMARTFAX #5012
1083 Austin Ave NE, Atlanta, GA 30307 (404) 577-1079. Profile: Non-profit organization that serves southeastern individual artists, theater, and dance companies.

GEORGIA SHAKESPEARE FESTIVAL, SMARTFAX #5098
4484 Peachtree Rd NE, Atlanta, GA 30319 (404) 688-8008. Profile: Produces a summer reperatory from June-August with 65 seasonal members.

ROBERT W. WOODRUFF ARTS CENTER, INC., SMARTFAX #8088
1280 Peachtree Street NE, Atlanta, GA 30309 (404) 733-4200. Profile: Parent company to the High Museum, the Alliance Theatre Company, Atlanta School of Arts and the Atlanta Symphony.

ZOO ATLANTA, SMARTFAX #5301
800 Cherokee Ave SE, Atlanta, GA 30315 (404) 624-5802. Profile: Atlanta's largest zoo.

Alliance Theatre Co.
SmartFax #8089
1280 Peachtree St NE,
Atlanta, GA 30309. (404)
733-4700.

Atlanta Botanical
Garden SmartFax #8090
Piedmont Ave @ The
Prado, Atlanta, GA
30309. (404) 765-5859.

Atlanta Cyclorama
SmartFax #8091
800-C Cherokee Ave SE,
Atlanta, GA 30315. (404)
658-7625.

Delmar Gardens of
Smyrna SmartFax #5645
404 King Springs Vill
Pkwy, Smyrna, GA
30082. (770) 432-4444.

Fernbank Museum of
Natural History
SmartFax #5945
767 Clifton Rd, Atlanta,
GA 30033. (404) 370-
8080.

High Museum of Art
SmartFax #8092
1280 Peachtree Street
Northeast, Atlanta, GA
30309. (404) 733-4400.

Social Services/Medical

AGENCY FOR TOXIC SUBSTANCES & DISEASE REGISTRY, SMARTFAX #5669
1600 Clifton Rd NE, Atlanta, GA 30333 (404) 639-3616. Profile: Public health service agency that works with the EPA and state health officials to ensure public safety.

AMERICAN CANCER SOCIETY, SMARTFAX #5670
1599 Clifton Rd NE, Atlanta, GA 30329 (404) 329-7561. Profile: Home office of the nationwide community-based voluntary health organization, employing 350+ in Atlanta.

AMERICAN RED CROSS, SMARTFAX #5365
1955 Monroe Drive NE, Atlanta, GA 30324 (404) 881-9800. Profile: Non-profit emergency assistance and blood bank, employing 700 in Southern Region.

ARTHRITIS FOUNDATION, SMARTFAX #5375
1314 Spring Street NW, Atlanta, GA 30309 (404) 872-7100. Profile: Non-profit organization providing educational and fund raising activities, with 125 employees.

ATLANTA UNION MISSION, THE, SMARTFAX #5033
PO Box 1807, Atlanta, GA 30301 (404) 588-4000. Profile: A Christian ministry that feeds and shelters homeless and poor men, women and children.

ATLANTA URBAN LEAGUE, INC., SMARTFAX #8095
100 Edgewood Ave NE, Suite 600, Atlanta, GA 30303 (404) 659-1150. Profile: National, non-profit political action group.

BOY SCOUTS OF AMERICA, SMARTFAX #8096
PO Box 440728, Kennesaw, GA 30144 (770) 421-1601. Profile: National, non-profit youth services organization.

BOYS & GIRLS CLUBS OF AMERICA, SMARTFAX #5402
1230 W Peachtree Street NW, Atlanta, GA 30309 (404) 815-5700. Profile: Moved corporate headquarters from NYC to Atlanta in 1994.

C A R E, SMARTFAX #5405

151 Ellis St NE, Atlanta, GA 30303-2439 (404) 681-2552. Profile: World's largest private international relief and development organization, employing 225 in Atlanta.

CENTER FOR DISEASE CONTROL & PREVENTION (CDC), SMARTFAX #5408

4770 Buford Hwy, Atlanta, GA 30341-3724 (770) 488-1700. Profile: Federal agency that provides national leadership for public health efforts to prevent disease. Employs over 3500 in Atlanta.

CHILDREN'S WISH FOUNDATION INTERNATIONAL INC, SMARTFAX #5064

PO Box 28785, Atlanta, GA 30358 (770) 393-9474. Profile: Fulfills wishes of terminally ill children.

CHRISTIAN CITY, SMARTFAX #5325

7290 Lester Rd, Union City, GA 30291-2317 (770) 964-3301. Profile: Provides for children, elderly and ill people in need, employing over 400 in Atlanta.

GA BAPTIST CHILDREN'S HOMES & FAMILY MINISTRIES, SMARTFAX #5095

2930 Flower, Atlanta, GA 30341 (770) 463-4092. Profile: Provides child care and other services for at-risk children and youth with developmental disabilities.

GOODWILL INDUSTRIES OF ATLANTA, INC., SMARTFAX #5944

2201 Glenwood Ave, Atlanta, GA 30316 (404) 377-0441. Profile: National, non-profit organization that provides social services to people with disabilities and other disadvantaged members of society.

GREATER ATLANTA CONSERVE CORPS, SMARTFAX #8097

250 Georgia Ave SE, Atlanta, GA 30312 (404) 522-4222. Profile: Non-profit organization taking action to further environmental welfare.

PEACE CORPS, SMARTFAX #5305

101 Marietta St NW, #2324, Atlanta, GA 30027 (404) 331-2601. Profile: Places skilled U.S. citizens in 94 developing countries in a variety of community development fields.

UNITED WAY OF METRO ATLANTA, SMARTFAX #8098

3081 Holcombe Bridge Rd, Norcross, GA 30071 (770) 446-0245. Profile: Non-profit organization that addresses the health and human care needs of millions of people in the U.S.

YMCA OF METRO ATLANTA, SMARTFAX #7505

100 Edgewood Ave NE, Atlanta, GA 30303 (404) 588-9622. Profile: Provides a wide range of low- or no-cost services in communities all over the country.

Other

Junior Achievement of GA SmartFax #5156
460 Abernathy Rd, Atlanta, GA 30087. (404) 257-1932.

Northwest GA Girl Scout Council SmartFax #5950
1000 Edgewood Ave NE,1100, Atlanta, GA . (404) 527-7551.

TECHNICAL

Aircraft/Aerospace

AERONAUTICAL SPECIALTIES, INC., SMARTFAX #8100
2220 Northwest Pkwy, Suite 200, Marietta, GA 30067 (770) 951-1398. Profile: Aerospace consulting firm.

AIRPORT GROUP INTERNATIONAL INC, SMARTFAX #5009
PO Box 45568, Atlanta, GA 30320 (404) 530-2090. Profile: Fixed base operator at Atlanta Hartsfield International Airport.

BARFIELD INSTRUMENT CORP., SMARTFAX #8103
1478 Central Ave, East Point, GA 30344 (404) 761-4321. Profile: Manufactures aircraft support test equipment.

ENGINEERED FABRICS CORP., SMARTFAX #8102
669 Goodyear Street, Rockmart, GA 30153 (770) 684-7855. Profile: Manufactures aircraft equipment.

GEC AVIONICS, SMARTFAX #8101
PO Box 81999, Atlanta, GA 30366 (770) 448-1947. Profile: Designs and manufactures electronic devices used in the aviation industry.

LOCKHEED MARTIN AERONAUTICAL SYSTEMS, SMARTFAX #5170
86 S Cobb Dr, Marietta, GA 30063-0530 (770) 494-5003. Profile: Defense contractor that develops and manufactures aircraft, employing 12,000 in Atlanta.

LOCKHEED MARTIN DISPLAY SYSTEMS, SMARTFAX #5171
6765 Peachtree Ind Blvd, Atlanta, GA 30360 (770) 448-1604. Profile: Designs, develops and manufactures airborne electronics display devices for the US government.

RELIABLE HYDRAULICS, SMARTFAX #5228
5550 South Cobb Drive, Smyrna, GA 30080 (404) 799-8554. Profile: A distributor of hydraulic lubrication equipment.

Sundstrand Aerospace SmartFax #8104
100 Harstfield Center Pkwy, Atlanta, GA 30354. (404) 761-2832.

Teledyne Continental Motors Aircraft
SmartFax #8105
370 Shadowland Rd, Marietta, GA 30067. (770) 952-6600.

Computer Hardware

AMERICAN MEGATRENDS, SMARTFAX #5671
6145-F Northbelt Pkwy, Norcross, GA 30071 (770) 263-8181. Profile: Designer and manufacturer of IBM and PC compatible hardware, employing 150.

CHECKMATE ELECTRONICS, SMARTFAX #5060
1003 Mansell Rd, Roswell, GA 30201 (770) 594-6000. Profile: Manufacturer of point-of-sales payment automation systems and terminals, employing 115.

GLOBAL COMPUTER SUPPLIES, SMARTFAX #5100
1050 Northbrook Pkwy, Suwanee, GA 30174 (770) 962-3300. Profile: Catalog company that sells computer supplies.

LASER LIFE INC, SMARTFAX #5165
1625 Williams Drive #206, Marietta, GA 30066 (770) 425-5928. Profile: Seller of printer and fax supplies.

LOTUS DEVELOPMENT CORP, W.P. DIVISION, SMARTFAX #5918
1000 Abernathy Rd, #1700, Atlanta, GA 30328 (770) 391-0011. Profile: Develops and markets a graphical word processor and an electronic documentation builder, employing 250.

Compubiz/Downtown Computers SmartFax #6031
161 Spring St NW, Atlanta, GA 30303. (404) 880-0340.

Hayes Microcomputer Products Inc. SmartFax #8112
5835 Peachtree Corners E, Norcross, GA 30092. (770) 840-9200.

Hewlett-Packard Co.
SmartFax #8113
20 Perimeter Summit Blvd, Atlanta, GA 30319. (770) 648-8052.

Intermec Corp.
SmartFax #5696
400 Northridge Rd, #260,
Atlanta, GA 30350. (770)
641-5030.

**N E C Technologies,
Inc.** SmartFax #6028
1 Nec Drive, Mcdonough,
GA 30253. (770) 957-
6600.

Computer Software

A.D.A.M. SOFTWARE, SMARTFAX #5005
1600 Riveredge Pkwy #800, Atlanta, GA 30328 (770) 980-0888. Profile: Healthcare software systems developer, employing 80.

AMERICAN SOFTWARE USA INC, SMARTFAX #5668
470 E Paces Fy Rd, Atlanta, GA 30305 (404) 264-5599. Profile: Develops, manufactures and markets software for business applications, employing 600 in Atlanta.

ATTACHMATE CORP., SMARTFAX #5035
1000 Alderman Dr, Alpharetta, GA 30202 (770) 442-4000. Profile: Fifth largest PC software company in the world, employing 350 in Atlanta.

BROCK CONTROL SYSTEMS, SMARTFAX #5336
2859 Paces Fy Rd, #1000, Atlanta, GA 30339 (770) 431-1200. Profile: Atlanta-based company in sales, marketing and customer service automation software, employing nearly 200.

CONSULTEC INC, SMARTFAX #5078
9040 Roswell Rd #700, Atlanta, GA 30350 (770) 594-7799. Profile: Data processing software company.

D & B SOFTWARE, SMARTFAX #5112
66 Perimeter Center East, Atlanta, GA 30326 (404) 239-2000. Profile: Subsidiary of Dun and Bradstreet that designs and manufactures business software systems, employing 800 in Atlanta.

DAUGHERTY SYSTEMS INC, SMARTFAX #5335
400 Interstate N Pkwy #500, Atlanta, GA 30339 (770) 618-5858. Profile: Client server software development company.

DIGITAL EQUIPMENT CORP., SMARTFAX #5492
5555 Windward Pkwy West, Alpharetta, GA 30201-7407 (770) 343-0000. Profile: World's second largest manufacturer of computer systems, with 1100 employees in Atlanta.

EMERGING MARKET TECHNOLOGIES INC, SMARTFAX #5085
1775 The Exchange, Suite 425, Atlanta, GA 30339 (770) 980-1400. Profile: Provides sales automation software, custom programming and training.

ENCORE SYSTEMS, SMARTFAX #5444
900 Circle 75 Pkwy, Suite 1700, Atlanta, GA 30339 (770) 612-3500. Profile: Developer and marketer of computerized property management systems.

HARBINGER E.D.I. SERVICES, SMARTFAX #5471
1055 Lenox Park Blvd, Atlanta, GA 30319 (404) 841-4334. Profile: Computer software development company, employing 140.

IMNET SYSTEMS, SMARTFAX #5485
8601 Dunwoody Pl, #420, Atlanta, GA 30350 (770) 998-2200. Profile: Makes PC software for networks used to convert documents into electronic images, employing 90.

IN HEALTH RECORD SYSTEMS, INC, SMARTFAX #5107
5076 Winters Chapel Rd, Atlanta, GA 30360 (770) 396-4994. Profile: Provides a variety of recordkeeping system products for the healthcare industry, employing 120.

INFORMATION SYSTEMS SERVICES CORP. (IBM), SMARTFAX #6023
3200 Windy Hill Rd 2nd Fl, Atlanta, GA 30339 (770) 835-7103. Profile: World leader in information technology, employing 5000 in Atlanta.

IQ SOFTWARE, SMARTFAX #5581
3295 River Exchange Drive, Norcross, GA 30092 (770) 446-8880. Profile: Develops software for data analysis, employing 100.

ISA/SUNGARD, SMARTFAX #5483
500 Northridge Rd, S400, Atlanta, GA 30350 (770) 587-6800. Profile: Develops software for the financial services industry, employing more than 100.

LYSIS CORP., SMARTFAX #5175

740 W Peachtree St, Atlanta, GA 30188 (404) 892-3301. Profile: Provides customer service support software products.

MEDICAL SOFTWARE INTEGRATORS, INC, SMARTFAX #5302

3939 Roswell Rd #300, Marietta, GA 30062 (770) 973-0173. Profile: Developer/vendor for health care/medical practice management software.

NUSTAR INTERNATIONAL INC, SMARTFAX #5225

3355 Breckinrdge Bvd #128, Duluth, GA 30136 (770) 806-1275,EXT 137. Profile: A software development/electronics publishing company.

PEACHTREE SOFTWARE, SMARTFAX #6020

1505-C Pavilion Place, Norcross, GA 30093 (770) 564-5800. Profile: Developer of accounting software.

THE SYSTEM WORKS, SMARTFAX #5617

3301 Windy Ridge Pkwy, Atlanta, GA 30339 (770) 952-8444. Profile: Manufactures plant performance systems, employing 225.

VBXTRAS, SMARTFAX #5284

1905 Powers Fy Rd #100, Atlanta, GA 30339 (770) 952-6388. Profile: Re-seller of Visual Basic add-on tools.

XCELLNET, SMARTFAX #5868

5 Concourse Pkwy, S 200, Atlanta, GA 30328 (770) 804-8100. Profile: Software developer, employing 160.

Alltel Information Services SmartFax #8106
200 Ashford Center N, Atlanta, GA 30338. (404) 847-5000.

American System & Programming Co., Inc.
SmartFax #5014
3834 Cardinal Drive, Tucker, GA 30084. (770) 938-9394.

GE Capital Technology Management Svcs
SmartFax #8111
6875 Jimmy Carter Blvd, Suite 3200, Norcross, GA 30071. (770) 246-6200.

HNS Software, Inc.
SmartFax #5478
7000 Central Pkwy #220, Atlanta, GA . (770) 396-5540.

Howard Systems International,Inc.
SmartFax #5482
Six Concourse Pkwy, #2140, Atlanta, GA 30328. (770) 394-5700.

Intecolor Corp.
SmartFax #8115

2150 Boggs Rd, Atlanta,
GA 30336. (770) 623-
9145.

**Lotus Development
Corp.** SmartFax #8116
1000 Abernathy Rd, Suite
1700, Atlanta, GA 30328.
(770) 391-0011.

MicroBilt Corp.
SmartFax #5195
6190 Powers Fy Rd,
Atlanta, GA 30339. (770)
955-0313.

**Nova Information
Systems** SmartFax #8150
5 Concourse Pkwy NE,
Atlanta, GA 30328. (770)
396-1456.

Palm Soft, Inc.
SmartFax #5976
4470 Cham-D'woody Rd
#270, Atlanta, GA . (770)
986-0073.

Sales Technologies Inc.
SmartFax #5871
3399 Peachtree Rd, Suite
700, Atlanta, GA 30326.
(404) 841-4000.

Servantis Systems, Inc.
SmartFax #5877
4411 E Jones Bridge Rd,
Norcross, GA 30092.
(770) 441-3387.

Sterling Software
SmartFax #5940
3340 Peachtree Rd South,
Atlanta, GA 30326. (404)
231-8575.

TSW International
SmartFax #8120
3301 Windy Ridge Pkwy,
Atlanta, GA 30339. (770)
952-8444.

Computer Services

ADVANCED COMPUTER DISTRIBUTORS, SMARTFAX #5007
2395 Pleasantdale Rd #13, Atlanta, GA 30340 (770) 453-9200. Profile: Wholesales
computer products.

AIRTOUCH CELLULAR, SMARTFAX #5315
4151 Ashford Dunwoody Rd, Atlanta, GA 30319 (404) 257-5000. Profile: Provides
cellular products, employing 550+ in Atlanta.

ARMKNECHT & ASSOCIATES, SMARTFAX #5020
35 Glenlake Pkwy #550, Atlanta, GA 30328 (770) 671-8929. Profile: Information
management consulting firm.

AUTOMATIC DATA PROCESSING, SMARTFAX #5391
5680 New Northside Drive, Atlanta, GA 30328 (770) 955-3600. Profile: Nation's
largest independent data services company, employing 350 in Atlanta.

CHEMTECH LIMITED, SMARTFAX #5059

550 Pharr Rd #207, Atlanta, GA 30305 (404) 262-9800. Profile: Full service provider of software solutions.

COMMAND CONTROL INC, SMARTFAX #5071
8800 Roswell Rd #130, Atlanta, GA 30350 (770) 992-8430. Profile: Provides systems analysis, engineering, programming and computer related training.

COMPUTER HORIZONS CORP., SMARTFAX #5333
3340 Peachtree St NE #160, Atlanta, GA 30326 (404) 814-3777. Profile: Information technology services company.

DATA GENERAL CORP., SMARTFAX #5434
4170 Ashford-Dunwoody Rd, #300, Atlanta, GA 30319 (404) 705-2500. Profile: Customer support center for Fortune 300 company that manufactures and sells computers and related services, employing 300 here.

DATAMATX, SMARTFAX #8123
3146 Northeast Expressway, Atlanta, GA 30341 (770) 936-5600. Profile: Provides data processing and related services.

DYNAMIC RESOURCES INCORPORATED, SMARTFAX #5343
1866 Independence Square, Atlanta, GA 30338 (770) 391-9330. Profile: Provides systems integration and other software development services.

GE CAPITAL COMPUTER & TELECOMMUNICATIONS SVCS, SMARTFAX #5458
1001 Windward Concourse, Alpharetta, GA 30202 (770) 442-6100 OR 6112. Profile: Computer support organization of GE Capital, employing 160.

GEORGIA U.S. DATA SERVICES, SMARTFAX #8124
2990 Gateway Drive, Norfolk, GA 30071 (770) 441-2110. Profile: Provides information and management services to the medical industry.

HBO & CO., SMARTFAX #5533
35 Herring Rd, Newnan, GA 30265 (770) 254-4400. Profile: Supplier of hospital information systems, second largest in US, with 1000 employees in atlanta.

HC ASSOCIATES INTERNATIONAL INC., SMARTFAX #5130

1455 Lincoln Pkwy #180, Atlanta, GA 30346 (770) 673-0543. Profile: Provides services for implementation in payroll, financial systems support, networking and related services.

INFORMATION AMERICA, INC, SMARTFAX #5487
600 W Peachtree Street NW, Suite 1200, Atlanta, GA 30308 (404) 892-1800. Profile: Purveyor of on-line information, employing 100 in Atlanta.

INFORMATION SYSTEMS & NETWORKS CORP., SMARTFAX #5110
210 Interstate N Pkwy 700, Atlanta, GA 30339 (770) 933-3760. Profile: Provides systems integration, hardware prototyping and a wide range of other computer related services.

INPUT SERVICES, INC., SMARTFAX #8121
1090 North Chase Pkwy, Suite 300, Marietta, GA 30067 (770) 952-8094. Profile: Data processing company.

INTELLIGENT SYSTEMS CORP., SMARTFAX #5523
4355 Shackleford Rd, Norcross, GA 30093 (770) 381-2900. Profile: Manufacturer of PC software and computer repair, employing 150 in Atlanta.

KCM INCORPORATED, SMARTFAX #5320
211 Per'm Cent Pkwy #1020, Atlanta, GA 30346 (770) 604-9727. Profile: Provides automated computer solutions.

KEANE, INC., SMARTFAX #5495
2000 Galleria Pkwy, S 400, Atlanta, GA 30339 (770) 850-7270. Profile: Provides information systems and applications development, employing 200 in Atlanta.

MICROBILT CORP., SMARTFAX #5195
1640 Airport Rd #115, Kennesaw, GA 30144 (770) 955-0313. Profile: Computer services company.

NATIONAL CITY PROCESSING CO., SMARTFAX #5214
3375 NE Expressway, Atlanta, GA 30341 (770) 454-4551. Profile: Processes credit card transactions for merchants and retailers.

NATIONAL DATA CORP., SMARTFAX #5215

2 Ndc Plaza, Atlanta, GA 30329-2010 (404) 728-2000. Profile: Provider of data exchange, processing and telecommunications services to a variety of financial and corporate clients.

NATIONAL MESSAGE CENTER INCORPORATED, SMARTFAX #5327
27 Oak Street, Roswell, GA 30075 (770) 993-4980. Profile: 24-hour inbound call center servicing large insurance companies, department stores, etc.

NIIT (USA) INCORPORATED, SMARTFAX #5332
1050 Crown Point Pkwy #900, Atlanta, GA 30338 (770) 551-9494. Profile: Multinational company specializing in computer training, consulting and application software development.

OAO SERVICES, INC., SMARTFAX #5205
3475 Lenox Rd #400, Atlanta, GA 30326 (404) 238-0524. Profile: Provides data processing consultants to IBM.

POWERCERV TECHNOLOGIES CORP, SMARTFAX #5591
3055 Breckinridge Bl #310, Duluth, GA 30136 (770) 931-3822. Profile: Provides client-server, graphical application design, development and deployment services.

SALES TECHNOLOGIES, SMARTFAX #5871
3399 Peachtree Rd NE,S700, Atlanta, GA 30326 (404) 841-4000. Profile: Designs, develops, installs, markets and supports software to large corporations.

SECUREWARE, INC, SMARTFAX #5242
2957 Clairmont Rd #350, Atlanta, GA 30329-1647 (404) 315-6296. Profile: Security software company.

SPECTRUM SOFTWARE, INC, SMARTFAX #5254
PO Box 920278, Norcross, GA 30071 (770) 448-8662. Profile: Software consulting and service company.

SUN DATA, SMARTFAX #5582
1300 Oakbrook Drive, Norcross, GA 30093 (770) 449-6116. Profile: Remarketer of IBM midrange computers and services, employing 160.

SUNTRUST SERVICES, SMARTFAX #5891

250 Piedmont Av #2000, Atlanta, GA 30302 (404) 588-8877. Profile: Handles programming operations for SunTrust Banks, employing 230.

SYSTEMATIC HEALTHCARE SERVICES, SMARTFAX #5979
200 Ashford Center N, Atlanta, GA 30338 (404) 847-5000. Profile: Develops, manufactures and markets hardware, software and services for hospital information systems, employing 275.

TELTECH CORP., SMARTFAX #5262
3295 River Exch Drive #360, Norcross, GA 30092 (770) 840-8850. Profile: Full-service consulting, education and software firm.

TOTAL SYSTEM SERVICES, INC., SMARTFAX #8122
1300 6th Ave, Columbus, GA 31901 (706) 649-4000. Profile: Provides card processing services and comprehensive on-line systems, with nearly 2,500 employees worldwide.

UNISYS - MARKETING REGIONAL HEADQUARTERS, SMARTFAX #5900
4151 Ashford Dunwoody Rd, Atlanta, GA 30319 (404) 851-3000. Profile: Handles direct sales of Unisys's hardware and software products and information services, employing 525.

UNISYS CORP. - ATLANTA DEVELOPMENT CTR, SMARTFAX #5515
5550-A Peachtree Pkwy, Norcross, GA 30092 (770) 368-6000. Profile: R&D center that develops applications software and provides information services for the financial industry.

WANG LABORATORIES INC, SMARTFAX #5292
2300 Lake Park Drive #400, Smyra, GA 30080 (770) 431-3049. Profile: Provider of integration and support services for client server networks and related products.

Advanced Control Systems Inc. SmartFax #8125
2755 Northwoods Pkwy, Norcross, GA 30071. (770) 446-8854.

Astechnologies Inc. SmartFax #8126
PO Box 395, Roswell, GA 30077. (770) 993-5100.

Buypass Corp. SmartFax #8127
360 Interstate North Pkwy, Suite 400, Atlanta, GA 30339. (770) 916-3222.

Computer Communications Specialists SmartFax #8128
6529 Jimmy Carter Blvd, Norcross, GA 30071. (770) 441-3114.

Computone Corp. SmartFax #8129
1100 Northmeadow Pkwy, Suite 150, Roswell, GA 30076. (770) 475-2725.

Convergent Media Systems Corp. SmartFax #8130
3490 Piedmont Rd NE, Suite 800, Atlanta, GA 30305. (404) 262-1555.

CPI, Inc. SmartFax #5538
7000 Central Pkwy #1730, Atlanta, GA 30328. (770) 393-8100.

Crown Andersen Inc. SmartFax #8131
306 Dividend Drive, Peachtree City, GA 30269. (770) 997-2000.

CryoLife Inc. SmartFax #8132
2211 New Market Pkwy, Suite 142, Marietta, GA 30067. (770) 952-1660.

Dateq Information Network Inc. SmartFax #8133
5555 Triangle Pkwy, Suite 400, Norcross, GA 30092. (770) 446-8282.

DayStar Digital Inc. SmartFax #8134
5556 Atlanta Highway, Flowery Branch, GA 30542. (770) 962-2077.

Dickens Data Systems SmartFax #8135
1175 Northmeadow Pkwy, Suite 150, Roswell, GA 30076. (770) 475-8860.

Digital Communications Associates SmartFax #8136
1000 Alderman Drive, Alpharetta, GA 30201. (770) 442-4000.

E3 Associates Ltd. SmartFax #8137
1800 Pkwy Place, Suite 600, Marietta, GA 30067. (770) 424-0100.

Electromagnetic Sciences SmartFax #5082
660 Engineering Drive, Norcross, GA 30092. (770) 448-5770.

ERDAS Inc. SmartFax #8139
2801 Buford Highway NE, Suite 300, Atlanta, GA 30329. (404) 248-9000.

First Data Corp. SmartFax #8140
3 Corporate Square, Suite 700, Atlanta, GA 30329. (404) 321-0120.

Inacom Computer Training Services SmartFax #5486
56 Perimeter Center E #103, Atlanta, GA 30346. (770) 391-0002.

Intecolor Inc. SmartFax #8115
2150 Boggs Rd, Berkeley Lake, GA 30136. (770) 623-9145.

Integrated Network Services Inc SmartFax #5695
1325 Northmeadow Pkwy 110, Roswell, GA 30076. (770) 751-8881.

Integrated Network Services Inc. SmartFax #5695
1325 Northmeadow Pkwy, Suite 110, Roswell, GA 30076. (770) 751-8881.

Inventory Locator Service SmartFax #8143
1229 Johnson Fy Rd, Marietta, GA 30068. (770) 973-1840.

IQ Software SmartFax #5581
3295 River Exchange Drive, Norcross, GA 30092. (770) 446-8880.

Isolyser Co. SmartFax #8145
4320 International Blvd, Norcross, GA 30093. (770) 381-7566.

Keane SmartFax #5495
2000 Galleria Pkwy NW, Atlanta, GA 30339. (770) 850-7270.

Marbil Co Inc. D/B/A Insol SmartFax #5969
2080 Peachtree Ind Blvd #102, Atlanta, GA . (770) 458-8658.

Melita International Corp. SmartFax #8147
6630 Bay Cir, Norcross, GA 30071. (770) 446-7800.

MicroHelp Inc.
SmartFax #8148
4359 Shallowford Indust Pkwy, Marietta, GA 30066. (770) 516-0899.

Micrometrics Instrument Corp.
SmartFax #8149
1 Micrometrics Drive, Norcross, GA 30093. (770) 662-3620.

Nova Information Systems Inc. SmartFax #8150
5 Concourse Pkwy, Suite 700, Atlanta, GA 30328. (770) 396-1456.

Perma-Fix Environmental Services SmartFax #8151
3406 Oakcliff Rd, Suite D-1, Atlanta, GA 30340. (770) 451-7990.

Purafil Inc. SmartFax #8152
2654 Weaver Way, Doraville, GA 30340. (770) 662-8545.

Scherer Healthcare Inc. SmartFax #8153
2859 Paces Fy Rd, Suite 300, Atlanta, GA 30339. (770) 333-0066.

Scientific Research Corp. SmartFax #8154
2300 Windy Ridge Pkwy, Suite 400 S, Atlanta, GA 30339. (770) 859-9161.

Shared Medical Systems SmartFax #8155
400 Northridge Rd, Suite 700, Atlanta, GA 30350. (770) 993-2490.

Softsense Computer Products, Inc. SmartFax #5881
1000 Alderman Drive #B, Alpharetta, GA . (770) 663-3400.

Tech Management Service SmartFax #5094
6875 Jimmy Carter, #3200, Norcross, GA 30071. (770) 246-6200.

TechForce Corp.
SmartFax #8157
3901 Roswell Rd NE, Marietta, GA 30607. (770) 977-5303.

Telecorp Systems Inc.
SmartFax #8158
1000 Holcomb Woods Pkwy, Suite 410A, Roswell, GA 30076. (770) 587-0700.

The Seydel Companies
SmartFax #8159
4200 Northside Pkwy, Atlanta, GA 30327. (404) 233-3496.

TSW International
SmartFax #8120
3301 Windy Ridge Pkwy, Marietta, GA 30067. (770) 952-8444.

UniComp Inc. SmartFax #8161
1800 Sandy Plains Pkwy, Suite 305, Marietta, GA 30066. (770) 424-3684.

Video Display Corp.
SmartFax #6008
1868 Tucker Industrial Blvd, Tucker, GA 30084. (770) 938-2080.

Wegener Corp.
SmartFax #8163
11350 Technology Cir, Duluth, GA 30136. (770) 623-0096.

Whitley Group
SmartFax #8164
4775 Cherrywood Lane
NE, Atlanta, GA 30342.
(404) 843-8550.

Electronic/Electrical

A.E.L. CROSS SYSTEMS, SMARTFAX #5349
1355 Blue Grass Lakes Pkwy, Alpharetta, GA 30202 (770) 475-3633. Profile: Designs and builds high tech military innovations, employing 145.

A.E.R. ENERGY RESOURCES, SMARTFAX #5561
1500 Wilson Way, Smyrna, GA 30082 (770) 431-2084. Profile: Developer and manufacture of long-life batteries, employing 70.

ADT SECURITY SYSTEMS-CUSTOMER SERVICE, SMARTFAX #5006
815 Park N Blvd #200, Atlanta, GA 30021 (404) 297-6297. Profile: Largest security company in world, employing 150 in Atlanta.

ARCHIMEDES SYSTEMS INC, SMARTFAX #5019
PO Box 48314, Doraville, GA 30340 (770) 986-0800. Profile: Manufactures commercial, municipal, irrigation, and fire protection booster pump stations, employing 14.

ARGENBRIGHT SECURITY INC, SMARTFAX #5038
3355 Lenox Rd #100, Atlanta, GA 30326 (404) 674-8910 PAGER. Profile: Contract security company employing 1,000.

AT&T TRIDOM, SMARTFAX #5599
840 Franklin Court, Marietta, GA 30067 (770) 426-4261. Profile: High-tech firm that designs, manufactures and monitors VSAT equipment used to provide digital data services via satellite.

AUTOMATED FIRE & PROTECTION SYSTEMS, SMARTFAX #5037
Box 48317, Doraville, GA 30362 (770) 242-7360 OR 446-8010. Profile: Designs and installs commercial fire alarm devices and related products and systems.

BEL TRONICS, SMARTFAX #5397
8100 Sagl Pkwy, Covington, GA 30209 (770) 787-6500. Profile: Manufacturer of consumer electronics and telecommunications hardware, employing 230.

DAWN ELECTRONICS, INC., SMARTFAX #5114
2575-D Cobb Int'l Blvd, Kennesaw, GA 30144 (770) 422-9490. Profile: Provides repair services on a wide range of computer-related products.

ELECTROMAGNETIC SCIENCES, SMARTFAX #5082
PO Box 7700, Norcross, GA 30091 (770) 263-9200. Profile: Designs, manufactures and sells microwave components and radio-link terminals, and handles staffing for their LXE subsidiary, employing 750.

GEC MARCONI AVIONICS, SMARTFAX #5585
PO Box 81999, Atlanta, GA 30366 (770) 448-1947. Profile: Manufactures electronics, with products including heads-up display for fighter aircraft, employing 275 in Atlanta.

HITACHI HOME ELECTRONICS, SMARTFAX #5475
3890 #ve Reynolds Blvd, Norcross, GA 30093 (770) 279-5600. Profile: Corporate HQ support and sales office for Hitachi subsidiary that manufactures and sells electronic equipment.

HITACHI TELECOM (USA), SMARTFAX #5692
2990 Gateway Drive, Norcross, GA 30071 (770) 446-8820. Profile: US corporate HQ for telecommunications operations of Hitachi.

INGLETT ESTUBBS INC, SMARTFAX #5111
PO Box 93007, Atlanta, GA 30318 (404) 881-1199. Profile: Electrical contractor, employing 500.

JOHNSON YOKOGAWA, SMARTFAX #5451
4 Dart Rd, Newnan, GA 30265-1040 (770) 254-0400. Profile: Supplies advanced instrumentation systems for continuous batch and discrete process industries, among other services, employing 325 in Atlanta.

LANIER WORLDWIDE, SMARTFAX #5164
2300 Parklake Drive NE, Atlanta, GA 30345 (770) 496-9500. Profile: The largest electronics company headquartered in the Southeast, employing 1000 in Atlanta.

MITSUBISHI CONSUMER ELECTRONICS OF AMERICA, SMARTFAX #5517

PO Box 299, Braselton, GA 30517 (706) 654-3011. Profile: Manufacturing facility producing cellular phones and color TVs.

MURATA ELECTRONICS NORTH AMERICA, SMARTFAX #5569

2200 Lake Park Drive, Smyrna, GA 30080 (770) 436-1300. Profile: Manufacturer of a wide variety of electronic components.

PAMECO CORP., SMARTFAX #5540

1000 Center Place, Norcross, GA 30093 (770) 798-0600. Profile: Nation's largest wholesale distributor of commercial refrigeration and air conditioning equipment, and one of the largest producers of high energy friction materials and components.

PANASONIC/MATSUSHITA ELEC. CORP OF AMERICA, SMARTFAX #5490

1225 Northbrook Pkwy, Suwanee, GA 30174 (770) 338-6700. Profile: Southeast regional sales and service office.

RADIO SHACK, SMARTFAX #5227

900 Circle 75 Pkwy #1320, Atlanta, GA 30339 (770) 850-9994. Profile: A national retailer of electronic equipment.

ROCKWELL INTERNATIONAL-TACTICAL SYSTEMS DIV, SMARTFAX #5232

1800 Satellite Blvd, Duluth, GA 30136 (770) 476-6474. Profile: Major defense contractor manufacturing high-tech components, including missile systems, sensors, seekers and subsystems.

RS ELECTRONICS, SMARTFAX #5238

1885-A Beaver Ridge Cir, Norcross, GA 30071 (770) 242-0520. Profile: Broadline electronic component distributor.

RUTLEDGE AND JACKSON ELECTRIC, SMARTFAX #5237

4371 Highway 78, Lilburn, GA 30247 (770) 972-1337. Profile: Residential electrical wiring and repair.

SCIENTIFIC ATLANTA, CORPORATE HEADQUARTERS,
SMARTFAX #5626

1 Technology Pkwy So, Norcross, GA 30092-2967 (770) 903-5000. Profile: Provides corporate staff support functions.

SCIENTIFIC ATLANTA, ELECTRONICS SYSTEMS DIV.,
SMARTFAX #5627

4261 Communications Drive, Norcross, GA 30093 (770) 903-3307. Profile: Manufactures remote sensing ground stations and support equipment.

SENTRY SURVEILLANCE, INC, SMARTFAX #5244

5064 Canton Rd NE, Marietta, GA 30066 (770) 592-0400. Profile: Sells and services closed circuit television systems.

SIEMENS - ATLANTA AREA SERVICE CENTER, SMARTFAX #5878

2140 Flintstone Drive, Tucker, GA 30084 (770) 493-1231. Profile: Manufactures commercial switchboards and panelboards, employing 225.

SIEMENS - RESIDENTIAL PRODUCTS DIVISION, SMARTFAX #5604

2037 Weems Rd, Tucker, GA 30084 (770) 939-7230. Profile: Manufactures residential circuit protection products, employing 350.

SIEMENS - SALES/MARKETING, SMARTFAX #5606

3333 State Bridge Rd, Alpharetta, GA 30202 (770) 751-2000. Profile: Handles hiring of sales and marketing personnel.

SIEMENS - SYSTEMS DIVISION, SMARTFAX #6018

100 Technology Drive, Alpharetta, GA 30202 (770) 740-3000. Profile: Manufactures AC and DC variable speed drives, programmable control products and industrial systems, employing 550.

SONY ELECTRONICS, SMARTFAX #5575

3175 Northwoods Pkwy, Norcross, GA 30071 (770) 263-9888. Profile: Sales office employing 150.

SONY MUSIC ENTERTAINMENT, INC., SMARTFAX #5883

PO Box 1528, Carrollton, GA 30117 . Profile: Manufactures audio tape and musical video cassettes, employing 1250.

SOUTHERN ELECTRONICS CORP., SMARTFAX #5633

4916 N Royal Atlanta Drive, Tucker, GA 30085 (770) 491-8962. Profile: Distributor of computers and cellular equipment, employing 400.

VANKIRK & ASSOCIATES, SMARTFAX #5318

5815-2d Live Oak Pkwy, Norcross, GA 30093 (770) 729-1148. Profile: Electrical contracting company.

Action Electric Co.
SmartFax #8165
2600 Collins Springs
Drivw, Smyrna, GA
30080. (404) 799-3551.

**All In One Electronic
Repair** SmartFax #5929
3196 Glenwood Rd,
Decatur, GA 30032.
(404) 284-8661.

Alta Telecom SmartFax
#8166
270 Scientific Drive,
Norcross, GA 30092.
(770) 662-0540.

Bryant Electric Co.
SmartFax #8167
2875 Northside Drive
NW, Atlanta, GA 30305.
(404) 605-0781.

Commercial Electric
SmartFax #5921
6065 Roswell Rd, #1448,
Atlanta, GA 30328. (404)
250-9733.

**Electronic Power
Technology, Inc.**
SmartFax #5661

6400 Atlantic Blvd #130,
Norcross, GA 30071.
(770) 449-1104.

Hicks Electric SmartFax
#8168
PO Box 1613, Norcross,
GA 30091. (770) 446-
6600.

Honeywell Inc.
SmartFax #8114
1190 West Druid Hills,
Atlanta, GA 30329. (404)
248-2300.

**Mark Henderson
Electric** SmartFax #8169
5322 Snapfinger Park
Drive, Decatur, GA
30035. (770) 987-6780.

Southwire SmartFax
#5885
1 Southwire Drive,
Carrollton, GA 30119.
(770) 832-4242.

Video Display Corp.
SmartFax #6008
1868 Tucker Ind Blvd,
Tucker, GA 30084. (770)
938-2080.

Sciences

AMOCO FOAM - TECHNOLOGY CENTER, SMARTFAX #5939
2907 Log Cabin Drive, Smyrna, GA 30080 (404) 350-1300. Profile: R&D center employing 75.

CYTRX, SMARTFAX #5651
154 Technology Pkwy, Norcross, GA 30092 (770) 368-9500. Profile: Pharmaceutical research and development company, employing 60 in Atlanta.

GEORGIA TECH RESEARCH INSTITUTE, SMARTFAX #5966
955 Fowler Street, Atlanta, GA 30332-0435 (404) 894-9412. Profile: Operates 8 research laboratories and employs 900.

SMITHKLINE BEECHAM CLINICAL LABORATORIES, SMARTFAX #5247
1777 Montreal Cir, Tucker, GA 30084 (770) 934-9205. Profile: Largest clinical lab in North America.

SOLVAY PHARMACEUTICALS, SMARTFAX #5605
901 Sawyer Rd, Marietta, GA 30062 (770) 578-9000. Profile: Clinical research and development center for major pharmaceutical firm, employing 400.

Galaxy Scientific Corp. SmartFax #5688
2310 Parklake Dr, #325, Atlanta, GA 30345. (770) 491-1100.

Telecommunications

AT&T, SMARTFAX #5025
1200 Peachtree St, Atlanta, GA 30309 (770) 934-8433. Profile: Southern area headquarters for long distance services, covering an 18-state territory and employing 20,000 in Atlanta.

AT&T NETWORK SYSTEMS, SMARTFAX #5637
6701 Roswell Rd NE, Atlanta, GA 30328 (404) 573-4000. Profile: Southern Region headquarters location, with more than 3000 employees.

BELL NORTHERN RESEARCH (BNR), SMARTFAX #5676

705 West Tech Drive, Norcross, GA 30092 (770) 246-2000. Profile: Northern Telecom subsidiary conducting research and development for telecommunications equipment and systems, employing 350.

BELLSOUTH CELLULAR CORP/BELLSOUTH MOBILITY, SMARTFAX #5677

1100 Peachtree Street NE, #1000, Atlanta, GA 30309 (404) 249-5000. Profile: Cellular service provider employing 500 in Atlanta.

BELLSOUTH INTERNATIONAL, SMARTFAX #5399

1100 Peachtree Street NE, #400, Atlanta, GA 30309 (404) 249-4800. Profile: Develops marketing and business opportunities for telecommunications services internationally, employing 200 here in Atlanta.

COMMUNICATIONS CENTRAL, INC., SMARTFAX #5577

1150 Northmeadow Pkwy, Roswell, GA 30076 (770) 751-1132. Profile: Provider of pay phones to institutions.

DIAL CALL COMMUNICATIONS, SMARTFAX #5624

6 W Druid Hills Dr, Suite 700, Atlanta, GA 30329 (770) 825-9000. Profile: Mobile radio company, subsidiary of Dial Page.

DIGITEL CORP., SMARTFAX #5448

2600 School Drive, Atlanta, GA 30360 (770) 451-1111. Profile: Provides telecommunications services with nearly 50 employees in Atlanta.

DULMISON, INC., SMARTFAX #5342

1725 Purcell Rd, Lawrenceville, GA 30243 (770) 339-3350. Profile: Supplier of support hardware to the telecommunications industry.

FULTON COMMUNICATIONS INC, SMARTFAX #5129

3146 Reps Miller Rd, Norcross, GA 30071 (770) 446-3100. Profile: Provides telecommunications systems and services.

GTE CUSTOMER NETWORK, SMARTFAX #5529

5897 Winward Pkwy #300, Alpharetta, GA 30202 (770) 772-5713. Profile: National headquarters location for GTE subsidiary that handles telecommunications equipment.

KEY FOUR INC, SMARTFAX #5158

5238 Royal Wds Pkwy #110, Tucker, GA 30084 (770) 908-4405. Profile:
Telecommunications company.

LUCENT TECHNOLOGIES, SMARTFAX #5380
2000 Northeast Expressway, Norcross, GA 30071 (770) 798-2600. Profile:
Manufacturing facility producing wire and fiber optics communications cable,
employing 2700.

M.C.I., SMARTFAX #5177
780 Johnson Fy Rd, Atlanta, GA 30342-1434 (404) 250-5938. Profile: Sales office
for telecommunications company with revenue exceeding $15 billion annually.

M.C.I. TELECOMMUNICATIONS CORP., SMARTFAX #5509
3 Ravinia Drive, Atlanta, GA 30346-2102 (770) 668-6000. Profile: MCI Business
Services Headquarters.

M.C.I. TELECOMMUNICATIONS, STONE MOUNTAIN, SMARTFAX #5178
7840 Roswell Rd Bldg 200, Stone Mountain, GA 30083 (770) 390-5331. Profile:
Handles the telemarketing operations for MCI products and services.

METRO TELECOM INC, SMARTFAX #5193
2000 Powers Fy Rd #510, Marietta, GA 30068 (770) 980-1000. Profile:
Communications company selling telephone systems and providing data networking
services.

MOBILE COMMUNICATIONS OF GWINNETT INC., SMARTFAX #5198
885 Cripple Creek Dr, Lawrenceville, GA 30243 (770) 963-3748. Profile:
Communications provider via two-way radios, cellular phones and pagers.

MOTOROLA - ENERGY PRODUCTS DIVISION, SMARTFAX #5646
1700 Belle Meade Court, Lawrenceville, GA 30243 (770) 338-3000. Profile:
Corporate headquarters for Motorola Corporation division.

NATIONAL HOME SERVICES INC, SMARTFAX #5216
3297 Northcrest Rd #210, Atlanta, GA 30340 (770) 621-9500. Profile: Call center
providing sales and customer service functions long distance telecommunications
clients.

NCR, SMARTFAX #5608
2651 Satellite Blvd, Duluth, GA 30136 (770) 623-7000. Profile: Designs, develops, and manufactures integrated software and hardware computer systems for retailers, employing 700+.

NCR-WORLD SVC PARTS CTR, SMARTFAX #5379
200 Hwy 74 South, Peachtree City, GA 30269 (770) 487-7000. Profile: Facility that handles national and international distribution of NCR parts, employing 700.

OVERLOOK COMMUNICATIONS INT'L, SMARTFAX #5206
2839 Paces Fy Rd #500, Atlanta, GA 30339 (770) 432-6800. Profile: Full service telecommunications service bureau.

PAGEMART WIRELESS, SMARTFAX #5207
6300 Jimmy Carter Bl #110, Norcross, GA 30071 (770) 416-8300. Profile: Provides wireless messaging services nationwide.

S.I.T.A., SMARTFAX #5618
3100 Cumberland, #200, Atlanta, GA 30339 (770) 850-4500. Profile: Telecommunication/data processing company.

SPRINT CORP., SMARTFAX #5887
3100 Cumberland Cir, Atlanta, GA 30339 (770) 849-5000. Profile: Third largest long distance carrier, employing 200 in Atlanta.

STANCOM, INC, SMARTFAX #5257
2615 Shallowford Rd, Atlanta, GA 30345 (404) 636-2179. Profile: Industrial communications company.

TECH SYSTEMS, INC, SMARTFAX #5273
1050 Northfield Ct #240, Roswell, GA 30076 (770) 667-3340. Profile: Design and install CCTV equipment for commercial organizations.

VSI ENTERPRISES INC, SMARTFAX #5288
5801 Gashen Springs Rd, Norcross, GA 30071 (770) 242-7566. Profile: Designs, manufactures and markets interactive videoconferencing systems.

AAA Paging SmartFax #8170
2810 New Spring Rd NW, Atlanta, GA 30339. (770) 437-9000.

Absolute Communications SmartFax #8171
334 Peachtree Rd NE, Suite 1800, Atlanta, GA 30326. (404) 848-7700.

Action Cellular SmartFax #8172
2145 Cobb Pkwy, Smyrna, GA 30080. (770) 952-1200.

Advantage Cellular SmartFax #8173
3059 Peachtree Rd, Atlanta, GA 30305. (404) 233-1186.

Advantage Communication SmartFax #8174
1289 Roswell Rd, Suite 100, Atlanta, GA 30328. (770) 565-5222.

AirTouch Paging SmartFax #8175
1975 Lakeside Pkwy, Suite 300, Tucker, GA 30032. (770) 493-8700.

All American Communications SmartFax #8176
82 Peachtree St NW, Atlanta, GA 30383. (404) 688-1719.

ALT Communications SmartFax #8177
3250 Peachtree Corner Cir, Suite E, Norcross, GA 30092. (770) 729-0800.

American Radio & Cellular Commun. SmartFax #8178
6000 Roswell Rd, Atlanta, GA 30328. (404) 255-3457.

Atlanta Cellular Services SmartFax #8183
2137 Roswell Rd, Marietta, GA 30062. (770) 428-3663.

Atlanta Mobile Communications SmartFax #8184
5200 Dallas Highway, Suite 300, Powder Springs, GA 30073. (404) 570-3606.

Atlanta Satellites and Beepers SmartFax #8185
2291 Austell Rd SW, Suite 104, Marietta, GA 30060. (770) 684-1804.

Atlanta Voice Page, Inc. SmartFax #8186
2700 Northeast Expressway, Suite C-550, Atlanta, GA 30345. (404) 634-5588.

BBA Communications SmartFax #8187

1040 Fairway Valley Drive, Woodstock, GA 30289. (770) 516-1515.

Beepers Etc. SmartFax #8188
2033 Stewart Ave, Suite D, Atlanta, GA 30315. (404) 559-7722.

BellSouth Communication Systems SmartFax #8189
1800 Century Blvd, Atlanta, GA 30345. (404) 982-6200.

Best Buy SmartFax #8190
1201 Hammond Drive, Atlanta, GA 30080. (770) 392-0454.

BTI SmartFax #8191
1117 Perimeter Center W, Suite 401, Atlanta, GA 30339. (770) 392-0046.

Budget Cellular SmartFax #8192
201 Allen Rd, Suite 404, Atlanta, GA 30328. (404) 843-0404.

Butler Telecom SmartFax #5580
4960 Peachtree Ind Blvd #210, Norcross, GA 30071. (770) 448-7738.

Cable & Wireless Inc. SmartFax #8193

2690 Cumberland Pkwy NW, Suite 490, Atlanta, GA 30339. (404) 434-4161.

Can We Talk Cellular SmartFax #8194
3479 Memorial Drive, Decatur, GA 30032. (404) 289-1496.

Capstone Communications SmartFax #8195
750 Hammond Drive, Bldg 16, Suite 350, Atlanta, GA 30328. (404) 257-1155.

Cellular Center SmartFax #8196
8540 Roswell Rd, Suite 700, Atlanta, GA 30350. (770) 993-9260.

Cellular Concepts SmartFax #8197
715 West Lanier Ave, Fayetteville, GA 30214. (770) 460-0087.

Cellular Network SmartFax #8199
3610 Milton Park Drive, Alpharetta, GA 30202. (770) 343-8649.

Cellular Solutions SmartFax #8200
4485 Lawrenceville Highway, Suite 301, Lilburn, GA 30247. (770) 931-9700.

Cellular South SmartFax #8201
5150 Buford Highway, Suite A-230, Doraville, GA 30340. (770) 451-6761.

Cellular Systems SmartFax #8202
552 Atlanta Rd, Cumming, GA 30130. (770) 781-5000.

Cellular Warehouse SmartFax #8203
3853 Green Industrial Way, Chamblee, GA 30341. (770) 457-7050.

Circuit City SmartFax #8204
3755 Atlanta Industrial Parkway, Atlanta, GA 30331. (404) 600-2109.

Custom Cellular SmartFax #8205
2100 Riverside Pkwy, Suite 117, Lawrenceville, GA 30245. (770) 682-9927.

Dial Page SmartFax #8206
585 Franklin Rd SE, Suite 160, Marietta, GA 30067. (770) 419-3060.

Diversified Communications SmartFax #8208
7390 Twin Branch Rd, Atlanta, GA 30328. (770) 399-9340.

Du Shaw Management Group Inc SmartFax #6026
2693 Northbrook Drive, Atlanta, GA 30340. (770) 938-4866.

Easy Communication SmartFax #8209
2179 Lawrenceville Highway, Decatur, GA 30033. (404) 325-1407.

Executone Information Systems Inc. SmartFax #8210
1090 Northchase Pkwy, Suite 100, Marietta, GA 30067. (770) 984-9977.

Fairchild Communications Services SmartFax #8213
1 Concourse Pkwy, Suite 190, Atlanta, GA 30328. (770) 395-3700.

Frontier Communications SmartFax #8214
100 Peachtree St, Suite 420, Atlanta, GA 30303. (404) 589-9119.

Full Spectrum Communications SmartFax #8215
4880 Lower Roswell Rd NE, Marietta, GA 30060. (770) 971-9005.

Future Cellular Inc. SmartFax #8217

2135 East Main St, Suite 190, Snellville, GA 30278. (770) 972-4122.

Futurepage SmartFax #8218
6360 Highway 85, Riverdale, GA 30274. (770) 907-8077.

Galaxy Telecommunications Inc. SmartFax #8219
1575 Northside Drive NW, Suite 105, Atlanta, GA 30318. (404) 352-8100.

Georgia Cellular Inc. SmartFax #8220
3385 West Hall Cir NW, Suite A, Duluth, GA 30136. (770) 813-8233.

Gold Coast Communication SmartFax #8221
5133 Old National Highway, College Park, GA 30349. (404) 767-9901.

GTE Mobilenet Communications SmartFax #5535
245 Perimeter Center Pkwy, Atlanta, GA 30346. (770) 391-8000.

High Tech Paging SmartFax #8224
3955 Pleasantdale Rd, Suite 102, Doraville, GA 30340. (770) 729-9400.

Inter-Tel SmartFax #8225
100 Pinnacle Way, Suite 140, Norcross, GA 30071. (770) 447-0707.

Interlink Telecommunications Inc. SmartFax #8226
1112 Elm St, Covington, GA 30209. (800) 488-5465.

Internet Communications SmartFax #8227
1780 Stewart Ave SW, Atlanta, GA 30315. (404) 765-0404.

Intl. Telecommun. Exchange Corp. SmartFax #8228
6040 Unity Drive, Suite F, Norcross, GA 30076. (770) 729-3700.

Kings Communications SmartFax #8230
5351-3 Buford Highway, Doraville, GA 30340. (770) 458-9744.

Last Stop Paging SmartFax #8232
2655-B N Decatur Rd, Decatur, GA 30033. (404) 687-9600.

LDDS WorldComm SmartFax #8233
1 Ravinia Drive, Suite 1300, Atlanta, GA 30346. (770) 395-0095.

Let's Talk Cellular SmartFax #8234
3393 Peachtree Rd, Atlanta, GA 30326. (404) 239-0444.

Line One Cellular SmartFax #8235
331 North Marietta Pkwy, Marietta, GA 30060. (770) 429-8800.

Metro Mobility SmartFax #8238
151 14th St, Suite 116, Atlanta, GA 30318. (404) 249-9355.

Metrocell Security SmartFax #8239
2160 Kingston Court, Suite M, Marietta, GA 30067. (770) 563-9000.

Metropolitan Commun. of Carrollton SmartFax #8240
103 Commercial Ave, Carrollton, GA 30117. (770) 834-7704.

Mobile Line Communication SmartFax #8242
334 S Main St, Alpharetta, GA 30201. (770) 475-3400.

Moon Communications SmartFax #8243
2484-40 Briarcliff Rd, Atlanta, GA 30329. (404) 634-4774.

Nationwide Communications SmartFax #8244
7040 Jimmy Carter Blvd, Suite 2, Norcross, GA 30092. (404) 261-5015.

NCR SmartFax #8179
1057 Lenox Park Blvd, Suite 400, Atlanta, GA 30319. (404) 426-2455.

Northern Telecom Atlanta SmartFax #5610
5555 Windward Pkwy, Alpharetta, GA 30201. (770) 661-5000.

Page Express SmartFax #8247
1107 Ralph David Abernathy Blv, Atlanta, GA 30310. (404) 753-7351.

Page One SmartFax #8248
245 Meriwether St, Griffin, GA 30223. (770) 229-1565.

Pagenet SmartFax #5208
3475 Lenox Rd #500, Atlanta, GA 30326. (404) 841-9100.

Peachtree Mobility SmartFax #5542
1220 Northpoint Cir, Alpharetta, GA 30202. (770) 751-1211.

Premier Cellular SmartFax #8251
425 Barret Pkwy, Suite C-1, Kennesaw, GA 30144. (770) 421-9999.

Robin Hood Telecommunications SmartFax #8256
2191 Northlake Pkwy, Bldg 11, Suite A, Tucker, GA 30084. (770) 939-5800.

Showcase SmartFax #8260
2323 Cheshire Bridge Rd NE, Atlanta, GA 30324. (404) 325-7676.

Sound Sensations SmartFax #8261
337 Cobb Pkwy, Marietta, GA 30062. (770) 429-1600.

Southeast Telecomm SmartFax #8262
120 Interstate North Pkwy E, Suite 200, Atlanta, GA 30346. (770) 955-1900.

Tell Call, Inc. SmartFax #5981
6000 Live Oak Pkwy #111-A, Norcross, GA 30093. (770) 368-9881.

The Edge In Electronics SmartFax #8263
142 Cumberland Mall, Atlanta, GA 30339. (770) 333-0996.

Total Mobile Commun. of Stockbridge SmartFax #8264
81 Highway 138, Stockbridge, GA 30281. (770) 507-1800.

U.S. Communications Inc. SmartFax #8265
6140-C Northbelt Pkwy, Norcross, GA 30071. (770) 840-8888.

Wolff Communications SmartFax #8266
6407-J Tara Blvd, Jonesboro, GA 30236. (770) 473-0079.

Environmental/Energy

ENVIRONMENTAL ENGINEERING CONSTRUCTION, SMARTFAX #5088
1896 Surrey Trail SE, Conyers, GA 30208 (770) 929-8154. Profile: Involved in hazardous waste and general contracting in 14 states.

INTERNATIONAL SERVICE SYSTEMS, SMARTFAX #8267
1955 Lake Park Drive, Suite 300, Smyrna, GA 30080 (770) 436-9900. Profile: Handles chemical and waste disposal.

JTM INDUSTRIES, INC., SMARTFAX #8269
1000 Cobb Place Blvd, Building 400, Kennesaw, GA 30144 (770) 424-1900. Profile: Waste management company.

PLANTATION PIPELINE CO., SMARTFAX #5912
945 E Paces Fy NE, Atlanta, GA 31126-0616 (404) 364-5880 (5924). Profile: Interstate pipeline transporter of liquid refined petroleum products.

REPUBLIC WASTE INDUSTRIES, INC., SMARTFAX #8268
2849 Paces Fy Rd NW, Suite 370, Atlanta, GA 30339 (770) 431-7140. Profile: Provides solid and hazardous waste disposal and handling.

ROLLINS, INC., SMARTFAX #5233
2170 Piedmont Rd NE, Atlanta, GA 30324 (404) 888-2125. Profile: Corporate headquarters for diversified service corporations, including Rollins Protective Services.

TENSAR CORP., SMARTFAX #5621
1210 Citizens Pkwy, Morrow, GA 30260 (770) 968-3255. Profile: Involved in the production and sale of geosynthetics for various environmental applications.

WESTINGHOUSE REMEDIATION SERVICES, INC., SMARTFAX #5904
675 Park N Blvd, Bldg F, Clarkston, GA 30021 (770) 299-4650. Profile: Remediates all hazardous waste sites except nuclear, employing 280.

ADS Environmental Services Inc. SmartFax #8270
1910 Providence Court, Atlanta, GA 30349. (770) 997-0446.

American Recycling Co. SmartFax #8271
4791 Mendel Court SW, Atlanta, GA 30336. (404) 691-1117.

ATEC Associates Inc. SmartFax #5558
1300 Williams Drive, Marietta, GA 30066. (770) 427-9456.

ATEC Associates, Inc. SmartFax #5558
1300 Williams Dr, Marietta, GA 30060. (770) 427-9456.

Atlanta Metal Inc. SmartFax #8273
75 Airline St, Atlanta, GA 30312. (404) 688-6278.

Black & Veatch Waste Science Inc. SmartFax #7148
400 Northridge Rd, Suite 350, Atlanta, GA 30350. (770) 594-2500.

Blaze Recycling & Metal SmartFax #8275
1882 Mitchell Rd, Norcross, GA 30071. (770) 447-0175.

Brown and Caldwell SmartFax #8276
53 Perimeter Center East, Suite 500, Atlanta, GA 30346. (770) 394-2997.

Browning-Ferris Industries of Ga SmartFax #8277
3045 Bankhead Highway, Atlanta, GA 30318. (404) 792-4471.

C H 2 M Hill SmartFax #5406
115 Perimeter Center Pl,S700, Atlanta, GA 30346. (770) 604-9095.

Camp Dresser & McKee Inc. SmartFax #8279
2100 RiverEdge Pkwy, Suite 500, Atlanta, GA 30305. (770) 952-8643.

Central Metals Co. SmartFax #8281
950 Marietta St NW, Atlanta, GA 30318. (404) 874-7564.

CFC Recovery Systems Inc. SmartFax #8282
1700 Cumberland Point Drive, Suite 13, Marietta, GA 30067. (770) 984-2292.

CH2M Hill Inc. SmartFax #7149
115 Perimeter Center Place NE, Suite 700, Atlanta, GA 30346. (770) 604-9095.

Chadwick Road Landfill SmartFax #8284
13700 Chadwick Farm Blvd, Woodstock, GA 30188. (770) 475-9868.

Choice Warehouses SmartFax #8285
6170 Duquesne Dr SW, Atlanta, GA 30336. (404) 346-0031.

Dames & Moore SmartFax #7151
6 Piedmont Center, Suite 500, Atlanta, GA 30305. (404) 262-2915.

Delta Environmental Consultants Inc SmartFax #8287
20 Technology Pkwy, Suite 160, Norcross, GA 30092. (770) 409-0454.

Donzi Lane Landfill SmartFax #8288
1060 Moreland Industrial Blvd, Atlanta, GA 30316. (404) 622-3389.

Dynamic Metals Inc. SmartFax #8289
584 Edgewood Ave, Atlanta, GA 30312. (404) 577-2398.

Emcon SmartFax #7154
1560 Oakbrook Pkwy, Suite 100, Norcross, GA 30093. (770) 447-4665.

224

Environmental Science & Engineering SmartFax #8291
1351 Dividend Drive, Suite C, Atlanta, GA 30067. (770) 955-2180.

Environmental Technology of North America SmartFax #8292
2264 Northwest Pkwy, Suite E, Marietta, GA 30067. (770) 850-0777.

Foster Wheeler Environmental SmartFax #8293
302 Research Drive, Norcross, GA 30092. (770) 825-7200.

Free-Flow Packaging Corp. SmartFax #8294
5800 Wheaton Drive SW, Atlanta, GA 30336. (404) 346-0696.

Geraghty & Miller Inc. SmartFax #8295
2675 Paces Fy Rd, Suite 200, Atlanta, GA 30339. (770) 434-9666.

Golder Associates SmartFax #5469
3730 Chamblee-Tucker Rd, Atlanta, GA 30341. (770) 496-1893.

Green Stone Industries SmartFax #8297
6057 Boat Rock Blvd, Atlanta, GA 30336. (404) 344-3590.

Gwinnett Clean & Beautiful SmartFax #8298
240 Oak St, Lawrenceville, GA 30245. (770) 822-5187.

Live Oak Land Fill SmartFax #8300
1189 Henrico Rd, Conley, GA 30027. (404) 361-1182.

Metro Alloys Inc. SmartFax #8301
717 Highland Ave, Atlanta, GA 30312. (404) 688-6063.

Newell Recycling Co. SmartFax #8302
1359 Central Ave, Atlanta, GA 30344. (404) 766-1621.

OHM Remediation Services Corp. SmartFax #8303
5335 Triangle Pkwy, Suite 450, Norcross, GA 30092. (770) 729-3900.

Parsons Engineering Science SmartFax #8304
57 Executive Park South NE, Atlanta, GA 30329. (404) 235-2300.

Perma-Fix Environmental Services SmartFax #8151

3406 Oakcliff Rd, Suite D-1, Atlanta, GA 30340. (770) 451-7990.

Pirkle Inc. SmartFax #8306
598 Wells St, Atlanta, GA 30312. (404) 525-1464.

PRC Environmental Management Inc. SmartFax #8307
285 Peachtree Center Ave, Suite 900, Atlanta, GA 30303. (404) 522-2867.

Radian Corp. SmartFax #8308
1979 Lakeside Pkwy, Suite 800, Tucker, GA 30084. (770) 414-4522.

Recycall Corp. SmartFax #8309
922 Memorial Drive, Atlanta, GA 30316. (404) 688-6824.

Recycle America of Atlanta SmartFax #8310
255 Ottley Drive NE, Atlanta, GA 30324. (404) 892-8480.

Recycled Fibers of GA SmartFax #8311
797 Wylie St, Atlanta, GA 30316. (404) 525-2021.

Roy F. Weston Inc. SmartFax #8312

1880-H Beaver Ridge Cir, Norcross, GA 30071. (770) 263-5400.

Rust Environment & Infrastructure SmartFax #8313
3980 DeKalb Technology Pkwy NE, Suite 700, Atlanta, GA 30340. (770) 458-9309.

Sandy Springs Clean and Beautiful SmartFax #8314
470 Morgan Falls Rd, Atlanta, GA 30350. (404) 551-7643.

Sanifill of GA SmartFax #8315
6201 Powers Fy Rd, Suite 150, Atlanta, GA 30339. (770) 953-0608.

Shred-All Document Processing SmartFax #8316
2625 Piedmont Rd, Suite 56, Atlanta, GA 30324. (404) 699-9100.

South States Environmental Service SmartFax #8317
317 Marble Mill Rd, Marietta, GA 30060. (770) 514-1884.

Southeast Recycling Corp. SmartFax #8319
2000 Powers Fy Rd, Suite 600, Marietta, GA 30067. (770) 951-7950.

United Waste Service Inc. SmartFax #8320
550 Six Flags Pkwy, Mableton, GA 30059. (770) 941-4363.

Waste Management of Atlanta SmartFax #8321
1591 Burks Dr, Morrow, GA 30260. (404) 361-2530.

Waste Recovery Inc. SmartFax #8322
1593 Huber St NW, Atlanta, GA 30318. (404) 355-0547.

Other

American Water Broom SmartFax #5015
3565 McCall Place, Atlanta, GA 30340. (770) 451-2000.

Applied Innovation, Inc. SmartFax #5373
5800 Innovation Drive, Dublin, OH 43016. 614) 798-2000.

Von Roll, Inc. SmartFax #5631
3025 Breckinridge Bl #170, Duluth, GA 30136. (770) 925-9997.

GOVERNMENT

COMPTROLLER OF THE CURRENCY, SMARTFAX #5680
245 Peachtree Center Av NE, Atlanta, GA 30303 (404) 659-8855. Profile: Government agency responsible for the soundness of national banks, employing 100 here.

DEKALB COUNTY MERIT SYSTEM, SMARTFAX #5115
1300 Commerce Drive #100, Decatur, GA 30030 (404) 371-2332. Profile: Local government employing over 6000.

GEORGIA DEPARTMENT OF LABOR, SMARTFAX #5096
148 Int'l Blvd NE #642, Atlanta, GA 30303 (404) 656-3032. Profile: Provides many employment-related services at no charge.

GEORGIA LOTTERY CORP., SMARTFAX #5908
250 Williams St, S 3000, Atlanta, GA 30303-1071 (404) 215-5000. Profile: Administers the GA lottery, employing 230.

City of College Park SmartFax #5066
3667 Main St, College Park, GA 30337. (404) 767-1537.

MISCELLANEOUS

Automotive

AKZO COATINGS INC., SMARTFAX #5367
5555 Spalding Drive, Norcross, GA 30092 (770) 662-8464. Profile: Manufacturer and distributor of technical paint and coatings for auto aftermarket, employing 250 in Atlanta.

ALLIED SIGNAL, INC. (FRICTION MATERIALS DIVISION), SMARTFAX #8331
1551 Mineral Springs Eoad, Elberton, GA 30635 (706) 283-7920. Profile: This division manufactures spark plugs.

BEARINGS & DRIVES INC, SMARTFAX #5041

PO Box 93447, Atlanta, GA 30318 (404) 875-9305. Profile: Industrial distributor in five Southeastern states.

COVINGTON MOULDING CO., SMARTFAX #8324
10116 Industrial Blvd NE, Covington, GA 30209 (770) 786-8182. Profile: Automotive stamping company.

DOUGLAS & LOMASON CO., SMARTFAX #8327
PO Box 489, Carrollton, GA 30177 (770) 834-6681. Profile: Manufactures and distributes auto parts.

FORD MOTOR CO. - ATLANTA ASSEMBLY PLANT 340, SMARTFAX #5687
340 Henry Ford Ii Ave, Hapeville, GA 30354 (404) 669-1547. Profile: This facility assembles various Ford and Mercury cars, employing 2700.

GENERAL MOTORS, SMARTFAX #5460
3900 Motors Industrial Wy, Doraville, GA 30360 (404) 455-5100. Profile: The Doraville manufacturing facility operates one shift, employing over 2000.

GENUINE PARTS CO., SMARTFAX #5461
2999 Circle 75 Pkwy, Atlanta, GA 30339 (770) 953-1700. Profile: Automotive parts distributor/wholesaler, employing 175.

LAGRANGE MOULDING CO., SMARTFAX #8326
Lukken Industrial Drive West, LaGrange, GA 30240 (706) 882-2901. Profile: Manufactures aluminum die-castings and automotive trim.

MACK SALES OF ATLANTA INC, SMARTFAX #5994
PO Box 18027, Atlanta, GA 30087 (404) 577-5230. Profile: Heavy duty truck dealership.

MDC, SMARTFAX #8328
3900 Motors Industrial Way, Doraville, GA 30360 (770) 455-5255. Profile: Manufactures auto bodies.

MOBIL CHEMICAL CO., SMARTFAX #5518
PO Box 71, Covington, GA 30210 (404) 786-5372. Profile: Manufactures and sells polyethylene and polystyrene disposable products.

NAPA AUTO PARTS, SmartFax #5213
PO Box 2000, Norcross, GA 30091 (770) 447-8233. Profile: Distributes automotive replacement parts and accessory items.

PEP BOYS, SmartFax #5913
2726a Candler Rd, Decatur, GA 30034 (404) 243-8805. Profile: World's largest automotive retailer of aftermarket parts and service sales.

RACETRAC PETROLEUM, INC, SmartFax #5226
PO Box 105035, Atlanta, GA 30348 (770) 431-7600. Profile: One of Atlanta's largest privately held firms, this office is headquarters for the gasoline convenience store chain with multi-billion dollar revenue.

ROBERT BOSCH CORP., SmartFax #5312
1600 Westfork Drive, Lithia Springs, GA 30057 (770) 944-4006. Profile: Re-manufacturer of starters and alternators for the automotive aftermarket.

ROSWELL INFINITI, INC., SmartFax #5317
11405 Alpharetta Hwy, Roswell, GA 30076 (770) 740-9500. Profile: New car dealership.

SAAB CARS USA, SmartFax #5643
4405-A Saab Dr, Box 900, Norcross, GA 30091 (770) 279-0100. Profile: US corporate headquarters for Swedish car company.

SNAPPER, SmartFax #5615
PO Box 777, Mcdonough, GA 30253 (770) 954-2500. Profile: Manufacturer of outdoor power equipment, employing 1450.

SUBARU OF AMERICA (SOUTHEAST REGION), SmartFax #8330
220 The Bluffs, Austell, GA 30001 (770) 732-3200. Profile: Regional distribution office for Subaru.

UNITED EQUIPMENT SALES CO., INC., SmartFax #8325
655 Memorial Drive SE, Atlanta, GA 30312 (404) 577-2691. Profile: Distributor of truck parts and equipment.

WILLIAMS, DETROIT, DIESEL, ALLISON, SmartFax #8329

2849 Moreland Ave, Atlanta, GA 30315 (404) 366-1070. Profile: Manufactures engines, transmissions and generators.

YAMAHA MOTOR MANUFACTURING CORP., SMARTFAX #5506

1000 Georgia Hwy 34, Newnan, GA 30265 (770) 254-4000. Profile: Manufacturing facility that makes golf cars and water vehicles, employing 450.

Capital Cadillac
SmartFax #5050
2210 Cobb Pkwy South, Smyrna, GA 30080. (770) 952-2277.

Centennial Industries Division SmartFax #8332
420 10th Ave, Columbus, GA 31901. (706) 323-6446.

CPC Group SmartFax #8333
3900 Motors Industrial Way, Atlanta, GA 30360. (770) 455-5255.

Dyer & Dyer Volvo
SmartFax #6007
5260 Peachtree Ind Blvd, Chamblee, GA 30341. (770) 452-0077.

Goetze Gasket Co.
SmartFax #8334
1641 Lukken Industrial Drive West, LaGrange, GA 30240. (706) 884-6011.

ITT Automotive
SmartFax #8335
29 Westside Industrial Blvd, Rome, GA 30165. (706) 235-6081.

LaGrange Plastics
SmartFax #8336
1501 Orchard Hill Rd, LaGrange, GA 30240. (706) 884-3341.

Leer Southeast
SmartFax #8337
2000 Dogwood Drive SE, Conyers, GA 30208. (770) 929-0042.

Lewis Steel Works
SmartFax #8338
Highway 1 South, Wrens, GA 30833. (706) 547-6561.

Mim Industries, Inc. A Brother Co. SmartFax #5516
1110 Airport Pkwy SW, Gainesville, GA . (770) 535-3122.

Piedmont Automotive Products SmartFax #8339
Rocky Branch Rd, Clarkesville, GA 30523. (706) 754-4147.

Southern Ambulance Builders SmartFax #8340

1507 Country Club Rd, Elberton, GA 30635. (706) 213-0900.

Supreme Corp.
SmartFax #8341
Highway 19, Griffin, GA 30223. (770) 228-6742.

Tune Up Clinic
SmartFax #5272
814 Livingston Ct #E, Marietta, GA 30067. (770) 422-9545 X303.

UT Automotive
SmartFax #8342
1884 Warrenton Highway, Thomson, GA 30824. (706) 595-5105.

Volvo of North America
SmartFax #5623
1125-A Northbrook Pkwy, Suwanee, GA 30174. (770) 995-1675.

Apparel and Textiles

AMOCO FABRICS AND FIBERS CO., SmartFax #8352
900 Circle 75 Pkwy, Atlanta, GA 30339 (404) 350-1330. Profile: Manufactures carpet backing and other nonwoven fabrics.

BARRY MANUFACTURING CO., SmartFax #8370
2303 John Glenn Drive, Chamblee, GA 30341 (770) 451-5476. Profile: Produces men's apparel.

BREMEN-BOWDON, SmartFax #8361
141 Commerce Street, Bowdon, GA 30108 (770) 258-3315. Profile: Manufactures men's apparel.

CARRIAGE INDUSTRIES, INC., SmartFax #8345
PO Box 12542, Calhoun, GA 30703 (706) 629-9234. Profile: Manufacturer of carpeting.

CHICOPEE, INC., SmartFax #8360
PO Box 2537, Gainesville, GA 30503 (770) 532-3161. Profile: Manufactures industrial and commercial fabrics.

CLUETT, PEABODY & CO, INC., SmartFax #5937
4150 Boulder Ridge Drive SW, Atlanta, GA 30336 (404) 346-5300. Profile: Manufactures Arrow-brand clothing, employing nearly 300 in Atlanta.

CMI INDUSTRIES, SmartFax #8344
PO Box 85, Clarksville, GA 30523 (706) 754-4118. Profile: Fabric manufacturer.

COATS AMERICAN, SmartFax #8366
1835 Shackleford, Suite 150, Norcross, GA 30093 (770) 925-3324. Profile: Manufactures yarns and threads.

CORONET INDUSTRIES, INC., SmartFax #8353
PO Box 1248, Dalton, GA 30722 (706) 259-4511. Profile: Manufactures carpeting.

CROWN CRAFTS, INC., SmartFax #8358

PO Box 12371, Calhoun, GA 30703 (770) 917-0037. Profile: Manufactures home furnishings and beddings.

DUNDEE MILLS, INC., SMARTFAX #8354
PO Box 100, Jackson, GA 30233 (770) 775-7842. Profile: Manufactures clothing for infants.

FUQUA ENTERPRISES, SMARTFAX #8372
1201 West Peachtree St NW, Suite 5000, Atalnta, GA 30309 (404) 815-2000. Profile: Tans and finishes leather for the apparel industry.

HUNTER DOUGLAS FABRICATION - SOUTHEAST, SMARTFAX #5143
2755-A Bankers Ind Dr, Atlanta, GA 30360 (770) 447-1440. Profile: One of the world's largest manufacturers of window coverings.

INTERFACE FLOORING SYSTEMS, INC., SMARTFAX #8346
PO Box 1503, LaGrange, GA 30241 (706) 882-1891. Profile: Manufacturer of carpeting.

LAMAR MANUFACTURING CO., SMARTFAX #8362
202 West College Street, Bowdon, GA 30108 (770) 258-7201. Profile: Manufactures men's apparel.

LAWLER HOSIERY MILLS, SMARTFAX #8359
940 Columbia Drive, Carollton, GA 30117 (770) 832-2477. Profile: Manufactures hosiery products.

LOVABLE CO., SMARTFAX #5632
2121 Peachtree Ind Blvd, Buford, GA 30518 (770) 945-2171. Profile: Atlanta-based maker of intimate apparel, employing 620.

MANNINGTON CARPET, INC., SMARTFAX #8343
PO Box 12281, Calhoun, GA 30703 (706) 629-7301. Profile: Carpet manufacturer.

MOHAWK INDUSTRIES, SMARTFAX #5519
1755 The Exchange, Atlanta, GA 30339 (770) 951-6000. Profile: Manufacturer of residential and commercial carpet.

OXFORD INDUSTRIES, SMARTFAX #5949
222 Piedmont Ave, Atlanta, GA 30308 (404) 659-2424. Profile: Fortune 500 apparel manufacturing and marketing company.

PRINCE STREET TECHNOLOGIES, LTD., SMARTFAX #8355
36 Enterprise Blvd, Atlanta, GA 30336 (404) 691-0507. Profile: Manufactures commercial carpets.

PRINTED FABRICS CORP., SMARTFAX #8356
PO Box 220, Carrollton, GA 30117 (770) 832-3561. Profile: Manufactures finished cotton and synthetic fabrics.

QUEEN CARPET CORP., SMARTFAX #8350
PO Box 1527, Dalton, GA 30722 (706) 277-1900. Profile: Manufactures and distributes carpeting internationally.

SEWELL MANUFACTURING CO., SMARTFAX #8368
115 Atlantic Ave, Bremen, GA 30110 (770) 537-3862. Profile: Produces and markets men's apparel.

SHAW INDUSTRIES, INC., SMARTFAX #8349
PO Box 1018, Newnan, GA 30264 (770) 253-5391. Profile: Manufacturers of carpeting.

SIMMONS CO., SMARTFAX #5653
1 Concourse Pkwy, S 600, Atlanta, GA 30328 (770) 512-7700. Profile: Manufacturer of bedding, with 3 facilities in Atlanta employing 300.

SPRINGS INDUSTRIES, INC., SMARTFAX #8364
PO Box 1328, Dalton, GA 30722 (706) 629-4541. Profile: Manufactures rugs and bedding materials.

SPRINGTOWN, SMARTFAX #8348
PO Box 2289, Cartersville, GA 30120 (770) 382-1520. Profile: Manufacturer of outerwear.

STONE MOUNTAIN HANDBAGS, SMARTFAX #8357
PO Box 325, Conley, GA 30027 (404) 366-9600. Profile: Manufactures handbags.

SWIFT TEXTILES, INC., SMARTFAX #8373
PO Box 1400, Columbus, GA 31994 (706) 324-3623. Profile: Textile mill producing cotton yarn and employing nearly 500.

THE ARROW COMPANIES, SMARTFAX #8369
4150 Bouldridge Drive, Atlanta, GA 30336 (404) 346-5300. Profile: Produces Arrow brand men's dress shirts.

THE WARREN FEATHERBONE CO., SMARTFAX #8347
PO Box 383, Gainesville, GA 30503 (770) 535-3000. Profile: Manufacturer of infant care and clothing products.

VERITEC, SMARTFAX #8367
336 Athena Drive, Athens, GA 30601 (706) 549-6561. Profile: Producers of nonwoven textiles.

WALTON FABRICS, INC., SMARTFAX #8365
PO Box 1046, Monroe, GA 30655 (770) 267-9411. Profile: Manufactures woven textiles.

WALTON MANUFACTURING CO., INC., SMARTFAX #8363
4601 Atlanta Highway 78, Loganville, GA 30249 (770) 466-4851. Profile: Manufactures men's suits.

WILKINS INDUSTRIES, INC., SMARTFAX #8351
PO Box 1512, Athens, GA 30603 (706) 546-7960. Profile: Manufactures and distributes ladies' apparel.

WILLIAM CARTER CO., SMARTFAX #5597
PO Box 937, Griffin, GA 30224 (770) 228-0930. Profile: Children's clothing manufacturer, employing 2000.

WORLD CARPETS CARTERSVILLE SPINNING PLANT, SMARTFAX #8371
PO Box 548, Cartersville, GA 30120 (770) 382-6485. Profile: Produces yarns for the manufacturing of carpeting.

Y K K USA, SMARTFAX #5557

1306 Cobb Industrial Dr, Marietta, GA 30066 (770) 427-5521. Profile: World's largest manufacturer of zippers, employing 100 in Atlanta.

American Nonwovens
SmartFax #8374
1020 Oak Chase Drive,
Tucker, GA 30084. (770)
414-1962.

American Polycraft
SmartFax #8375
PO Box 3603, Dalton,
GA 30719. (706) 277-
9524.

Apache Mills SmartFax
#8376
417 S River St, Calhoun,
GA 30701. (706) 629-
7791.

Apex Samples SmartFax
#8377
442 N Hamilton St,
Dalton, GA 30720. (706)
226-1908.

Apparel Finishers
SmartFax #8378
150 Fritz Mar Lane,
Athens, GA 30607. (706)
546-1314.

Aratex Services
SmartFax #8379
401 Glen Iris Drive NE,
Atlanta, GA 30308. (404)
521-2454.

Barret Carpet Mills
SmartFax #8380

2216 Abutment Rd
#2045, Dalton, GA
30721. (706) 277-2114.

Barrow Manufacturing
SmartFax #8381
PO Box 460, Winder, GA
30680. (706) 867-2121.

Bates Fabrics SmartFax
#8382
36 Avery Drive NE,
Atlanta, GA 30309. (404)
876-8913.

Beaulieu of America
SmartFax #8383
600 5th Ave, Dalton, GA
30721. (706) 278-6666.

Beaver Manufacturing
SmartFax #8384
12 Pine St, Mansfield,
GA 30255. (770) 786-
1622.

Bleyle SmartFax #8385
14 Saint John Cir,
Newnan, GA 30265.
(770) 253-2792.

Collins & Aikman Floor
SmartFax #8386
PO Box 1447, Dalton,
GA 30722. (706) 256-
9711.

Colormasters SmartFax
#8387

200 S Fair St, Calhoun,
GA 30701. (706) 629-
8244.

Custom Graphics
SmartFax #8388
300A Springdale Rd,
Dalton, GA 30721. (706)
278-3021.

Dawnville Tufters
SmartFax #8389
5211 Mitchell Bridge Rd
E, Dalton, GA 30721.
(706) 259-6490.

Dellinger SmartFax
#8390
1943 N Broad St, Rome,
GA 30161. (706) 291-
4447.

Designer Rugs Limited
SmartFax #8391
3510 Corporate Drive,
Dalton, GA 30721. (706)
277-8593.

Dorsett Carpet Mills
SmartFax #8392
502 11th Ave, Dalton,
GA 30721. (706) 278-
1961.

DuPont SmartFax #8393
PO Box 1808, Athens,
GA 30603. (706) 353-
4600.

Durkan Pattern Carpet
SmartFax #8394

POBox 1006, Dalton, GA 30722. (706) 278-7037.

Estex Manufacturing Co. SmartFax #8395
402 E Broad St, Fairburn, GA 30213. (770) 964-3322.

Focus Carpet Co. SmartFax #8396
1627 Abutment Rd Dalton, Dalton, GA 30721. (706) 278-1234.

Georgia Commercial Carpters SmartFax #8397
303 Tuftco Drive, Dalton, GA 30721. (706) 277-2223.

Globaltex Carpet Mills, Ltd. SmartFax #8398
3515 Corporate Drive, Dalton, GA 30721. (706) 277-2660.

Golden City Hosiery mills SmartFax #8399
106 Temple Street, Villa Rica, GA 30180. (770) 459-4481.

Guilford Mills SmartFax #8400
PO Box 1055, Gainesville, GA 30503. (770) 532-1228.

Helios SmartFax #8401
South Industrial Blvd, Calhoun, GA 30701. (706) 629-5311.

Henson Garment Co.
SmartFax #8402
125 Paradise Blvd, Athens, GA 30607. (706) 548-2268.

Heritage Carpets
SmartFax #8403
1502 Coronet Drive, Dalton, GA 30720. (706) 256-9771.

Hi-Tech Industries
SmartFax #8404
110 E Walnut Ave, Dalton, GA 30721. (706) 226-7635.

Hickory Tufters
SmartFax #8405
1617 Abutment Rd, Dalton, GA 30721. (706) 277-3499.

HTC Tufters SmartFax #8407
3618A Chatsworth Rd SE, Dalton, GA 30721. (706) 275-0972.

Hubbard Co. SmartFax #8408
202 Georgia Ave N, Bremen, GA 30110. (770) 537-2341.

Image Industries
SmartFax #8409
Highway 100 Summerville Ind Pk, Summerville, GA 30747. (706) 857-6481.

In-Xs Carpets SmartFax #8410
2619 S Dixie Rd, Dalton, GA 30720. (706) 277-6255.

J&J Industries
SmartFax #8411
PO Box 1287, Dalton, GA 30722. (706) 278-4454.

J. Belk SmartFax #8412
601 Callahan Rd SE, Dalton, GA 30721. (706) 277-4747.

Kane Industries
SmartFax #8413
PO Box 1647, Athens, GA 30603.

Kinnaird & Franke Carpets SmartFax #8414
3021 Dug Gap Rd, SW, Dalton, GA 30720. (706) 277-2599.

Kym Co. SmartFax #8416
325 Alabama Blvd, Jackson, GA 30233. (770) 775-5220.
Lady Madison SmartFax #8417
1318 Underwood Street, Dalton, GA 30721. (706) 278-8028.

LAT Sportswear
SmartFax #8418
1200 Airport Dr, Ball Ground, GA 30107. (404) 521-0142.

Lee Apparel Co.
SmartFax #8419
813 Legion Drive,
Dalton, GA 30721. (706)
278-2340.

Liberty Carpet Co.
SmartFax #8420
3514 US Highway 41 s,
Dalton, GA 30720. (706)
277-9700.

Marietta Drapery Co.
SmartFax #8421
PO Box 569, Marietta,
GA 30061. (770) 428-
3335.

**Multitex Corp. of
America** SmartFax
#8422
PO Box 628, Dalton, GA
30722. (706) 277-2770.

Nantucket Industries
SmartFax #8423
200 Cook Street,
Cartersville, GA 30120.
(770) 382-3505.

Newmark & James
SmartFax #8424
PO Box 3637, Dalton,
GA 30719. (706) 278-
8661.

**Nonpareil Finish
Division** SmartFax #8425
121 Goodwill Drive,
Dalton, GA 30721. (706)
226-8005.

NPC South SmartFax
#8426
203 S Easterlind Street,
Dalton, GA 30721. (706)
278-5911.

**Outside Carpets
Internationsl** SmartFax
#8427
906 E Hermitage Rd NE,
Rome, GA 30161. (706)
295-4565.

Patercraft SmartFax
#8428
PO Box 1087, Dalton,
GA 30722. (706) 277-
2133.

Peds Products SmartFax
#8429
225 Lovvorn Rd,
Carrollton, GA 30177.
(770) 834-4495.

**Pelham Manufacturing
Winer Industries**
SmartFax #8430
712 Winer Industrial
Way, Lawrenceville, GA
30245. (770) 963-9285.

Pietrafesa Co. SmartFax
#8431
1000 Columbia Drive,
Carrollton, GA 30177.
(770) 834-4141.

Playtex Apparel
SmartFax #8432
PO Box 429, Newnan,
GA 30264. (770) 253-
2121.

**R&R Manufacturing
Co.** SmartFax #8433
1247 4th Ave, Auburn,
GA 30203. (770) 963-
4846.

**Rome Manufacturing
Co.** SmartFax #8434
208 E 2nd Street, Rome,
GA 30161. (706) 291-
6970.

Rus of Griffin SmartFax
#8435
1156 Uniform Rd,
Griffin, GA 30223. (770)
229-0620.

Russell Corp. SmartFax
#8436
330 W Maple Street,
Cumming, GA 30130.
(706) 889-9266.

Simpson SmartFax
#8437
55 Zena Drive SE,
Cartersville, GA 30120.
(770) 386-2822.

Southern Mills
SmartFax #8438
6501 Shannon Mall Blvd,
Union City, GA 30291.
(770) 969-1000.

Southern Tufters
SmartFax #8440
1704 Waring Rd NW,
Dalton, GA 30721. (706)
259-3400.

SPZ SmartFax #8441

2375 Button Gwinnett Drive, Atlanta, GA 30340. (770) 409-8999.

Syntec Industries
SmartFax #8442
101 Watson Street, Rome, GA 30165. (706) 235-1158.

T&S Tufting Co.
SmartFax #8443
4303 Perry Drive SW, Dalton, GA 30720. (706) 277-3309.

Terry Southern
SmartFax #8444
1581 Southern Drive, Griffin, GA 30223. (770) 229-2361.

Textile Marketing
SmartFax #8445
107 Brooker Drive, Dalton, GA 30721. (706) 259-7445.

Turner-Prichard Clothing SmartFax #8446
131 Alabama Ave S, Bremen, GA 30110. (770) 537-9077.

Wonalancet Co.
SmartFax #8447
1711 Tille Cir NE, Suite 104, Atlanta, GA 30329. (404) 633-4551.

Young's Tufters
SmartFax #8448
101 Hollywood Drive, Dalton, GA 30721. (706) 259-7874.

Pulp and Paper

CARAUSTAR INDUSTRIES INC, SMARTFAX #5051
PO Box 115, Austell, GA 30001 (770) 948-3101. Profile: Manufacturer and converter of paperboard products, employing 450 in Atlanta.

GEORGIA PACIFIC CORP., SMARTFAX #5464
133 Peachtree St NW, Atlanta, GA 30303 (404) 652-4000. Profile: Fortune 50 forest products company and Atlanta's largest Fortune 500 firm, employing 300.

INDUSTRIAL PAPER CORP., SMARTFAX #5109

300 Villanova Drive SW, Atlanta, GA 30336 (404) 346-5800. Profile: Distributor of packaging products and related materials, employing 50.

KIMBERLY-CLARK CORP., SMARTFAX #5498
1400 Holcomb Bridge Rd, Roswell, GA 30076 (770) 587-8000. Profile: HQ for diversified manufacturer, supplying administrative support to several businesses, employs 1300.

METRO LABEL COPORATION, SMARTFAX #5192
1395 Chattahoochee Ave NW, Atlanta, GA 30318 (404) 351-3310. Profile: Manufacturer of pressure sensitive labels.

RIVERWOOD INTERNATIONAL, SMARTFAX #5609
3350 Cumberland C NW,1400, Atlanta, GA 30339 (770) 644-3000. Profile: Manufacturer of paperboard and coated board products.

ROVEMA PACKAGING MACHINES, SMARTFAX #5234
650 Old Norcross Place, Lawrenceville, GA 30245 (770) 513-9604. Profile: Services, sells and manufactures packaging machinery.

UNION CAMP CORP., SMARTFAX #5277
1975 Lakeside Pkwy #314, Tucker, GA 30084 (770) 621-2227. Profile: Manufacturer of corrugated containers and other paper products.

Agriculture

AGCO, SMARTFAX #6021
4830 River Green Pkwy, Duluth, GA 30136 (770) 813-9200. Profile: Manufacturer of farm machinery and equipment, employing 1200.

GOLD KIST, INC., SMARTFAX #5532
244 Perimeter Center Pkwy, Atlanta, GA 30346 (770) 393-5000. Profile: Atlanta-based farm cooperative, employing 750.

Enforcer Products
SmartFax #8449
Highway 41 North,
Emerson, GA 30137.
(770) 386-0801.

Scott/Hyponex Corp.
SmartFax #8450

Highway 42 North,
Jackson, GA 30233.
(770) 775-5081.

Metals/Mining

ALL METALS SERVICES & WAREHOUSE INC, SMARTFAX #5010
848 Damar Drive N E, Marietta, GA 30062 (770) 421-6680. Profile: Specializes in metal processing and steel warehousing, employing 40.

ALUMAX, INC., SMARTFAX #5361
5655 Peachtree Pkwy, Norcross, GA 30092 (770) 246-6600. Profile: World's fifth-largest aluminum producer, employing 120 in Atlanta.

ATLANTA WIRE WORKS, INC., SMARTFAX #8454
1117 Battle Creek Rd, Jonesboro, GA 30236 (770) 471-0660. Profile: Produces a variety of wire products.

ATLANTIC STEEL, SMARTFAX #5390
PO Box 1714, Atlanta, GA 30301 (404) 897-4500. Profile: Steel producer employing 750.

BEKAERT STEEL WIRE CORP., SMARTFAX #8452
PO Box 1205, ROme, GA 30162 (706) 235-4481. Profile: Manufactures a wide range of wire products.

BROWN STEEL CONTRACTORS, SMARTFAX #8457
PO Box 549, Newnan, GA 30264 (770) 253-3232. Profile: Produces steel products.

E.C.C INTERNATIONAL, SMARTFAX #5932
5775 Peachtree-Dunwoody #200, Atlanta, GA 30342 (404) 843-1551. Profile: Produces and markets kaolin and clay, employing 180 in Atlanta headquarters.

GEORGIA MARBLE, SMARTFAX #5547
1201 Roberts Blvd, Bg 100, Kennesaw, GA 30144 (770) 421-6500. Profile: Involved in mining and quarrying of marble, which is then processed for the end-user.

INTERMET CORP., SMARTFAX #8456
2859 Paces Fy Rd, Atlanta, GA 30339 (770) 431-6000. Profile: Produces iron castings.

J.M. TULL METALS CO., INC., SMARTFAX #8451

4400 Peachtree Industrial Blvd, Norcross, GA 30091 (770) 368-4311. Profile: Distributor of a variety of metal products.

MONITOR MANUFACTURING CO, SMARTFAX #5201
1820 South Cobb Ind Blvd, Smyrna, GA 30080 (770) 433-0763. Profile: Metal stamping company that manufactures industrial wheels.

OWEN STEEL CO. OF GEORGIA, INC., SMARTFAX #8453
PO Box 368, Lawrenceville, GA 30246 (770) 963-6251. Profile: Manufactures structural and reinforcement steel.

TRENT TUBE, SMARTFAX #8455
141 Hammond St, Carrollton, GA 30117 (770) 832-9047. Profile: Produces and distributes various stainless steel products.

Alcan Cable SmartFax #8458
3 Ravinia Dr, Suite 1600, Atlanta, GA 30346. (770) 394-9886.

Armco Advanced Materials Co. SmartFax #8459
4715 N Springs Ct, Atlanta, GA 30338. (770) 394-9263.

Cambridge-Lee Industries SmartFax #8460
2312 Peachford Rd, Atlanta, GA 30338. (770) 455-0500.

Cerro Copper Products SmartFax #8461
5325 Dividend Dr, Decatur, GA 30035. (770) 987-8282.

Cobb Wire Rope & Sling Co. SmartFax #8462
525 Frederick Ct SW, Atlanta, GA 30336. (404) 691-8847.

Crown Cork & Seal Co. SmartFax #8463
125 Ottley Dr NE, Atlanta, GA 30324. (404) 892-1988.

Foster Co. SmartFax #8464
6455 Old Peachtree Rd, Norcross, GA 30071. (770) 662-7700.

Herman Miller SmartFax #8465
5650 E Ponce De Leon Ave, Stone Mountain, GA 30083. (770) 496-1726.

Hoover Precision Products SmartFax #8466
2200 Pendley Rd, Cumming, GA 30131. (770) 889-9223.

Hopson-Broker SmartFax #8467
PO Box 7295, Marietta, GA 30065. (770) 578-2400.

Indalex SmartFax #8468
2905 Old oakwood Rd, Gainesville, GA 30504. (770) 535-1349.

Kato Spring SmartFax #8469
2590 Breckinridge Blvd, Duluth, GA 30136. (770) 381-5255.

Knox Co. SmartFax #8470

4865 Martin Ct, Smyrna, GA 30082. (770) 434-7401.

Metal Building Compnonents SmartFax #8471
2280 Monier Ave, Lithia Springs, GA 30057. (770) 948-7568.

MM Systems Corp. SmartFax #8472
4520 Elmdale Dr, Tucker, GA 30084. (770) 938-7570.

Namasco SmartFax #8473
3775 Industrial Ct, Suwanee, GA 30174. (770) 271-9948.

Oneda Corp. SmartFax #8474
4000 Oneda Dr, Columbus, GA 31907. (706) 569-7030.

P&F Sales SmartFax #8476
4575 Stonegate Industrial Blvd, Stone Mountain, GA 30083. (404) 297-9400.

Pacesetter Steel Service SmartFax #8477
PO Box 1729, Woodstock, GA 30188. (770) 926-8900.

Perkins Engineers SmartFax #8478
2386 Flower St, Suite 2000, Snellville, GA 30278. (770) 979-7055.

Preussag International Corp. SmartFax #8479
5780 Peachtree Dunwoody Rd NE, Atlanta, GA 30342. (404) 257-9373.

Reynolds Aluminum SmartFax #8480
3451 Atlanta Industrial Pkwy NW, Atlanta, GA 30331. (404) 699-0726.

Unimast SmartFax #8481
6839 Southlake Pkwy, Morrow, GA 30260. (770) 961-4110.

USG Interiors SmartFax #8482
1000 Donn Dr, Cartersville, GA 30120. (770) 386-4410.

Other

HOSHIZAKI AMERICA, SMARTFAX #5481
618 North Highway 74, Peachtree City, GA 30269 (770) 487-2331. Profile: Manufacturer of commercial ice-making machines, employing 250.

J & M Concrete Construction Inc SmartFax #5150
360 Martin Ct SE, Marietta, GA 30060. (770) 499-8535.

Oldcastle, Inc. SmartFax #5975
375 Northridge Rd #350, Atlanta, GA . (770) 804-3363.

Spinalight SmartFax #5886
320-A Bell Park Dr, Woodstock, GA . (770) 928-0366.

Trindel America Corp. SmartFax #5271
2831 Peterson Place, Norcross, GA 30071-1812. (770) 368-2003.

UCB, Inc. SmartFax #5607
2000 Lake Park Drive, Atlanta, GA 30080. (770) 801-3262.

William L Bonnell SmartFax #5453
PO Box 428, Newnan, GA 30264. (770) 253-2020.

Plastics, Chemicals and Petroleum

ALPHA PRODUCTS, SMARTFAX #5360
500 Interstate W Pkwy, Lithia Springs, GA 30057 (770) 941-5000. Profile: Manufacturer of plastic cups, employing 250.

AMREP, INC., SMARTFAX #5556
990 Industrial Park Drive, Marietta, GA 30062 (770) 422-2071. Profile: Manufacturer of specialty chemicals, employing 90.

ATCO INTERNATIONAL, SMARTFAX #5026
1820 Water Pl #250, Atlanta, GA 30339 (770) 952-1233. Profile: Industrial specialty chemical company, employs 80+.

ATLANTA THERMOPLASTIC PRODUCTS, SMARTFAX #5032
6032 N Royal Atlanta Dr, Tucker, GA 30084 (770) 938-1900. Profile: Custom provider of light-gauge plastics products and services with over 50 employees.

AUTO CHLOR SYSTEM, SMARTFAX #5036
640 Angier Ave NE, Atlanta, GA 30308 (404) 522-1585. Profile: Commercial dishwashing and laundry chemical service company.

CFC RECOVERY SYSTEMS INC, SMARTFAX #5054
1935-G Delk Indl Blvd, Marietta, GA 30067 (770) 984-2292. Profile: Recovers, recycles, buys and sells refrigerants.

CHEMENCE INC, SMARTFAX #5058
6425 Industrial Way, Alpharetta, GA 30201 (770) 664-6624. Profile: Manufacturer of adhesive materials.

COLONIAL PIPELINE, SMARTFAX #5414
PO Box 18855, Atlanta, GA 31126-8855 (404) 841-2306. Profile: Nation's largest petroleum pipeline company.

COLUMBIAN CHEMICALS CO., SMARTFAX #8487

1600 Parkwood Cir, Suite 400, Atlanta, GA 30339 (770) 951-5785. Profile: Manufactures furnace carbon block and iron oxides.

CONSTAR INTERNATIONAL, SMARTFAX #5418
PO Box 43325, Atlanta, GA 30336 (404) 691-4256. Profile: Division of Crown Cork & Seal that manufactures plastics.

ENPLAS U.S.A., INC., SMARTFAX #8489
1901 West Oak Cir, Marietta, GA 30062 (770) 435-3131. Profile: Manufactures plastic engineering parts.

ERB INDUSTRIES, SMARTFAX #8493
PO Box 1237, Woodstock, GA 30188 (770) 926-7944. Profile: Provides a range of custom molding services and related equipment.

FLEXEL INC., SMARTFAX #5531
115 Perimeter Center Pl 1100, Atlanta, GA 30346 (770) 393-0696. Profile: Manufacturer of flexible materials and specialty films.

FLEXIBLE PRODUCTS CO., SMARTFAX #8490
1007 Industrial Park Drive, Marietta, GA 30062 (770) 428-2684. Profile: Manufactures polyurethane and vinyl compounds.

HERCULES, INC., SMARTFAX #8484
3169 Holcombe Bridge Rd, Suite 700, Norcross, GA 30071 (770) 447-9120. Profile: Manufactures and distributes a wide range of chemicals.

KAWNEER CO., INC., SMARTFAX #8494
PO Box 150, Highway 54, Jonesboro, GA 30237 (770) 478-8841. Profile: Subsidiary of Alumax, one of the largest aluminum producers in North America.

MAXELL CORP. OF AMERICA, SMARTFAX #5184
1400 Parker Rd, Conyers, GA 30207 (770) 922-1000. Profile: U.S. headquarters, manufacturing videocassettes at this location.

NORDSON CORP., SMARTFAX #5223
11475 Lakefield Drive, Duluth, GA 30155 (770) 497-3548. Profile: North American Division Headquarters manufacturing finishing and adhesive application equipment.

OLSONITE CORP., SMARTFAX #8488
PO Box 340, Newnan, GA 30264 (770) 253-3930. Profile: Manufactures plastic and vinyl toilet seats.

PPG INDUSTRIES, INC., SMARTFAX #8483
1377 Oakleigh Drive, East Point, GA 30344 (404) 761-7771. Profile: Manufactures a wide variety of coatings, resins, glass and chemicals.

PRINTPACK INC, SMARTFAX #5952
PO Box 43687, Atlanta, GA 30378 (404) 691-5830. Profile: Nation's fourth largest converter of unprinted, unlaminated packaging film.

PURITAN CHURCHILL CHEMICAL CO., SMARTFAX #8491
916 Ashby Street NW, Atlanta, GA 30318 (404) 875-7331. Profile: Manufactures specialty chemicals.

RECKITT AND COLEMAN, SMARTFAX #8485
4111 Pleasantdale Rd, Atlanta, GA 30340 (770) 448-7670. Profile: Manufactures and distributes a wide variety of chemical products for home use.

SELIG CHEMICAL INDUSTRIES, SMARTFAX #8492
PO Box 43106, Atlanta, GA 30378 (404) 691-9220. Profile: Manufactures specialty cleaning products.

TRINTEX CORP., SMARTFAX #8486
PO Box 309, Bowdon, GA 30108 (770) 258-5551. Profile: Manufactures and distributors a variety of rubber and plastic products.

UNITED PROMOTIONS, INC, SMARTFAX #5282
2951 Flowers Rd S #102, Atlanta, GA 30341 (770) 451-6415. Profile: Distributes its own chemical products.

ZEP MANUFACTURING CO., SMARTFAX #5300
1310 Seabord Ind Blvd, Atlanta, GA 30318 (404) 352-1680. Profile: Manufactures and sells specialty chemicals, employing 450 in Atlanta.

Aqualon Co. SmartFax #8496

8300 Dunwoody Place, Atlanta, GA 30350. (770) 642-8040.

Arizona Chemical Co. SmartFax #8497

5323 Oconnel Court, Stone Mountain, GA 30088. (770) 498-3869.

Ashland Chemical SmartFax #8498
17 Executive Park Drive NE, Atlanta, GA 30329. (404) 320-4950.

Atco Rubber Products SmartFax #8499
765 S Erwin St, Cartersville, GA 30120. (770) 386-7968.

Atlanta Pest Control SmartFax #8500
PO Box 965094, Marietta, GA 30066-0002. (770) 591-1892.

Bagcraft Corp. of America SmartFax #8501
18 Royal Drive, Forest Park, GA 30050. (404) 363-6116.

Bandag SmartFax #8502
801 Greenbelt parkway, Griffin, GA 30223. (770) 228-9602.

Borden Packaging SmartFax #8503
1201 S Pine Hill Rd, Griffin, GA 30223. (770) 228-4600.

Bundy Corp. SmartFax #8504

2 Swisher Drive, Cartersville, GA 30120. (770) 382-3260.

Cabot Corp. SmartFax #8505
690 Village Trace, Marietta, GA 30067. (770) 850-9700.

Cellofoam North America SmartFax #8506
1961 Industrial Blvd NW, Conyers, GA 30207. (770) 483-4491.

Clorox Co. SmartFax #8507
17 Lake Mirror Rd, Forest Park, GA 30050. (404) 36.-8300.

Clowhite Co. SmartFax #8508
75 Georgia Pacific Way, Hampton, GA 30228. (770) 946-4216.

Columbus Rubber & Gasket SmartFax #8509
4863 Milgen Rd, Columbus, GA 31907. (706) 563-4400.

Cook's Pest Control SmartFax #8510
203 Highway 411 E SE, Rome, GA 30161. (706) 234-2666.

Dart Container Corp. SmartFax #8511

2120 Lithonia Industrial Blvd, Lithonia, GA 30058. (770) 482-8851.

Dynatron Bondo Corp. SmartFax #8512
3700 Atlanta Industrial Pkwy NW, Atlanta, GA 30331. (404) 696-2730.

Elkay Plastics Co. SmartFax #8513
5290 Westgate Drive SW, Suite D, Atlanta, GA 30336. (404) 346-7776.

Evanite Fiber Corp. SmartFax #8514
1000 Abernathy Rd NE, Suite 7700, Atlanta, GA 30328. (770) 668-880.
Evco Plastics SmartFax #8515
100 Evco Drive SE, Calhoun, GA 30701. (706) 625-2300.

Focal Point SmartFax #8516
3051 Olympic Industrial Drive, Smyrna, GA 30080. (404) 351-0820.

Georgia Duck & Cordage Mill SmartFax #8517
21 Laredo Drive, Scottdale, GA 30079. (404) 294-5272.

Georgia Gulf Corp. SmartFax #6005

400 Perimeter Center Tr #595, Atlanta, GA 30346. (770) 395-4500.

Grafco Atlanta SmartFax #8518
6880 Barton Eoad, Morrow, GA 30260. (770) 960-0220.

Henkel Corp. SmartFax #8519
701 Wissahickon Ave, Cedartown, GA 30125. (770) 748-1200.

Holox Ltd. SmartFax #8520
2186 Marietta Blvd NW, Atlanta, GA 30318. (404) 355-8628.

Hoover Hanes Rubber Custom Mix SmartFax #8521
280 Pequanic Drive, Tallapoosa, GA 30176. (770) 574-2341.

King Packaging Co. SmartFax #8522
PO Box 1197, Bremen, GA 30110. (770) 537-5548.

Klockner Pentaplast America SmartFax #8523
260 N 5th Ave, Rome, GA 30165. (706) 291-3981.

Lever Brothers Co. SmartFax #8524

218 Industrial Park Drive, Cartersville, GA 30120. (770) 382-8660.

Mayo Chemical Co. SmartFax #8525
5544 Oakdale Rd, Smyrna, GA 30082. (404) 696-6711.

Medical Disposables Co. SmartFax #8526
PO Box 1181, Marietta, GA 30061. (770) 422-3036.

Medical Packaging Technology SmartFax #8527
4385 International Blvd, Norcross, GA 30093. (770) 925-4811.

Momar SmartFax #8528
1830 Wllsworth Industrial Drive NW, Atlanta, GA 30318. (404) 355-4580.

Newsome Pest Control SmartFax #8529
3635 Steinhauer Rd, Marietta, GA 30066. (770) 928-9392.

Novi American SmartFax #8530
6195 Purdue Drive SW, Atlanta, GA 30336. (404) 344-5600.

Novus International SmartFax #8531

135 Terrell Mill Rd, Marietta, GA 30067. (770) 933-9700.

Owens-Brockway Plastic Products SmartFax #8532
3490 Hamilton Blvd SW, Atlanta, GA 30354. (404) 766-9613.

Pave-Mark Corp. SmartFax #8533
1855 Plymouth Rd NW, Atlanta, GA 30318. (404) 351-9780.

Pax Industries SmartFax #8534
6610 Jimmy Carter Blvd, Norcross, GA 30071. (770) 242-8949.

Penford Products Co. SmartFax #8535
1534 Dunwoody Village Pkwy, Atlanta, GA 30338. (770) 394-3281.

Plaid Enterprises, Inc. SmartFax #8536
1649 International Court, Norcross, GA 30093. (770) 923-8200.

Plastics Marketing, Inc. SmartFax #5578
PO Box 2791, Norcross, GA 30091. (770) 446-2281.

Plicon Corp. SmartFax #8537

6001 River Rd, Suite
300, Columbus, GA
31904. (706) 322-0067.

Primex Plastics Corp.
SmartFax #8538
3435 Old Oakwood Rd,
Oakwood, GA 30566.
(770) 534-0223.

Ralph Wilson Plastics
SmartFax #8539
2323 Park Central Blvd,
Decatur, GA 30035.
(770) 593-2424.

Rhone-Poulenc
SmartFax #8540
1525 Church Street,
Marietta, GA 30060.
(770) 422-1250.

**Sears Treatment & Pest
Control** SmartFax #8541
2958 Miller Rd, Lithonia,
GA 30038. (770) 593-
2052.

Spurlin Industries
SmartFax #8542
625 Main Street,
Palmetto, GA 30268.
(770) 463-1644.

Standridge Color Corp.
SmartFax #8543
832 E Hightower Trail,
Social Circle, GA 30279.
(770) 464-3362.

Synthetic Industries
SmartFax #8544

PO Box 977, Gainesville,
GA 30503. (770) 532-
9756.

**Textile Rubber &
Chemical Co.** SmartFax
#8545
1400 Tiarco Drive SW,
Dalton, GA 30720. (706)
277-1400.

Vantage Products Corp.
SmartFax #8546
1715 Dogwood Drive
SW, Conyers, GA 30207.
(770) 483-0915.

Wattyl Paint Corp.
SmartFax #8547
5275 Peachtree Industrial
Blvd, Atlanta, GA 30341.
(770) 455-7000.

Win Cup SmartFax
#8548
4604 Lewis Rd, Stone
Mountain, GA 30083.
(770) 938-5281.

Wright Plastics Co.
SmartFax #8549
3315 McGaw Drive,
Atlanta, GA 30341. (770)
451-0226.

Food and Beverages

ALL AMERICAN GOURMET CO., SMARTFAX #8561
5475 Bucknell Dr SW, Atlanta, GA 30336 (404) 349-1226. Profile: Manufactures the frozen meals "Budget Gourmet".

ALLIED FOODS, INC., SMARTFAX #8557
1450 Hills Place NW, Atlanta, GA 30318 (404) 351-2400. Profile: Manufactures and distributes canned pet food.

ANHEUSER-BUSCH, SMARTFAX #5371
PO Box 200248, Cartersville, GA 30210 (770) 386-2000. Profile: Brewery employing 400+.

ATHENS PACKAGING, SMARTFAX #8566
8771 Macon Hwy, Athens, GA 30606 (706) 354-1837. Profile: Packages snack foods manufactured and distributed by its' parent company, Keebler Company.

ATLANTA COCA-COLA BOTTLING CO., SMARTFAX #5029
PO Box 723040, Atlanta, GA 31139-0040 (770) 989-3100. Profile: As Atlanta Regional office, this location bottles and distributes Coca-Cola products, with over 1800 employees.

CAGLE'S INC., SMARTFAX #8570
2000 Hills Ave NW, Atlanta, GA 30318 (404) 355-2820. Profile: Produces and distributes a variety of poultry products.

COCA-COLA ENTERPRISES, SMARTFAX #5413
PO Drawer 1734, Atlanta, GA 30301 (404) 676-2665. Profile: Second largest Fortune 500 company headquartered in Atlanta, employing over 3500 here.

CONAGRA, SMARTFAX #8558
PO Box 1810, Gainesville, GA 30503 (770) 536-3413. Profile: Manufactures and distributes various poultry products.

CRYSTAL FARMS, INC., SMARTFAX #8556
PO Box 7101, Chestnut Mountain, GA 30502 (770) 967-6152. Profile: Largest egg producer in the state of Georgia.

EDWARDS BAKING CO., SMARTFAX #5986
One Lemon Lane, NE, Atlanta, GA 30307-2899 (404) 377-0511. Profile: Manufacturer of frozen pies.

EPI DE FRANCE BAKERY, SMARTFAX #5089
1771 Tullie Cir, Atlanta, GA 30329 (404) 325-1016. Profile: National wholesale bakery.

FINE PRODUCTS CO., INC., SMARTFAX #8559
317 North Ave NE, Atlanta, GA 30308 (404) 874-0868. Profile: Manufactures candy products.

FRITO-LAY, INC., SMARTFAX #8576
2299 Perimeter Park Drive, Suite 100, Atlanta, GA 30341 (404) 344-7921. Profile: Worldwide manufacturer of snack products.

GOLDEN PEANUT CO., SMARTFAX #8565
1100 Johnson Fy Rd NE, Suite 900, Atlanta, GA 30342 (404) 843-7850. Profile: One of the largest handlers of raw peanuts in the country.

GOLDEN POULTRY CO., SMARTFAX #8568
244 Perimeter Center Pkwy NE, Atlanta, GA 30346 (770) 393-5000. Profile: Processes poultry parts for the food service and retail food industries.

GOLDEN STATE FOODS CORP., SMARTFAX #8571
1525 Old Covington Rd NE, Conyers, GA 30208 (770) 483-0711. Profile: Produces sausages and other prepared meat products.

GOODE BROTHERS POULTRY CO., INC., SMARTFAX #8567
5550 Mallory Rd, College Park, GA 30337 (404) 766-0921. Profile: Processes and markets poultry products.

INTERSTATE DISTRIBUTORS, INC., SMARTFAX #8552
4101 Blue Ridge Industrial Pk, Norcross, GA 30071 (770) 476-0103. Profile: Food distributors.

KEEBLER CO., SMARTFAX #8562

111 Hollow Tree Lane SW, Atlanta, GA 30354 (404) 768-5990. Profile: National manufacturer and marketer of snack products.

KELLOGG CO., SMARTFAX #8555
5601 Bucknell Dr, Atlanta, GA 30336 (404) 344-6065. Profile: Kellogg is an international manufacturer and marketer of breakfast cereals, with this location producing frozen waffles.

KRAFT GENERAL FOODS, INC., SMARTFAX #8572
PO Box 1046, Atlanta, GA 30301 (404) 897-2500. Profile: This location handles the manufacturing and distribution of dairy products for the international parent company.

LEON FARMER & CO., SMARTFAX #8574
PO Box 1352, Athens, GA 30603 (706) 353-1166. Profile: Wholesale beverage distributor.

MAPPELI FOODS, SMARTFAX #8563
PO Box 43684, Atlanta, GA 30336 (404) 344-9851. Profile: National producer and marketer of meat products.

MAR-JAC, INC., SMARTFAX #8553
PO Box 1017, Gainesville, GA 30503 (770) 536-0561. Profile: Handles poultry processing.

MERICO, INC., SMARTFAX #8569
273 Central Ave, Forest Park, GA 30050 (404) 361-7211. Profile: Produces a variety of bakery products.

MODERN WAREHOUSING/MODERN PACKAGING, SMARTFAX #5200
1030 Norcross Ind Ct, Norcross, GA 30071 (770) 448-9675. Profile: A warehousing, food processing and packaging facility.

NABISCO BRANDS, INC., SMARTFAX #8564
1400 Murphy Ave SW, Atlanta, GA 30310 (404) 756-6000. Profile: One of the largest consumer food manufacturers in the country.

NATIONAL DISTRIBUTING CO., INC., SMARTFAX #8575

1 National Dr SW, Atlanta, GA 30336 (404) 696-9440. Profile: Wholesale distributor of beverages.

PARMALAT NEW ATLANTA DAIRIES, INC., SMARTFAX #8551
777 Memorial Dr SE, Atlanta, GA 30316 (404) 688-2671. Profile: Dairy processing facility.

PEPSI COLA, SMARTFAX #5501
1480 Chattahoochee Ave, Atlanta, GA 30318 (404) 355-1480. Profile: Bottles and distributes Pepsi Cola brands of soft drinks.

PEPSI-COLA BOTTLERS OF ATLANTA, SMARTFAX #8554
1480 Chattachoochee Ave, Atlanta, GA 30318 (404) 355-1480. Profile: International bottler of Pepsi-Cola products.

ROYAL CROWN BOTTLING CO., SMARTFAX #8550
2429 Victory Dr, Columbus, GA 31901 (706) 689-8203. Profile: bottler of carbonated beverages, mainly RC Cola.

STORK GAMCO, SMARTFAX #8560
PO Box 1258, Gainesville, GA 30503 (770) 532-7041. Profile: Manufactures products used in poultry processing.

TYSON FOODS, INC., SMARTFAX #8573
PO Box 247, Cumming, GA 30130 (770) 887-2344. Profile: This location processes chickens for one of the world's largest handlers of poultry-based food products.

Atlanta Baking Co.
SmartFax #8577
PO Box 4996, Atlanta,
GA 30302. (404) 653-9700.

B & B Spirits Inc
SmartFax #5039
4689 Memorial Dr,
Decatur, GA 30032.
(404) 296-8273.

Harry's Farmer's Market SmartFax #6014

PO Box 567, Alpharetta,
GA . (770) 751-3359.

Southern Tea/Tetley USA, Inc SmartFax #5252
1267 Cobb Industrial Dr,
Marietta, GA 30066.
(770) 428-5555.

Sweetheart Cup Co.
SmartFax #8578

PO Box 380, Conyers,
GA 30207. (770) 483-9556.

252

EMPLOYMENT AGENCIES

A-ONE SERVICE PERSONNEL, SMARTFAX #1532
1718 Peachtree Street NW, #157, Atlanta, GA 30309 (404) 885-9675. offsup, fin

AAA EMPLOYMENT, SMARTFAX #1535
2814 New Spring Rd #306, Atlanta, GA 30339 (770) 434-9232. mgmt

ACCESS, INC., SMARTFAX #1001
PO Drawer 566428, Atlanta, GA 31156 (770) 587-1234. dp

ACCOUNTANTS & BOOKKEEPERS PERSONNEL INC, SMARTFAX #1002
1841 Montreal Rd #212, Tucker, GA 30084 (770) 938-7730. actg, fin

ACCOUNTANTS ON CALL, SMARTFAX #1520

3355 Lenox Rd NE, Atlanta, GA 30326 (404) 261-4800. actg, fin

ACCOUNTEMPS, SMARTFAX #1003
1816 Independence Sq, Dunwoody, GA 30338 (770) 392-0540. actg

ACCOUNTING ALLIANCE GROUP, SMARTFAX #1005
3500 Piedmont Rd NE #500, Atlanta, GA 30305 (404) 231-0828. actg, fin

ACCURATE MEDICAL PLACEMENT, SMARTFAX #1007
5046 Chestnut Forest Lane, Doraville, GA 30360 (770) 452-0443. med

ACTION TEMPORARIES INC, SMARTFAX #1008

6015-D Atlantic Blvd, Norcross, GA 30071 (770) 417-1780. hosp, LI, sales

AD OPTIONS, SMARTFAX #1547
PO Box 7778, Marietta, GA 30065 (770) 424-7778. mktg

AD-VANCE PERSONNEL SERVICES, SMARTFAX #1010
627-E Holcomb Bridge Rd, Roswell, GA 30076 (770) 552-0120. LI, offup

ADIA PERSONNEL SERVICES, SMARTFAX #1009
400 Perimeter Center Tr #100, Atlanta, GA 30346 (770) 399-7741. offsup, sales

AGRI PERSONNEL, SMARTFAX #1530
5120 Old Bill Cook Rd, Atlanta, GA

30349 (404) 768-5701. offsup

ALL MEDICAL PERSONNEL, SMARTFAX #1525 1961 North Druid Hills Rd, #104B, Atlanta, GA 30329 (404) 320-9125. med

ALTERNATIVE STAFFING, INC., SMARTFAX #1548 2181 Northlake Pkwy, Bldg 6 #122, Tucker, GA 30084 (770) 491-3397. offsup

AMH EMPLOYEE LEASING INC, SMARTFAX #1058 1234 Moreland Ave SE #206, Atlanta, GA 30316 (404) 622-8449. offsup, LI

APEX TECHNICAL RESOURCES, SMARTFAX #1181 2100 Powers Fy Rd #150, Atlanta, GA 30339 (770) 933-0707. dp

ARTHUR SLOAN & ASSOCIATES, SMARTFAX #1180 8283 Dunwoody Pl NE 400, Atlanta, GA 30350 (770) 393-1040. MBA's

ASHFORD MANAGEMENT GROUP INC, SMARTFAX #1303 2295 Parklake Drive #425, Atlanta, GA 30345 (770) 938-6260. retail

ASHLEY-NOLAN INTERNATIONAL, SMARTFAX #1015 2000 Powers Fy Rd Center, Marietta, GA 30067 (770) 956-8010. mortgage

ATC HEALTHCARE SERVICES, SMARTFAX #1556 1895 Phoenix Blvd #162, Atlanta, GA 30349 (770) 991-2515. med

ATLANTA TECHNICAL SUPPORT INC, SMARTFAX #1018

One Concourse Pkwy #100, Atlanta, GA 30328-6111 (770) 390-9888. dp

ATLANTA TEMPORARY PERSONNEL, SMARTFAX #1076 PO Box 191746, Atlanta, GA 31119 (404) 239-9775. hosp

ATLANTA TEMPORARY STAFFING, SMARTFAX #1326 841 Memorial Drive SE, Atlanta, GA 30316 (404) 523-6374. offsup

ATS STAFFING, ATLANTA, SMARTFAX #1017 7875 Roswell Rd #D, Atlanta, GA 30350 (770) 551-0777. offsup, actg, LI

ATS STAFFING, NORCROSS, SMARTFAX #1372 3380 Holcomb Bridge Rd, #7, Norcross, GA 30092

(770) 448-2090. offsup, actg, LI

BAILEY & QUINN INC, SMARTFAX #1020
6045 Atlantic Blvd, Norcross, GA 30071 (770) 662-1557. dp

BASES CONSULTING GROUP, INC., SMARTFAX #1021
1100 Circle 75 Pkwy #800, Atlanta, GA 30339 (770) 933-1622. dp

BETTY THOMAS ASSOCIATES, SMARTFAX #1186
2020 Howell Mill Rd, #C283, Atlanta, GA 30318-1732 (404) 352-2569. med

BOREHAM INTERNATIONAL, SMARTFAX #1187
275 Carpenter Dr, S 309, Atlanta, GA 30328 (404) 252-2199. offsup, mgmt, sales

BRIGGS LEGAL STAFFING, SMARTFAX #1022
1275 Peachtree St NE #590, Atlanta, GA 30309-3572 (404) 885-1993. legal

BROCK & ASSOCIATES, SMARTFAX #1023
3190 N E Expwy #210, Atlanta, GA 30341 (770) 525-2525. offsup

CAD CAM, INC., SMARTFAX #1190
6095 Barfield Rd NE, #206, Atlanta, GA 30328 (404) 303-8525. tech

CADTECH STAFFING SERVICE INC, SMARTFAX #1024
2211 Newmarket Pkwy #154, Marietta, GA 30067 (770) 933-0170. tech

CAMBRIDGE PLACEMENTS INC, SMARTFAX #1027

One Piedmont Center #510, Atlanta, GA 30305 (404) 842-2800. legal

CARRIE YORK ASSOC / HALLMARK RECRUITING, SMARTFAX #1028
5696 Peachtree Pkwy, Norcross, GA 30092 (770) 263-3747. fin

CARSON ASSOCIATES, INC., SMARTFAX #1029
6075 Roswell Rd #523, Atlanta, GA 30328 (404) 255-0039. dp

CHART CONSULTING GROUP, SMARTFAX #1030
30 Woodstock St, Roswell, GA 30075 (770) 645-4650. paper

CHASE MEDICAL STAFFING, SMARTFAX #1013
750 Hammond Drive NE, Atlanta, GA

255

30328 (404) 250-9519. med

CHILDCARE RESOURCES INC, SMARTFAX #1031
10945 StreetBrd Rd #401-150, Alpharetta, GA 30202 (770) 495-1328. nannies

CLAREMONT-BRANAN INC, SMARTFAX #1032
1298 Rockbridge Rd #B, Stone Mountain, GA 30087 (770) 928-2915. tech

CLIENTLINK CORP., SMARTFAX #1570
4800 Northpoint Pkwy #300, Alpharetta, GA 30202 (770) 663-3900. dp

CMA CONSULTING SERVICES, SMARTFAX #1199
2971 Flowers Rd So, #280, Atlanta, GA 30341 (770) 454-1137. dp

COMMS PEOPLE INC, SMARTFAX #1033
3340 Peachtree St NE #1410, Atlanta, GA 30326 (404) 812-7626. dp

COMPAID CONSULTING SERVICES INC, SMARTFAX #1571
7840 Roswell Rd #320, Atlanta, GA 30350 (770) 394-1200. dp

COMPREHENSIVE COMPUTER CONSULTANTS, INC., SMARTFAX #1198
7000 Central Pkwy, #1000, Atlanta, GA 30328 (770) 512-0100. dp

COMPUTER AID INC, SMARTFAX #1572
3600 Dallas Hwy #B4-392, Marietta, GA 30064 (770) 419-0197. dp

COMPUTER PEOPLE INC, SMARTFAX #1329

200 Galleria Pkwy #450, Atlanta, GA 30339-5944 (770) 951-1772. dp, offsup

COMPUTER STAFFING SOLUTIONS INC, SMARTFAX #1034
2520 E Piedmont Av #F250, Marietta, GA 30066 (770) 578-6677. dp

COMPUTER XPERTS, INC., SMARTFAX #1016
1360 Peachtree Street#444, Atlanta, GA 30309 (404) 888-0800. dp, offsup

COMSYS TECHNICAL SERVICES/CUTLER/WILLIAMS INC, SMARTFAX #1573
6 Concourse Pkwy #2990, Atlanta, GA 30328 (770) 393-7420. eng
CORPORATE RECRUITING GROUP, INC., SMARTFAX #1036
5 Concourse Pkwy #3100, Atlanta, GA

30328 (404) 252-5656. sales, mktg

DATANOMICS, INC., SMARTFAX #1112
6425 Powers Fy Rd #255, Atlanta, GA 30339 (770) 850-9005. dp, tech

DIXIE STAFFING SERVICES, STONE MOUNTAIN, SMARTFAX #1324
4960-F Redan Rd, Stone Mountain, GA 30088 (404) 299-1050. offsup, LI

DOCTOR'S CHOICE, INC., SMARTFAX #1325
5250-A Highway Nine, Alpharetta, GA 30201 (770) 475-0504. med

DOROTHY LONG SEARCH, SMARTFAX #1521
6065 Roswell Rd NE #416, Atlanta, GA 30328 (404) 252-3787. real estate

DSA-DIXIE SEARCH ASSOCIATES, SMARTFAX #1545
501 Village Trace, Bldg 9, Marietta, GA 30067 (770) 850-0250. hosp

DURHAM STAFFING, SMARTFAX #1388
4485-K Fulton Ind Blvd, Atlanta, GA 30336 (404) 691-1404. offsup, LI

DXI CORP., SMARTFAX #1166
1110 Spring Street#308, Atlanta, GA 30309 (404) 873-5221. dp

ELITE STAFFING SERVICES, INC., SMARTFAX #1295
230 Peachtree St NW #2125, Atlanta, GA 30303 (404) 577-4511. offsup, LI

EVIE KREISLER & ASSOCIATES, SMARTFAX #1289
2575 Peachtree Rd #300, Atlanta, GA

30305 (404) 262-0599. man

EXCEL TECHNICAL SERVICES, SMARTFAX #1042
1117 Perimeter Center W #W03, Atlanta, GA 30338 (770) 392-9340. dp

EXCEL TEMPORARY SERVICES, SMARTFAX #1043
4772 Ashford Dunwoody Rd, Suite 310, Atlanta, GA 30338 (770) 393-0532. offsup, LI

EXECUTIVE PLACEMENT SERVICES, SMARTFAX #1044
5901 Peachtree Dunwoody #498, Atlanta, GA 30328 (770) 396-9114. hosp, retail

EXECUTIVE RESOURCE GROUP, ATLANTA, SMARTFAX #1045

127 Peachtree Street #1122, Atlanta, GA 30303 (404) 522-0888. high level executives

EXECUTIVE STRATEGIES INC, SMARTFAX #1519
1425 Market Blvd #1320 N7, Roswell, GA 30076 (770) 552-3085. dp, mgmt

FIRST IMPRESSIONS STAFFING AGENCY, SMARTFAX #1294
3390 Peachtree Rd #900, Atlanta, GA 30326 (404) 238-0867. hosp

FOCUS ENTERPRISES, INC., SMARTFAX #1293
3 Corporate Sq, Ste 340, Atlanta, GA 30329 (404) 321-5400. dp, tech

FSA INC, SMARTFAX #1115
PO Box 448, Marietta, GA 30061-0448 (770) 427-8813. ins

GEORGE MARTIN ASSOCIATES, INC., SMARTFAX #1049
12 Executive Park Drive NE, Atlanta, GA 30329 (404) 325-7101. dp

GMW AGENCY, SMARTFAX #1047
4303 Suite D Memorial Dr, Decatur, GA 30032 (404) 296-2360. hosp

GYNN ASSOCIATES, INC, SMARTFAX #1291
3 Piedmont Center, #312, Atlanta, GA 30305 (404) 237-8208. real estate

H & H CONSULTING GROUP INC, SMARTFAX #1537
1456-C McLendon Dr, Decatur, GA 30033 (770) 414-0045. dp

HALL MANAGEMENT GROUP, SMARTFAX #1332
736 Green Street NE, Gainesville, GA 30501 (770) 531-5568. mgmt

HAPPY HELPERS, THE, SMARTFAX #1120
1360 Powers Fy Rd, Suite 150, Marietta, GA 30067 (770) 952-5933. nannies

HIRE INTELLECT, INC., SMARTFAX #1168
1810 Water Place, #240, Atlanta, GA 30339 (770) 850-8502. mktg, graph

HORIZONS RESOURCES, INC., SMARTFAX #1121
1375 Peachtree St NE #179, Atlanta, GA 30309 (404) 885-9556. offsup

HOWIE AND ASSOCIATES, SMARTFAX #1333
875 Old Roswell Rd F100, Roswell, GA 30076 (770) 998-0099. dp, tech

HUEY GERALD ASSOCIATES, SMARTFAX #1123
3636 Autumn Ridge Pk #100, Marietta, GA 30066 (770) 973-8944. dp, tech

INFORMATION TECHNOLOGY RESOURCES, INC, SMARTFAX #1052
220 Renaissance Pkwy NE #2313, Atlanta, GA 30308 (404) 888-9945. dp

INFORMATION TECHNOLOGY STAFFING INC, SMARTFAX #####
3350 Cumberland Cir #1900, Atlanta, GA 30339 (770) 984-9400. dp

INTERIM PERSONNEL, SMARTFAX #1054

5975 Roswell Rd, #109, Atlanta, GA 30328 (404) 252-5528. offsup

INTERNATIONAL MEDICAL AND DENTAL ASSOC. INC., SMARTFAX #1557
6255 GA Hwy 85, Riverdale, GA 30274 (770) 997-4637. med

INTERSOURCE LTD, SMARTFAX #1056
72 Sloan Street, Roswell, GA 30075 (770) 645-0015. HR, dp, tech

IOA STAFFING, SMARTFAX #1057
8290 Roswell Rd #200, Atlanta, GA 30350 (770) 552-7771. offsup

IPR, SMARTFAX #1055
8097 B Roswell Rd, Atlanta, GA 30350 (770) 396-7500. ins

J E S SEARCH FIRM, INC., SMARTFAX #1292

3475 Lenox Rd, Ste 970, Atlanta, GA 30326 (404) 262-7222. dp

JACOBSON ASSOCIATES, SMARTFAX #1159
1775 The Exchange #240, Atlanta, GA 30339 (770) 952-3877. ins

JSA INC, SMARTFAX #1231
2900 Delk Rd #700-290, Marietta, GA 30067 (770) 973-7771. dp

KAUFFMAN & CO, SMARTFAX #1061
PO Box 53218, Atlanta, GA 30355 (404) 233-3530. hosp

KELLY SERVICES, SMARTFAX #1063
2839 Paces Fy Rd #670, Atlanta, GA 30339 (770) 801-7246. offsup

KELLY TECHNICAL

SERVICES,
SMARTFAX #1544
1995 N Park Place
#270, Atlanta, GA
30339 (770) 850-
1333. dp

KELLY
TEMPORARY
SERVICES,
SMARTFAX #1081
1995 N Park Place
#330, Atlanta, GA
30339 (770) 952-
4797. offsup

KEY
TEMPORARIES,
SMARTFAX #1065
1100 Circle 75 Pkwy
#1500, Atlanta, GA
30339 (770) 984-
6760. offsup

LAWSTAF, INC.,
SMARTFAX #1301
1201 W Peachtree
Street, Ste 4830,
Atlanta, GA 30309
(404) 872-6672.
legal

LEADER
INSTITUTE,
SMARTFAX #1066
340 Interstate N
Pkwy #250, Atlanta,

GA 30339 (770) 984-
2700. dp

LEAFSTONE
STAFFING INC,
SMARTFAX #1067
3 Piedmont Center
Suite 200, Atlanta,
GA 30075 (404) 816-
7575. offsup

LEGAL
PROFESSIONAL
STAFFING INC,
SMARTFAX #1068
2 Ravinia Drive
#380, Atlanta, GA
30346 (770) 392-
7181. Legal

LUCAS
FINANCIAL
SEARCH,
SMARTFAX #1069
3384 Peachtree Rd
#710, Atlanta, GA
30326 (404) 239-
5620. fin

M.S.I.
CONSULTING,
SMARTFAX #1518
6151 Powers Fy Rd
#545, Atlanta, GA
30339 (770) 850-
6465. dp
MAC TEMPS,
SMARTFAX #1075

1830 1st Union 999
Peachtree, Atlanta,
GA 30309 800) 622-
8367. dp, graph

MALCOM
GROUP, THE,
SMARTFAX #1077
53 Office Park 13350
Hwy 53 E, Marble
Hill, GA 30148 (770)
893-3485. ins

MANAGEMENT
ANALYSIS &
UTILIZATION,
SMARTFAX #1078
501 Greene St,
Augusta, GA 30901
706) 722-6806. dp,
offsup, eng

MANAGEMENT
RECRUITERS OF
ATLANTA, WEST,
SMARTFAX #1079
685 Thornton Way,
Lithia Springs, GA
30057 (770) 948-
5560. mgmt

MANAGEMENT
RECRUITERS OF
NORTH FULTON,
SMARTFAX #1082
21 N Main St,
Alpharetta, GA

Date _____   Signed _____

Date _____   Signed _____

AFFIX VOIDED OR CANCELLED CHECK BELOW

Attachment B

The Sports Section, Inc.

Group Photo Products

8/5/03

TSS Order #:

Franchisee:

Franchise Order #:

Group Name:

Special Instructions:

Logo File:

Roll	Frame	TSS Item	Order Qty	Name	Slate

Total Qty: Subject ID:

AUTHORIZATION AGREEMENT FOR AUTOMATIC DEPOSTS
(ACH CREDITS)

Company Name: The Sports Section. Inc. / B & H Products. Inc.

I(We) do hereby authorize the above named company, hereinafter referred to as the Originator, to initiate credit entries to the account indicated below, and to initiate corrective reversal entries (debits) to the account indicated below in the event any credit entries are originated in error.

Name of Depository
Financial Institution _____

Location of Depository Financial Institution:

City _____ State _____ Zip _____

Transit / ABA number (nine digits) ___ ___ ___

Account Number _____

This authority is to remain in effect until the Originator has received my(our) written notification of its termination in such time and in such manner as to afford the Originator a reasonable opportunity to

30201 (770) 664-5512. pkg, mgmt

**MARISTAFF,
FOREST PARK,**
SMARTFAX #1086
5300 Frontage Rd,
Forest Park, GA
30050 (404) 361-7433. dp, LI, offsup

**MATRIX
RESOURCES,**
SMARTFAX #1539
115 Permeter Center
Pl, Atlanta, GA
30346 (770) 677-2400. dp

MED STAT, INC,
SMARTFAX #1125
551 N Main St,
Alpharetta, GA
30201 (770) 772-4418. med

**MEDICAL
OFFICE
STAFFING/DENT
AL PERSONNEL,**
SMARTFAX #1243
865 Holcomb Bridge
Rd #230, Atlanta,
GA 30076 (770) 998-7779. med
**MEDPRO
PERSONNEL,**

INC, SMARTFAX
#1528
1955 Cliff Vly Way,
#116, Atlanta, GA
30329 (404) 633-8280. med

**MEDWORLD
STAFFING
SERVICES,**
SMARTFAX #1127
8601 Dunwoody
Place #636, Atlanta,
GA 30350 (770) 587-5602. med

**MERLIN
SERVICES
GROUP,**
SMARTFAX #1559
10825 Stroup Rd,
Roswell, GA 30075
(770) 643-3000. med

**METRO
EMPLOYMENT/M
EDICAL
EMPLOYMENT
GROUP,**
SMARTFAX #1128
4056 Wetherburn
Way #1, Norcross,
GA 30092 (770) 662-8700. med

**MICHAEL
ALEXANDER**

GROUP,
SMARTFAX #1327
333 Sandy Springs
Cir NE #131,
Atlanta, GA 30328
(404) 256-7848. med

**MILLARD &
ASSOC,**
SMARTFAX #1130
2141 Kingston Court
#103, Marietta, GA
30067 (770) 984-8771. exec

**MONARCH
SERVICES,**
SMARTFAX #1131
3340 Peachtree Rd
NE, #119, Atlanta,
GA 30326 (404) 261-8474. offsup

**MULLING
GROUP, THE,**
SMARTFAX #1576
990 Hammond Drive
#900, Atlanta, GA
30328 7(770) 395-3131. mgmt

**NATIONAL
LABOR GROUP
INC,** SMARTFAX
#1088
1579 F Monroe Drive
#134, Atlanta, GA

30324 (404) 724-9980. LI

NELL RICH & ASSOCIATES, SMARTFAX #1560
PO Box 6363, Marietta, GA 30065 (770) 974-7567. const, real estate

NORRELL FINANCIAL STAFFING, SMARTFAX #1092
3535 Piedmont Rd NE, Atlanta, GA 30305 (404) 240-3600. Fin

NORRELL SERVICES, ATLANTA, SMARTFAX #1041
3535 Piedmont Rd, Atlanta, GA 30305 (404) 240-3000. Atlanta is the corporate headquarters for the fifth largest temporary help company in the U.S., with 14 offices here and over 300 nationwide.

NORRELL SERVICES, ATLANTA/PIEDMONT, SMARTFAX #1095
3535 Piedmont Rd NE, Atlanta, GA 30305 (404) 240-3000. full service

NORRELL SERVICES, LAWRENCEVILLE, SMARTFAX #1093
575 W Pike Street, Lawrenceville, GA 30245 (770) 995-7603. full service

NORRELL SERVICES, NORCROSS, SMARTFAX #1094
3150 Holcolmb Bridge Rd #110, Norcross, GA 30071 (770) 449-8084. full service

NORRELL SERVICES, PIEDMONT ROAD, SMARTFAX #1285
3535 Piedmont Rd NE, Atlanta, GA 30305 (404) 240-3000. full service

NPS OF ATLANTA, HAMMOND DRIVE, SMARTFAX #1096
750 Hammond Drive B15 #200, Atlanta, GA 30328 (404) 843-3758. full service

NPS OF ATLANTA, SOUTHLAKE, SMARTFAX #1383
118 North Ave, #A, Jonesboro, GA 30236 (770) 471-9033. full service

NPS OF ATLANTA, TUCKER, SMARTFAX #1097
2374 Main Street #A, Tucker, GA 30084 (770) 493-8353. full service

OFFICE SPECIALISTS, BUCKHEAD, SMARTFAX #1531
3500 Piedmont Rd NE, #112, Atlanta,

GA 30305 (404) 814-9865. full service

OFFICE SPECIALISTS, SANDY SPRINGS, SMARTFAX #1134
6623 Roswell Rd, Atlanta, GA 30328 (404) 843-0177. full service

OLIVER SEARCH, SMARTFAX #1540
PO Box 81092, Conyers, GA 30208 (770) 760-7661. mgmt

OLSTEN STAFFING SERVICES, SMARTFAX #1297
6065 Roswell Rd, #220, Atlanta, GA 30328 (404) 255-4222. offsup

OMNI RECRUITING GROUP, SMARTFAX #1553
1950 Spectrum Cir #A405, Marietta, GA 30067 (770) 988-2788. sales

P.J. REDA & ASSOCIATES, INC, SMARTFAX #1098
1955 Cliff Valley Way, #117, Atlanta, GA 30329 (404) 325-8812. hosp, med

PEOPLE NETWORK INC, SMARTFAX #1175
35 Glenlake Pkwy #225, Atlanta, GA 30328 (770) 392-1700. dp

PERSONALIZED MANAGEMENT ASSOCIATES, SMARTFAX #1546
1950 Spectrum Cir #B-310, Marietta, GA 30067-6059 (770) 916-1668. hosp

PREMIER STAFFING-THE LUCAS GROUP, SMARTFAX #1533
1100 Abernathy Rd, #L-10, Atlanta, GA 30328 (770) 396-9224. offsup

PRIDESTAFF, GALLERIA, SMARTFAX #1549
300 Galleria Pkwy #740, Atlanta, GA 30339 (770) 955-3377. offsup

PRIME STAFFING INC, SMARTFAX #1287
6000 Lake Forrest Dr, Atlanta, GA 30328 (404) 252-5855. offsup

PRIORITY ONE STAFFING SERVICES, SMARTFAX #1543
5805 State Bridge Rd #N, Duluth, GA 30136 (770) 813-1877. offsup

PRO STAFF ACCOUNTING SERVICES, SMARTFAX #1152
4 Concourse Pkwy #165, Atlanta, GA 30328 (770) 673-0900. actg

PRO STAFF PERSONNEL SERVICES, SMARTFAX #1176

4 Concourse Pkwy #150, Atlanta, GA 30328 (770) 393-9200. offsup

PROFESSIONAL MEDICAL RESOURCES, SMARTFAX #1148
5901 Peachtree Dunwoody Rd, Bldg10, Atlanta, GA 30174 (770) 698-1864 X116. med

QUEST SYSTEMS INCORPORATED, SMARTFAX #1154
3 Corporate Square #210, Atlanta, GA 30329 (404) 636-3000. dp

RANDSTAD STAFFING SERVICES, CLAIRMONT ROAD, SMARTFAX #1340
2970 Clairmont Rd, #1000, Atlanta, GA 30329 (404) 325-7000. offsup

REYNOLDS EDP ASSOCIATES, INC, SMARTFAX #1101

561 Pike Street #209, Lawrenceville, GA 30245 (770) 962-5447. dp

ROLLINS SEARCH GROUP, SMARTFAX #1103
216 Pkwy 575, Woodstock, GA 30188 (770) 516-6042. ins

ROWLAND MT. & ASSOCIATES, SMARTFAX #1104
4-E Executive Pk NE #100, Atlanta, GA 30329 (404) 325-2189. sales

S.C.I OF ATLANTA, INC., SMARTFAX #1106
1874 Independence Sq #B, Atlanta, GA 30338 (770) 396-7788. tech, sales, dp, med

SANFORD ROSE ASSOC, NORCROSS, SMARTFAX #1107
3525 Holcomb Bridge Rd #2b, Norcross, GA 30092 (770) 449-7200. tele

SBB & ASSOCIATES, SMARTFAX #1105
3107a Medlock Bridge Rd, Norcross, GA 30071 (770) 449-7610. hosp

SNELLING PERSONNEL, MARIETTA, SMARTFAX #1108
1337 Canton Rd #D3, Marietta, GA 30066 (770) 423-1177. offsup

SOFTWARE SEARCH, SMARTFAX #1109
2163 Northlake Pkwy #100, Tucker, GA 30084 (770) 934-5138. dp

SOFTWARE SERVICE CORP., SMARTFAX #1561
Three Piedmont Center #204, Atlanta, GA 30305 (404) 816-2520. dp

SOLUTION SOURCE, INC, SMARTFAX #1562

3761 Venture Drive #115, Duluth, GA 30136 (770) 418-1051. dp, tech

SONDRA SEARCH, SMARTFAX #1156
PO Box 101, Roswell, GA 30077 (770) 552-1910. sales, med, hosp

SOUTHERN CRESCENT PERSONNEL, INC, SMARTFAX #1113
7179 Jonesboro Rd #101, Morrow, GA 30260 (770) 968-4602. offsup, med, eg

SOUTHERN INDUSTRIAL EMPLOYEES, INC., SMARTFAX #1051
156-A Forsyth St, Atlanta, GA 30303 (404) 577-0239. LI

SPECIALTY EMPLOYMENT GROUP, SMARTFAX #1174
7390 Twin Branch Rd, Atlanta, GA

30328 (770) 399-9350. travel

STAFFING SOLUTIONS, INC, SMARTFAX #1116
1040 Crown Pt Pkwy #690, Atlanta, GA 30342 (770) 671-9333. offsup, LI

SUMMIT TEMPORARIES, ATLANTA, SMARTFAX #1118
5605 Glenridge Dr, #1060, Atlanta, GA 30342 (404) 256-3042. offup, LI

SUMMIT TEMPORARIES, MARIETTA, SMARTFAX #1162
1165 N'chase Pkwy SE, 150, Marietta, GA 30067 (770) 859-0400. offsup, LI

SUPERIOR/CORE STAFF STAFFING SERVICES, SMARTFAX #1119
One Concourse Pkwy, #150, Atlanta, GA 30318 (770) 394-8367. offsup, dp, actg

SYSTEM ONE TECHNICAL STAFFING, SMARTFAX #1122
5775 Peachtree-Dunwoody Rd, #B220, Atlanta, GA 30342 (404) 252-0099. dp

SYSTEMP (A SVC OF BRANDON ENGINEERS), SMARTFAX #1377
1050 Crown Point Pkwy #1180, Atlanta, GA 30338 (770) 399-5220. dp

SYSTEMS & PROGRAMMING CONSULTANTS, SMARTFAX #1512
100 Galleria Pkwy, Ste 690, Atlanta, GA 30339 (770) 612-4999. dp

SYSTEMS ENGINEERING SERVICES CORP., SMARTFAX #1267
400 Perimeter Center Ter, #900, Atlanta, GA 30346 (770) 804-6490. dp, tech

265

SYSTEMWARE PROFESSIONAL SERVICES, SMARTFAX #1268
990 Hammond Drive, #610, Atlanta, GA 30028 (770) 671-0900. dp

TAC TEMPS, ATLANTA, SMARTFAX #1161
900 Circle 75 Pkwy NW, #700, Atlanta, GA 30339 (770) 955-5340. offsup

TAC TEMPS, NORCROSS, SMARTFAX #1138
3150 Holcomb Bridge Rd, #340, Norcross, GA 30071 (770) 242-9484. offsup

TALENT TREE, SMARTFAX #1269
1 Coca-Cola Plaza #600, Atlanta, GA 30313 (404) 676-4026. In-house temporary agency for The Coca-Cola Company, filling 500+ positions weekly.

TALENT TREE STAFFING SERVICES, SMARTFAX #1356
Two Ravinia Drive, #320, Atlanta, GA 30346 (770) 395-0147. offsup

TANNER PERSONNEL, ATLANTA, SMARTFAX #1139
3312 Piedmont Rd, #340, Atlanta, GA 30305 (404) 231-9303. med

TEAM RESOURCES, INC, SMARTFAX #1132
5500 Interstate Pkwy #425, Atlanta, GA 30328 . exec, sales

TECH SPECIALISTS ATLANTA, SMARTFAX #1143
6151 Powers Fy Rd, Atlanta, GA 30339 (770) 933-0111. dp, tech, R&D

TECHNICAL ADVISORY

GROUP, SMARTFAX #1141
6855 Jimmy Carter Blvd, #2120, Norcross, GA 30071 (770) 246-0362. dp

TECHNICAL CONSULTING GROUP, SMARTFAX #1142
2856 Johnson Fy Rd, #200, Marietta, GA 30062 (770) 552-8885. dp

TECHNISOURCE, SMARTFAX #1514
3355 Lenox Rd, #810, Atlanta, GA 30326 (404) 816-9141. tech

TEL TEK SOLUTIONS, INC, SMARTFAX #1563
29B South Peachtree, NW, Norcross, GA 30071 (770) 446-3176. dp

TEMP WORLD, SMARTFAX #1170
600 Embassy Row, #260, Atlanta, GA 30328 (770) 901-5000. offsup, LI

266

TEMPORARY SPECIALTIES, ATLANTA, SMARTFAX #1133
4920 Roswell Rd, #35, Atlanta, GA 30305 (404) 303-8611. offsup

TEMPORARY SPECIALTIES, KENNESAW, SMARTFAX #1366
4200 Wade Green Rd, Kennesaw, GA 30144 (770) 426-7219. offsup

TRC STAFFING, DUNWOODY, SMARTFAX #1352
100 Ashford Center N #500, Dunwoody, GA 30338 (770) 392-1411. offsup, LI

TRC STAFFING, NORCROSS, SMARTFAX #1137
3091 Holcomb Bridge Rd, Norcross, GA 30071 (770) 242-1936. offsup, LI

TRIAD DATA INC, SMARTFAX #1564
1117 Perimeter Center W #114,
Atlanta, GA 30335 (770) 395-1222. dp

UNITED CONSULTING GROUP, LTD, SMARTFAX #1565
808 Park North Bld #100, Clarkston, GA 30021 (404) 294-3919. tech

UNIVERSAL DATA CONSULTANTS INC, SMARTFAX #1566
6630 Bay Cir, Norcross, GA 30071 (770) 446-6733. dp, tech

VOLT TEMPORARY SERVICES, SMARTFAX #1147
3575 Koger Blvd NW #170, Duluth, GA 30136 (770) 925-7314. offsup

WEGMAN ASSOICATES, INC., SMARTFAX #1567
1852 Enterprise Drive, Norcross, GA 30093 (770) 368-
0101. offsup, LI, const

WESSON, TAYLOR, WELLS & ASSOCIATES, INC., SMARTFAX #1517
1800 Pkwy Place Suite 300, Marietta, GA 30067 (770) 795-9945. dp

WHITTAKER AND ASSOCIATES, SMARTFAX #1568
2675 Cumberland Pkwy #263, Atlanta, GA 30339 (770) 434-3779. food, man

WINDWARD EXECUTIVE SEARCH, SMARTFAX #1151
58 South Park Square, #B, Marietta, GA 30060 (770) 425-6788. paper

267

A Temporary Solution SmartFax #1169
1396 Howell Mill Rd NW, Atlanta, GA 30318. (404) 352-9722.

A.R.M. Search
SmartFax #1541
38 South Park Sq, #1, Marietta, GA 30060. (770) 795-1553.

America Employment Incorporated
SmartFax #1554
1950 Spectrum Cir, Suite 405A, Marietta, GA 30067. (770) 980-3401.

Anesthesia Solutions
SmartFax #1179
100 Crescent Center Pkwy #525, Tucker, GA 30084. (770) 723-3780.

Anne Williams/Omni Associates SmartFax #1526
One Piedmont Center, #120, Atlanta, GA 30305. (404) 266-2663.

Ashley Staffing Services SmartFax #1341
1819 Peachtree Rd Ne/450, Atlanta, GA 30309. (404) 352-2200.

ASI Services Corp.
SmartFax #5024
1475 Peachtree Street NE #210, Atlanta, GA 30309. (404) 888-5555.

Automation Temporary Services Inc SmartFax #1019
305 Bucknel Ct, Atlanta, GA 30336. (404) 629-1751.

Bell Oaks Co.
SmartFax #1524
3390 Peachtree Rd, #1124, Atlanta, GA 30326. (404) 261-2170.

Bradley-Morris, Inc. SmartFax #1380
200 Galleria Pkwy, #220, Atlanta, GA 30339. (770) 612-4950.

Brandt & Associates
SmartFax #1359
8097-B Roswell Rd, Atlanta, GA 30350. (770) 396-0505.

Brannon & Tully
SmartFax #1382
5690 Holcomb Bridge Rd #S10, Norcross, GA 30092. (770) 447-8773.

Brookes & Associates SmartFax #5549
550 Keeler Woods Dr, Marietta, GA 30064. (770) 499-2199.

Business Professional Group
SmartFax #1334
3490 Piedmont Rd,1 SecCr, Atlanta, GA 30305. (404) 262-2577.

Butler Service Group, Inc.
SmartFax #1371
4960 Peachtree Ind Blvd, Norcross, GA 30092. (770) 448-9220.

C-Peck Co.
SmartFax #1523

169 Interlochen Drive, Atlanta, GA 30342. (404) 843-3183.

Caldwell Services SmartFax #1191 1540 Powers Fy Rd, #15, Marietta, GA 30067. (770) 955-1767.

Caldwell Services/Atlanta SmartFax #1025 200 Galleria Pkwy #905, Atlanta, GA 30339. (770) 955-1767.

Caldwell Services/Lithia Springs SmartFax #1026 561 Thornton Rd #S, Lithia Springs, GA 30057. (770) 739-0796.

Catherine Bishop Consulting SmartFax #1165 320 Interstate Pkwy, #490, Atlanta, GA 30339. (770) 850-8030.

CDI Information Services SmartFax #1193 22 Perimeter Center E #2200, Atlanta, GA 30346. (770) 394-2441.

Cella Associates of Atlanta SmartFax #1194 4045 Weberburn Wy,Ste 4, Norcross, GA 30092. (770) 242-3040.

Chandler Consultants SmartFax #1527 PO Box 741, Commerce, GA 30529. (404) 577-2485.

Charlotte Cody Consultants SmartFax #1552 1487 Panola Rd, Ellenwood, GA 30049. (770) 981-0431.

Citicare, Inc. SmartFax #1555 1950 Spectrum Cir, #A405, Marietta, GA 30067-6059. (770) 989-2811.

Claims Overload Systems SmartFax #1300 100 Colony Sq, #1220, Atlanta, GA 30361. (404) 892-2900.

Coe & Associates SmartFax #1370 2675 Paces Fy Rd, #160, Atlanta, GA 30339. (770) 434-3710.

Corporate Search Consultants SmartFax #1037 47 Perimeter Center E #260, Atlanta, GA 30346. (770) 399-6205.

Corporate Solutions SmartFax #1358 5901 Peachtree-Dun NE #A360, Atlanta, GA 30328. (770) 396-1115.

Crown Temporary Services, Inc. SmartFax #1385 2785 Lawrenceville Hwy, Decatur, GA 30033. (770) 621-0123.

Cubbage &
Associates SmartFax
#1172
3651 Canton Hwy,
#205, Marietta, GA
30066. (770) 926-
5095.

David C. Cooper &
Associates SmartFax
#1357
400 Perimeter Center
Tr/950, Atlanta, GA
30346. (770) 395-
0014.

DCW Group (The)
SmartFax #1379
1530 Dunwoody Vil
Pk #206, Atlanta, GA
30338. (770) 604-
9600.

Don Richard
Associates of GA
SmartFax #1343
3475 Lenox Rd NE,
#210, Atlanta, GA
30326. (404) 231-
2688.

Dunbar Associates
SmartFax #1536
5955 Jimmy Carter
Bld #20, Norcross,
GA 30071. (770)
441-2428.

Dunhill Professional
Search SmartFax
#1550
2110 Powers Fy Rd
#110, Atlanta, GA
30339. (770) 952-
0009.

Dunhill Temporary
Services SmartFax
#1202
3340 Peachtree Rd,
#2570, Atlanta, GA
30326. (404) 261-
7557.

Dynamic People
SmartFax #1529
260 Peachtree St
#1750, Atlanta, GA
30303. (404) 688-
1124.

Ecco Staffing
SmartFax #1284
5975 Roswell Rd,
#109, Atlanta, GA
30328. (404) 252-
5528.

Eden Group, Inc.
SmartFax #1203
1837 Mallard Lake
Dr, Marietta, GA
30068. (770) 640-
9577.

Emerging
Technology Search
SmartFax #1204
1080 Holcomb
Bridge Rd #100,
Roswell, GA 30076.
(770) 643-4994.

Emjay Computer
Careers SmartFax
#1205
3390 Peachtree Rd
NE, #100, Atlanta,
GA 30305. (404)
875-6003.

Engineering Group
SmartFax #1039
3000 Langford Rd
#700, Norcross, GA
30071. (770) 441-
2729.

Etcon, Inc.
SmartFax #1206
PO Box 1376,
Gainesville, GA
30503. (770) 532-
8449.

Evans & James
Executive Search
SmartFax #1040
PO Box 862232,
Marietta, GA 30062.
(770) 992-4299.

Executive Search Consultants
SmartFax #1542
5050 P'chtree Pkwy
340-118, Norcross,
GA 30092. (404)
4976-6677.

Expressdata Corp.
SmartFax #1208
1800 Sandy Plains
Rd #304, Marietta,
GA 30066. (770)
421-8883.

First Investors Corp. SmartFax #1210
3300 Holcomb
Bridge Rd, #290,
Norcross, GA . (770)
447-1108.

Firstaff SmartFax #1211
1175 Peachtree S NE
#1120, Atlanta, GA
30361. (404) 876-
2788.

Fox-Morris
SmartFax #1114
9000 Central Pk
#150, Atlanta, GA
30328. (770) 399-
4497.

G&K Services, Inc.
SmartFax #1213

PO Box 448, Atlanta,
GA . (404) 349-2863.

Garland Group (The) SmartFax #1215
PO Box 957435,
Duluth, GA 30136-
9524. (770) 497-
1871.

General Employment Enterprises
SmartFax #1522
260 Peachtree St
NW, #890, Atlanta,
GA 30303. (404)
255-5255.

General Personnel Consultants of Atlanta SmartFax #1048
4501 Circle 75 Pkwy
A1225, Atlanta, GA
30339. (770) 937-
0555.

Graphic Resources
SmartFax #1050
2265 Roswell Rd
#100, Marietta, GA
30062. (770) 509-
2295.

Hillary Group, The
SmartFax #1219

3675 Crestwood
Pkwy, Duluth, GA
30136. (770) 923-
4336.

HL Yoh Co.
SmartFax #5565
2400 Lake Park
Drive #315, Smyrna,
GA 30080. (770)
432-5200.

Home Health & Hospital Recruiters
SmartFax #1221
3020 Roswell Rd NE,
S 200, Marietta, GA
30062. (770) 578-
1884.

Hygun Group, Inc.
SmartFax #1378
3020 Roswell Rd,
#200, Marietta, GA
30062. (770) 973-
0838.

Interstaff, Inc.
SmartFax #1226
804 Pkwy 575, #802,
Woodstock, GA
30188. (770) 928-
8791.

ISC of Atlanta, Inc
SmartFax #1381
1200 Ashwood Pkwy,
#138, Atlanta, GA

30338. (770) 673-6800.

Jackie Glover Associates, Inc
SmartFax #1330
5825 Glenridge Drive #2/108, Atlanta, GA 30328. (404) 250-1538.

Jean Cody Associates, Inc.
SmartFax #1228
1000 Abernathy R#400/156, Atlanta, GA 30328. (770) 668-8868.

Jim Nixon & Associates SmartFax #1229
2900 Chamblee Tuck Rd #3, Atlanta, GA 30341. (770) 458-9963.

Jordan Temporaries
SmartFax #1230
1065 Spring St NW, Atlanta, GA 30309. (404) 892-1008.

K. Murphy & Associates SmartFax #1339
2557 Burnt Leaf Lane, Decatur, GA

30033. (404) 315-9859.

Keystone Consulting Group, Inc.
SmartFax #1167
1950 Spectrum Cir,A405, Marietta, GA 30067. (770) 563-1206.

Kindercare Learning Center
SmartFax #1232
850 Le Croy Drive, Marietta, GA . (770) 973-0696.

KL Stevens & Associates SmartFax #1233
#5 Concourse Pkwy, Atlanta, GA 30328. (770) 399-5157.

Knight & Associates
SmartFax #1234
PO Box 248, Kennesaw, GA 30144. (404) 423-9836.
Lanier Employment Services SmartFax #1235
PO Box 699, Gainesville, GA . (770) 536-2884.

Lucas Associates
SmartFax #1236
5901a Peachtree D'wdy Rd 525, Atlanta, GA 30328. (770) 901-5570.

M A & A Group
SmartFax #1071
35 Glenlake Pkwy #550, Atlanta, GA 30328. (770) 671-0844.

Management Decisions SmartFax #1238
3060 Holcomb Bridge Rd, #J, Norcross, GA 30071. (770) 416-7949.

Management Recruiters of Atlanta, North
SmartFax #1558
30 Woodstock Street, Roswell, GA 30075. (770) 998-1555.

Manpower International, Norcross SmartFax #1239
3150 Holcomb Bridge Rd, #330, Norcross, GA 30071. (770) 449-4822.

Manpower International, Perimeter SmartFax #1080
41 Perimeter Center E #150, Atlanta, GA 30346. (770) 399-6422.

Manpower Temporary Services, Atlanta
SmartFax #5511
260 Peachtree St NW, #900, Atlanta, GA . (404) 659-3565.

Manpower Temporary Services, Marietta
SmartFax #1240
3000 Windy Hill Rd, #1, Marietta, GA 30067. (770) 951-8983.

Maristaff, Atlanta
SmartFax #1085
PO Box 76082, Atlanta, GA 30358. (770) 393-2718.

Martin & Assoc
SmartFax #1087
2850 Delk Rd 41-G, Marietta, GA 30067. (770) 952-2472.

Meridian USA, Inc
SmartFax #1244
1266 W Paces Fy Rd, #455, Atlanta, GA 30327. (404) 848-7777.

Milam Design Services, Inc.
SmartFax #1368
2625 Cumberland Pkwy #120, Atlanta, GA 30339. (770) 432-4505.

More Personnel Services SmartFax #1551
4501 Circle 75 Pkwy A1190, Atlanta, GA 30339. (770) 955-0985.

MRC Resources
SmartFax #1344
400 Colony Square #200, Atlanta, GA 30361. (404) 877-9162.

MSI (Formerly Temps & Co)
SmartFax #1245
245 Peachtree Center Ave, #2500, Atlanta, GA 30303. (404) 659-5236.

MSI Consulting
SmartFax #1072
6151 Powers Fy Rd #540, Atlanta, GA 30339. (770) 850-6465.

MSI Services, Atlanta SmartFax #1328
4151 Ashford-Dun Rd, #290, Atlanta, GA 30319. (404) 255-1177.

MSI Services, Duluth SmartFax #1073
3500 Gwinnett Place Dr#4, Duluth, GA 30136. (770) 232-9600.

MSI Services, Inc.
SmartFax #1074
5901-A Peachtree Dunwoody Rd #410, Atlanta, GA 30328. (770) 901-9030.

Mullinax Temporary Services
SmartFax #1538
200 Cobb Pkwy North NE, #139, Marietta, GA 30062. (770) 499-8407.

National Personnel Recruiters SmartFax #1089
6520 Powers Fy Rd, Atlanta, GA 30339. (770) 955-4221.

NBI Staffing
SmartFax #1090
243 W Ponce De Leon Ave, Decatur, GA 30030. (404) 377-0500.

New Boston Select Group SmartFax #1091
3423 Piedmont Rd NE #100, Atlanta, GA 30305. (404) 848-9400.

Outsource Staffing
SmartFax #1288
3451 Peachtree Rd NE, #B, Atlanta, GA 30326. (404) 816-1820.

Paces Personnel, Inc. SmartFax #1249
235 Peachtree St,Ne #603, Atlanta, GA 30303. (404) 688-5307.

Paragon Protective Services, Inc.
SmartFax #5541
2470 Windy Hill Rd, #300, Marietta, GA . (770) 618-3019.

Paragon Resources
SmartFax #1360
4085 Chestnut Ridge Drive, Dunwoody, GA 30338. (770) 396-9774.

Pathfinders, Inc.
SmartFax #1251
229 Peachtree St NE #1500, Atlanta, GA 30303. (404) 688-5940.

Premier Staffing
SmartFax #1253
1827 Powers Fy Rd #2, Marietta, GA 30067. (770) 932-2775.

Pridestaff, Duluth
SmartFax #1144
3700 Crestwood Pkwy, Duluth, GA 30136. (770) 923-1000.

Pridestaff, Sandy Springs SmartFax #1145

1000 Abernathy Rd, Atlanta, GA 30328. (770) 662-8900.

Professional Options
SmartFax #1323
5671 Peachtree-Dun Rd, #550, Atlanta, GA 30342. (404) 843-6000.

Progressive Personnel Services
SmartFax #1286
1349 W Peachtree St, #1625, Atlanta, GA 30309. (404) 870-8240.

Quality Personnel
SmartFax #1255
1655 Peachtree St NE, #916, Atlanta, GA 30309. (404) 873-5223.

Quest Health Care Associates SmartFax #1155
2244 Mohawk Trail, Acworth, GA 30102.

Randstad Staffing Services, Park Place
SmartFax #1100
2015 South Park Place, Atlanta, GA 30339. (770) 937-7000.

Randstad Staffing Services, Roswell Road SmartFax #1099
6681-E Roswell Rd, Atlanta, GA 30328. (404) 250-1008.

Rannou & Associates, Inc. SmartFax #1158
1900 The Exchange, #370, Atlanta, GA 30339. (770) 956-8225.

Redden Associates SmartFax #1384
PO Box 2417, Peachtree City, GA 30269. (770) 487-8929.

Remedy, The Intellegent Temporary SmartFax #1153
990 Hammond Drive NE #820, Atlanta, GA 30328. (404) 512-3300.

Ridley And Associates SmartFax #1256
100 Galleria Pkwy #400, Atlanta, GA . (770) 859-9722.

Right Choice Staffing Services, Inc SmartFax #1102
1000 Parkwood Cr #140, Atlanta, GA 30339. (770) 988-9544.

Romac International SmartFax #1575
Three Ravinia Drive, Suite 1460, Atlanta, GA 30346. (770) 604-3880.

Search Atlanta, Inc. SmartFax #1258
PO Drawer 674899, Marietta, GA 30067. (770) 984-0880.

Search Financial, Inc SmartFax #1164
210 Interstate N Pkwy,#700, Atlanta, GA 30339. (770) 980-6672.

Sizemore Personnel SmartFax #1259
1369 Reynolds Street, Augusta, GA 30901. (706) 724-5629.

Snelling Personnel, Gainesville SmartFax #1110
PO Box 2729, Gainesville, GA 30503. (770) 534-0001.

Snelling Temporaries SmartFax #1157
1309 Powers Fy Rd SE, Marietta, GA 30067. (770) 952-0909.

Source Services Corp-Accountant Sourcetemps SmartFax #1260
4170 Ashfd-D'wdy Rd #285, Atlanta, GA . (404) 250-4444.

Southeast Research, Inc SmartFax #1510
1215 Hightower Trail D200, Atlanta, GA 30350-2915. (770) 992-2177.

Staff Builders Health Care Services SmartFax #5594
1835 Savoy Drive, Atlanta, GA 30341. (770) 457-1245.

Staff Demand of GA, Inc. SmartFax #1511
1700a Marietta Blvd, Atlanta, GA 30318. (404) 605-0058.

Staff Management SmartFax #1117
1800 Peachtree StreetSte 510, Atlanta, GA 30309. (404) 351-5510.

Staffing Technologies SmartFax #1261
5825 Glenridge Drive #3 #101, Atlanta, GA . (404) 705-6777.

Standard Coffee Service SmartFax #1262
6265 Mcdonough Drive, Norcross, GA . (770) 449-3211.

Sterling Legal Search, Inc.
SmartFax #1263
5180 Roswell Rd NW #202 S, Atlanta, GA 30342. (404) 250-9766.

Symonds & Smythe Associates SmartFax #1265
PO Box 941635, Atlanta, GA 31141. (770) 381-7880.

Tanner Personnel, Lawrenceville
SmartFax #1163
698 Highway 120, Lawrenceville, GA 30245. (770) 682-5646.

Taurus Personnel Consultants,Inc
SmartFax #1126
2110 Powers Fy Rd, #280, Atlanta, GA 30339. (770) 951-2461.

Team Builders
SmartFax #1140
6035 Atlantic Blvd #G, Norcross, GA 30071. (770) 416-0996.

Tech Source
SmartFax #1513
PO Box 191641, Atlanta, GA 31119-1641. (770) 452-8558.

Temp Choice, Inc.
SmartFax #1178

5150 Buford Hwy, #1306, Norcross, GA 30071. (770) 447-4199.

Temporary Talent SmartFax #1336
3475 Lenox Rd NE, #275, Atlanta, GA 30326. (404) 365-8367.

Tempworld Staffing Service, Atlanta
SmartFax #1515
8343 Roswell Rd, Atlanta, GA . (770) 992-9976.

Tempworld Staffing Services, Tucker
SmartFax #1135
4450 Hugh Howell Rd #7, Tucker, GA 30084. (770) 939-1143.

The Registry, Inc.
SmartFax #1516
5605 Glenridge Drive, #250, Atlanta, GA 30342. (404) 252-9119.

Toar Consulting Inc
SmartFax #1136
1176 Grimes Bridge Rd#200, Roswell,

GA 30075. (770)
993-7663.

**Top Notch
Personnel** SmartFax
#1171
75 Arcado Rd, #B,
Lilburn, GA 30247.
(770) 923-8858.

**Turknett Associates
Leadership Group**
SmartFax #5474
2310 Parklake Dr,
#500, Atlanta, GA
30345. (770) 270-
1723.

**Tyler Staffing
Svcs/Chase Medical
Staffing** SmartFax
#1197
750 Hammond Dr,
Bldg 4, Atlanta, GA
30328. (404) 250-
4448.

**United Consumers
Club of Nw Atlanta**
SmartFax #5280
1395 S Marietta
Pkwy #212, Marietta,
GA 30067. (770)
428-9999.

Victor Personnel
SmartFax #1177
1050 Crowne Pt
Pkwy #330, Atlanta,

GA 30338. (770)
399-0439.

Vistech SmartFax
#1277
5881 Glenridge Drive
#105, Atlanta, GA
30328. (404) 705-
9414.

**Volt Service Group,
Technical Services**
SmartFax #1278
5300 Oakbrook Pkwy
#245, Norcross, GA
30093. (770) 931-
5454.

Volt Services Group
SmartFax #1146
4771 Britt Rd #E-4,
Norcross, GA 30093.
(770) 496-9900.

Wanda Haynes
SmartFax #1376
258 Old Norton Rd,
Fayetteville, GA
30215. (770) 460-
6088.

**Western Staff
Services** SmartFax
#1149
999 Peachtree St NE
#760, Atlanta, GA
30309. (404) 888-
0003.

**Western Technical
Services** SmartFax
#1150
7094 Peachtree Ind
Blvd #201, Norcross,
GA 30071. (770)
263-6022.

**Western Temporary
Services** SmartFax
#1064
999 Peachtree St,
Suite 760, Atlanta,
GA 30309. (404)
892-6722.

**Windsor
International**
SmartFax #1569
3350 Cumberland Cir
#1900, Atlanta, GA
30339-3363. (770)
438-2300.

**Word Processors
Personnel, Atlanta**
SmartFax #1331
1100 Johnson Fy Rd
#588, Atlanta, GA
30339. (404) 257-
1303.

**Word Processors
Personnel, P'tree St.**
SmartFax #1281
230 Peachtree St NW
#1514, Atlanta, GA
30303. (404) 588-
9100.

Worldwide Temporary Resources SmartFax #1387 3260 Pointe Pkwy NW, #200, Norcross, GA 30092. (770) 729-1400.

PROFESSIONAL AND TRADE ASSOCIATIONS

AD 2/ATLANTA, SMARTFAX **#4039** 404/848-2717. Profile: Career Network Director handles job and applicant match-up, but job seeker must be a member.

AMER ASSOC of OCCUPATIONAL HEALTH NURSES, SMARTFAX **#4030** 404/262-1162. Profile: Maintains resume file for interested employers and applicants are coded to preserve anonymity.

AMER SOC of HEATING, REFRIG, AND AIR COND ENGINEERS, SMARTFAX **#4022** 770/419-7533. Profile: Local chapter publishes monthly newsletter whic lists synopses of job seekers, available free to members only.

AMERICAN INSTITUTE of CPA's/GEORGIA SOCIETY of CPA's, SMARTFAX **#4040** 404/231-8676. Profile: Membership Services Assistant maintains Job Bank for job seekers and job openings for both CPA's and non-CPA's.

AMERICAN INSTITUTE of GRAPHIC ARTS, SMARTFAX **#4010** 404/237-4957. Profile: Contact chapter president to be included in the resume bank.

AMERICAN MARKETING ASSOCIATION, SMARTFAX **#4011** 770/270-0619. Profile: Offers job seekers several excellent programs under their Employment Referral Service.

AMERICAN PRODUCTION AND INVENTORY CONTROL SOCIETY, SMARTFAX **#4031** 770/952-0009. Profile: Maintains resume file for employers. Contact Placement Coordinator.

AMERICAN SOC OF MECHANICAL ENGINEERS, SMARTFAX **#4012** 770/497-3718. Profile: Contact Editor for information on the monthly newsletter, which includes job seekers.

AMERICAN SOCIETY FOR QUALITY CONTROL, SMARTFAX **#4041** 770/830-1703. Profile: Has resume file and includes job seekers in monthly newsletter.

AMERICAN SOCIETY FOR TRAINING AND DEVELOPMENT, SMARTFAX #4042 404/845-0522. Profile: Has Job Hotline for members only. Contact chapter administrator.

AMERICAN SOCIETY of WOMEN ACCOUNTANTS, SMARTFAX #4043 770/427-3101. Profile: Publishes monthly newsletter including job seekers and job openings.

ASSOCIATION FOR SYSTEMS MANAGEMENT, SMARTFAX #4034 770/677-9097. Profile: No formal job assistance, but good networking opportunity.

ASSOCIATION of RECORDS MANAGERS AND ADMINISTRATORS, SMARTFAX #4032 770/648-8761. Profile: Career placement Chairman maintains a confidential file of job seekers, and applicants are notified before being referred to companies.

ATLANTA AD CLUB, SMARTFAX #4013 770/458-3181. Profile: Publishes monthly newsletter shich includes employment columns "Positions Wanted" and "Positions Available."

ATLANTA CHAMBER OF COMMERCE, SMARTFAX #5672 235 International Blvd NE, Atlanta, GA 30303 (404) 880-9000. Profile: Has limited turnover with only 75 employees.

BLACK DATA PROCESSING ASSOCIATES, SMARTFAX #4044 404/828-4605. Profile: Has job coordinator who maintains resume file.

BUILDING OWNERS AND MANAGERS of ATLANTA, SMARTFAX #4045 770/825-0116. Profile: Maintains resume file for employers.

BUSINESS MARKETING ASSOCIATION, SMARTFAX #4046 770/432-3666. Profile: Maintains Professional Assitance Network (PAN) to help members with job search.

COMMERCIAL REAL ESTATE WOMEN, SMARTFAX #4047 770/393-9030. Profile: Has Job Bank newsletter that includes job openings and seekers.

CREATIVE CLUB of ATLANTA, SMARTFAX #4015 404/874-0908. Profile: Publishes monthly newsletter which includes job information.

FINANCIAL EXECUTIVES INSTITUTE, SMARTFAX #4048 770/521-9393. Profile: Has Member Career Services Committe which serves as liaison with search firms, companies and applications; membership required.

GA SOCIETY FOR PROFESSIONAL ENGINEERS, SMARTFAX #4004 404/355-0177. Profile: Maintains resume bank and refers resumes on file to interested employers. Contact executive director.

GA SOCIETY of ASSOCIATION EXECUTIVES, SMARTFAX #4049 770/986-0700. Profile: Send resume to office for perusal by interested employers.

INSTITUTE of INTERNAL AUDITORS, SMARTFAX #4050 404/529-8419. Profile: Job Coordinator maintains resume file, matching applicants and openings.

INSTITUTE of MANAGEMENT ACCOUNTANTS, SMARTFAX #4051 404/679-2966. Profile: Has Employment Director who maintains resume file and matches resumes with company job requests.

INSTITUTE OF NUCLEAR POWER OPERATIONS, SMARTFAX #4035
700 Galleria Pkwy, Atlanta, GA 30339 (770) 644-8000. Profile: Trade association whose members are electric utilities with nuclear interests, employing 350.

INSTITUTE OF PAPER SCIENCE AND TECHNOLOGY, SMARTFAX #5958
500 10th Street NW, Atlanta, GA 30318 (404) 894-5700. Profile: University information and research service for the pulp and paper industry, employing 180.

INTERNATIONAL ASSOCIATION of BUSINESS COMMUNICATORS, SMARTFAX #4052
PO Box 2692, Atlanta, GA 30371 . Profile: Publishes monthly newsletter that includes employment section listing job seekers and job openings; $15 for non-members.

INTERNATIONAL CUSTOMER SERVICE ASSOCIATION,
SMARTFAX #4053 770/925-1774. Profile: Maintains resume bank for employers to review.

INTERNATIONAL FOUNDATION of EMPLOYEE BENEFIT PLANS, SMARTFAX #4021 404/840-8696. Profile: Job coordinator announces job openings at meetings or over the phone, and maintains a resume file for prospective employers. Membership required.

LIFE OFFICE MANAGEMENT ASSOCIATION (LOMA),
SMARTFAX #4037
5770 Powers Fy Rd, Atlanta, GA 30327 (770) 951-1770. Profile: Trade association that sponsors training to promote insurance companies, employing close to 200.

MEETING PROFESSIONALS INTERNATIONAL, SMARTFAX #4054
770/973-0071. Profile: Has Resume Library that collects resume and makes them available to potential employers.

NATIONAL ASSOCIATION of BLACK ACCOUNTANTS,
SMARTFAX #4055 404/587-4082. Profile: The Career Development Chairpersons maintain a job bank of resumes for interested employers.

NATIONAL ASSOCIATION of LEGAL SECRETARIES, SMARTFAX
#4056 404/815-6558. Profile: Has Employment Chairman who refers applicants to existing openings.

NATIONAL ASSOCIATION OF PURCHASING MANAGEMENT,
SMARTFAX #4018 770/606-3070. Profile: Contact for local job openings.

NATIONAL ASSOCIATION OF WOMEN IN CONSTRUCTION,
SMARTFAX #4057 770/850-6743. Profile: Operates Occupational Research and Referral Service, matching jobs and applicants.

NATIONAL CONTRACT MANAGEMENT ASSOCIATION,
SMARTFAX #4019 770/903-2204. Profile: Employment Chairman maintains resume file and refers to interested employers.

NON-PROFIT RESOURCE CENTER, SMARTFAX #4058 404/572-9694.
Profile: Job assistance is called Opportunity Knocks.

**PROFESSIONAL ENVIRONMENTAL MARKETING
ASSOCIATION**, SMARTFAX #4059 404/223-5700. Profile: Publishes Job Bank
newsletter which includes job vacancies. Job seekers should contact chapter
administrator.

PUBLIC RELATIONS SOCIETY of AMERICA, SMARTFAX #4060
5108 Victor Trail, Norcross, GA 30071 770/449-6369. Profile: Monthly newsletter
includes section "People Pointers," which lists job openings and job seekers. Free for
members.

SOCIETY FOR HUMAN RESOURCE MANAGEMENT, SMARTFAX
#4020 770/886-1800. Profile: Has resume referral service that maintains a resume
file for interested employers. Contact chapter administrator.

SOCIETY FOR PROFESSIONAL SERVICES, SMARTFAX #4061
404/633-8998. Profile: Employment Opportunity Committe maintains file of job
openings and applicants, and acts as clearing house for employers and applicants.

SOCIETY FOR TECHNICAL COMMUNICATION, SMARTFAX #4062
770/922-2047. Profile: Maintains resume database available to companies.

SOCIETY of LOGISTIC ENGINEERS, SMARTFAX #4008 770/793-0508.
Profile: Membership chairman maintains resume bank and monthly newsletter lists job
openings.

**TECHNICAL ASSOCIATION OF THE PULP & PAPER
INDUSTRY**, SMARTFAX #4036
15 Technology Pkwy South, Norcross, GA 30092 (770) 446-1400. Profile: Trade
association employing 85.

WOMEN IN COMMUNICATIONS, SMARTFAX #4063
7722 Pool Mill Rd, Douglasville, GA 30135 . Profile: Maintains Job Bank, matching
job openings with job seekers; free for members.

WORKING IN EMPLOYEE BENEFITS, SMARTFAX **#4064** 404/329-5757. Profile: To have resume on file for interested employers, contact Job Bank coordinator.

Atlanta Regional Commission SmartFax #4038. (404) 656-7700.

Financial Women International SmartFax #4017. (404) 875-4896.

National Assoc of Insurance Women SmartFax #4005 (770) 399-7169.

INDEX

CAPITALIZED selections indicate profiled companies.

285

287

288

289

290

292

293

295

302

311

—Y—

—Z—